JOHN MARINO'S
Bicycling
BOOK

JOHN MARINO'S
Bicycling
BOOK

JOHN MARINO
LAWRENCE MAY, M.D.
HAL Z. BENNETT

Published by
J. P. Tarcher, Inc.
Los Angeles
Distributed by
Houghton Mifflin Company
Boston

J. P. Tarcher, Inc.
9110 Sunset Blvd.
Los Angeles, CA 90069
Library of Congress Catalog Card No.: 79-57652

Design by Jane Moorman

Manufactured in the United States of America

First Edition

I dedicate this book to

My parents, John and Josephine Marino, for loving support and continuous recognition no matter how small the accomplishment.

My sisters Nina and Maria for offering encouragement for as long as I can remember.

Peter Rosten, for believing enough in me to make this book and the film on my '80 world record ride a reality.

Mr. Robert Hills and Gordon W. Smith, Jr., two prime motivators in my life. Without them I would never have had the desire nor the belief that I could set a world record.

And to my wife Joni, for being my biggest fan and best friend.

CONTENTS

PREFACE

I
n a very real way I owe the quality of my life today to a bike. Let me tell you how that came about.

When I was a 19-year-old college sophomore, I was drafted by the Los Angeles Dodgers. Having played baseball all my life, this seemed like a dream come true. Then, toward the end of my first baseball season, my life took a sudden tragic turn.

As part of my regular training program, I was lifting weights to build strength. I attempted to lift 525 pounds, which was too much for my physical condition at that time. Suddenly there was a loud crack that sounded as though a gun had gone off in the weightroom. My back exploded with pain, an electric shock raced down my spine. My toes curled, my legs shook uncontrollably, and I collapsed to the floor.

I had suffered a severe compression fracture of the lower lumbar vertebrae. My doctors informed me I had a permanent disability and from that day on for the rest of my life, my activities would have to be severely restricted.

The implications of this were almost unbearable. I was an athlete by nature. The accident had robbed me of my most important form of self-expression, and a central source of pride and self-esteem.

I visited one medical specialist after another, searching for that magic remedy that would give me back a normal life. But this search proved futile. Time and again I was told that nothing could be done.

For the next five years my physical and mental state declined. I gave up all forms of exercise and consoled myself with food. I gained weight and grew lazier by the day.

Then in 1973, another dramatic change took place in my life. I met a doctor with a holistic approach to health who urged me to stop looking for miracle cures and start taking care of myself. He told me that the human body has regenerating powers greater than anything the medical world can offer. His prescription for getting my body back to health started with diet—low fats, no sugar, no alcohol, no tobacco, no refined food products of any kind, and no red meat. It seemed to me like a severe sacrifice, but I was desperate enough to try anything.

I followed the doctor's recommendations to the letter, and though I was skeptical in the beginning my body definitely began to respond. By simply purifying my diet, my back began to show the first signs of improvement. For the first time in years I allowed myself to daydream about being active in sports again.

Running was out of the question, and that eliminated most types of sports. I needed something gentle, an activity that wouldn't put any stress on my back. When a friend suggested a bicycle, I knew that was it!

I started riding one or two miles a day. The more I rode the better I felt. And the better I felt the more I wanted to ride. Soon I was riding 10 and 20 miles at a stretch. My back relaxed and the painful muscle spasms that had once kept me a slave to my injuries began to subside. And along with my physical improvements I noticed that my attitude was picking up as well. Until that time I'd never realized how much the two were intertwined.

As I started losing weight, my self-esteem soared. My body, that miraculous self-regenerating machine, was again becoming a source of pleasure to me. Though the pain persisted—and persists even to this day—I found I could deal with it because I felt good about my life.

As the months passed, bicycling became a way of life for me. And eventually my love for the sport motivated me to do something special. I set the biggest goal I'd ever set in my life—to pedal from Los Angeles to New York City, a distance of nearly 3,000 miles. This challenge has been compared to running 43 consecutive marathons or swimming the English Channel 18 times in a row. This would be my tribute to the bike, to which I owed so much.

Looking through the *Guinness Book of World Records* one day I discovered that the official record for the transcontinental ride was 13 days 5 hours and 20 minutes. That was an average of well over 200 miles a day. I really didn't know how I was going to pull this off, but I was determined to break that record. I trained for 2½ years, one step at a time. During that time I learned that I could become an increasingly better and more efficient rider, and still have fun in the process. There was always something to keep me interested: constantly changing terrain, developing different riding techniques, making small changes on the bicycle itself that improved it and even made it more personal to me.

Finally, I was ready for the challenge. I set my date of departure: August 13, 1978.

At 4:50 A.M. on the morning of the big day, I left Santa Monica City Hall on my bike, and began the most challenging experience I'd ever confronted.

The miles rolled by. My performance was proving to be even better than I had expected. My body and mind worked together in perfect harmony—my mind nudging me on when my body grew tired, my body nudging me on when my mind grew tired.

I have to confess, the journey was much tougher than I had ever imagined. But on August 28, I arrived at City Hall in New York City with a new world's record to my credit. My riding time: 13 days 1 hour and 20 minutes.

The next year I tried to break my own record. I was in for a whole new set of experiences. Mother Nature beat me up. It rained—not just a gentle shower but a downpour!—for the last six days of the ride. I sloshed through flash floods, suffered through pelting hail and fought wind storms that under other circumstances would have sent me indoors. Sixty miles short of New York I stopped the ride when I ran out of time. Finishing the ride would have been an empty formality.

My failure to break my own record was a disappointment but also a challenge to try again the following year.

On June 16, 1980, I again left Santa Monica City Hall on my third challenge of the record. Twelve days 3 hours and 41 minutes later, I arrived in New York, having broken my record by nearly a full day.

Sometime during this third ride I got the idea for writing a book. I wanted to share my enthusiasm with others, encourage them to discover in bicycling some of the rewards and pleasures this sport has given me. At first I thought of writing about my own experiences. But then I realized that wasn't enough. Instead, I decided to do a complete, step-by-step guidebook to help every rider or potential rider get off to the right start or improve his or her performance. This book is no longer a dream. Like my cross-country challenge, it is a reality. These pages contain a broad program for improving every aspect of your physical and mental well-being as you embark on the exciting adventure of bicycling.

I'm neither a professional writer nor a trained professional in the field of health. I'm a bicyclist who knows what cycling has done for my body and mind. To communicate what I've learned, two experts joined me in making this book possible.

First, Dr. Lawrence May, a specialist in preventive medicine, joined the team. After my first ride, Larry conducted medical tests on me as part of a research project at the University of California, testing out his hypothesis that I must have special physical attributes, greater than the average person's, that allowed me to do what I've done. But after exhaustive tests on me, his hypothesis had to be scrapped. Physiologically I tested out average. There was nothing superhuman about me at all.

The results of his tests on me gave Larry impetus to seek out a different explanation for my accomplishments. His conclusion, based on a traditional medical approach, was that my success resulted simply from my lifestyle—a daily program that integrated exercise, diet, and positive mental attitudes. In other words, my accomplishments were within everyone's reach. Anyone could do what I have done if they only applied themselves.

Hal Bennett, a widely published writer of health-oriented books, is the second contributor. An avid cyclist himself, Hal had the demanding task of weaving it all together in words that cover not only the basic nuts and bolts information, but also the thrill and pleasure bicycling can bring into your life.

Finally, as you read on you'll meet—through their own stories—a larger community of cyclists, friends of mine, Larry's, and Hal's, who contributed their bicycling experiences and wisdom to this book. I owe a special debt of gratitude to all of these people. Their generous sharing helped to enrich and enliven these pages.

JOHN MARINO'S Bicycling BOOK

ONE

THE BICYCLE—A HUMAN-POWERED DREAM COME TRUE

The ranks of bicyclists in America are expanding in unprecedented numbers. According to the Department of Transportation, 105 million bicycle enthusiasts are riding the road today. That number has tripled over the last 20 years. Ten million new bikes were sold in the United States last year alone. That means that for the first time since World War I there are actually more bicycles than automobiles in this country. Half a million people are now using their two-wheeled, muscle-powered vehicles for commuting to their jobs each day. And, for pure recreation, government surveys rank bicycling second only to walking as the most popular activity in the world.

What has fueled this new passion for pedal power? Certainly the high cost of gas and a desire for physical fitness head the list. For many of us, however, beneath the practical concerns lies an old and enduring romance dating back to childhood. No doubt a bicycle was your first major possession—unlike anything you'd ever owned before. It fulfilled a wide range of fantasies. It could be a motorcycle zipping over a race course, a horse galloping across an open plain in pursuit of bandits, or even an airplane buzzing imaginary rooftops.

Mastering the awesome two-wheeler brought with it your first taste of youthful freedom. Suddenly you could ride to a friend's house half a mile away or race off to a park twice that distance from home. In moving around in the world without your parents for the first time, you experienced a new sense of control over your life. You learned how to take care of yourself in traffic. And you learned, perhaps through the bitter experience of loss, that personal property requires responsibility and protection.

Maybe these childhood attachments to our bicycles are what draw us back to them now. Perhaps it is true that the wind rushing past as we sail along on two wheels, under our own power, reawakens something rare and wonderful in all of us. Once again we savor the freedom, independence, and self-reliance we first discovered as children.

But beyond the bicycle's romantic, even nostalgic, attraction we find a down-to-earth practicality of equal appeal. Through the years bicycle power has been used to generate electricity, run sewing machines, plow fields, pump water, transport agricultural goods to market, saw wood . . . the list goes on and on. For the individual, the bicycle can simultaneously fulfill needs for recreation, physical fitness, and inexpensive transportation. No other activity can make such a claim. On a bicycle, even the most mundane errand can turn into pleasure as you pedal through the neighborhood or countryside without metal and windshield inhibiting your direct experience of the environment. And the distance you can travel by bike is almost without limit. You can ride off to the neighborhood grocery store for a loaf of bread or a bottle of wine, or, like me, capture the world's record for riding across the continent.

CYCLING FOR THE BODY, MIND, AND SPIRIT

For getting in shape and keeping fit, bicycling has the unique advantage of providing a thorough physical workout while still being gentle to your body. For this reason, bicycling is often the preferred sport for people with spine or joint problems. Moreover, with a bicycle you can get in your exercise without having to recruit a partner, assemble a team, reserve a court, or join a club.

Like other vigorous activities, a regular cycling program can bring about dramatic changes in your physical and mental well-being. Sharon Weber, a schoolteacher in Michigan, spends her summers bicycle touring. When the weather permits, she commutes five miles each way from home to her classroom. In spite of being a self-confessed foodaholic, she now manages to stay trim and fit. "Diets," she said, "never worked for me. I enjoy eating good food, and dieting was always a major deprivation. After a couple of days of counting calories, I would begin to get depressed and then give up." Bicycling allows Sharon to have her cake and eat it too, burning away the traces of her gourmet delights at the average rate of 16 calories per minute—or nearly a thousand per hour—while feasting on the pleasures of the great out-of-doors.

Shedding extra pounds and firming up flabby tissue are only part of the story of why bicycling can be so beneficial to your health. The internal changes are no less significant than the external, cosmetic ones. Over a period of time, a regular cycling program can increase the capacity of your lungs by as much as 20 percent. At the same time, your heart can become healthier and stronger because you'll grow vast new networks of capillaries to carry nutrients to the heart muscle itself. As your heart muscle improves in this way, the rate at which it will need to pump in order to perform a particular task will decrease.

Commenting about the training of competitive cyclists in *Bicycling* magazine, William Sanders observes that the healthier heart "can thump along in the 50s and 60s [beats per minute] at rest, and this means it doesn't wear out as fast as a heart that runs 80 or 90 all the time." In a report to the American Heart Association, Ralph S. Paffenburger, M.D., of the Stanford University School of Medicine, states that if people can burn up to 2,000 calories per week (about two hours of bike riding, depending on speed and terrain) they can reduce their risk of heart attack by 64 percent.

Many doctors today regard bicycling not only as a valuable means of building health and preventing disease, but also as an excellent means of rehabilitation. Bicycling is recommended for insomnia, hypertension, indigestion, anxiety, and even for recuperation from major heart attacks. Writing in the prestigious *L.A.W. Bulletin* about techniques doctors might apply to help survivors of myocardial infarction, Dr. Robert E. Bond relates his medical knowledge to his own personal experience: "Five years have elapsed since I suffered a heart attack . . . . Since that tin   I have ridden many miles in many states and several countries over widely varied terrain. I enjoy every mile and I look forward to every weekend."

Similarly, a cardiac patient by the name of Lee Walton, after two years of training at the Cardiac Rehabilitation Unit of Rancho Los Amigos Hospital in Downey, California, rode a "triple century" (300 miles) in 22 hours. His average speed was just under 14 miles per hour. Like others who have become extraordinary cyclists after suffering severe heart attacks, Lee is a member of the Specialized Coronary Outpatient Rehabilitation (SCOR) Cardiac Cyclists Club of Los Angeles.

Staying physically active greatly enhances your enjoyment of health in your later years. That bicycle riding—or anything else—increases longevity is impossible to prove scientifically. But looking at the number of cyclists who are still going strong, touring and even racing after passing their seventh decade, I am convinced that there's something to it. Writing in *Bicycling* Magazine, Dr. David L. Smith states: "Active exercising people are granted the benefit of an active old age. For most, active exercise like cycling will lead to a longer life span, and the extra years will be vigorous ones. There are many cyclists in their 70s, still vigorous and capable of long miles every day. Ed Delano and Clifford Graves (who are both in their 70s) are still riding centuries [100 miles in a day]."

Medical scientists measure growth through physical exercise in terms of increased numbers of red blood cells, greater lung capacity, a lower at-rest heart rate, and healthier tissue throughout your body. You will measure your growth in terms of a slimmer figure, better sleeping habits, greater resistance to disease, and more energy in everything you do—and also in terms of feelings of accomplishment and heightened self-esteem and a growing sense of inner serenity with which to face life's tensions and trials.

Not too much is known scientifically about the impact of exercise on the mind. Yet more often than not it is the initially hidden mental rewards that turn the average, everyday person into an avid cyclist. Margaret Marple, a West Coast book editor, wouldn't dream of facing the daily barrage of demands and pressures without her morning "hit." "Twenty minutes of pedaling along the palisades with my dog Henry running beside me usually sets me up for the day, giving me extra energy and a peace of mind that no tranquilizer could ever provide. Then, if things really get to me and I blow my cool, I just take another ride after work so that I can have a serene and productive evening."

Writing in *Psychology Today*, Dr. A. H. Ismail of Purdue University discusses his study of a group of middle-aged administrators and college professors. He found that after 20 minutes of exercise their blood levels of glucose, testosterone, and catecholamines—substances associated with aggression, depression, and anxiety—were radically changed. After only ten weeks of regular exercise, Dr. Ismail reports, "They become more open and extroverted. And their whole demeanor seemed more stable and self-confident." In a related field of inquiry, Dr. John H. Geist directed a project to compare physical exercise and psychotherapy as treatments for moderately depressed people. As reported in *Behavioral Medicine*, he was able to show that the exercise program was considerably more effective than psychotherapy. People in the exercise program developed new confidence in themselves. Having accomplished physical feats they never thought possible, they felt capable of taking fuller control of their lives in general.

These are just a few of the reasons why ten million people in the United States bought new bikes last year.

TOURING THE WORLD ON TWO WHEELS

For sheer romance, there is nothing to compare with bicycle touring. Imagine a summer of bicycling through France—wheeling through the countryside, a cool breeze on your face. Today you visit a vineyard near Lyon. Next week you'll be sleeping beneath a down comforter in a 17th-century inn at Bourg-en-Brasse, and a few days later you'll enjoy a folk festival in Dijon. No matter where you go, bike touring makes the experience seem richer, clearer, and more personal than any other mode of travel. Writing in *Quest* magazine, the novelist John A. Gould describes his bicycle touring experiences: "While pedaling I am so close to the land that I not only see but smell, hear, and touch it; I become a part of it—strong, patient, enduring."

Family touring is growing in popularity too. In 1977, Steve and Lena Johnson, who work as computer programmers in Berkeley, California, rented out their home, took leaves from their jobs, and struck out for Baja California on their bikes. Traveling with them was their two-year-old son, Tigran, who enjoyed the tour from a lightweight trailer attached to his father's bike. The family spent an adventurous year touring Baja. Now back at their jobs, they commute to work every day on their bikes. They have never owned a car—though they do own two houses—and have no plans to acquire one.

COMMUTING BY BIKE

Bicycles are ideal commuting machines. Energy-efficient, they burn between 12 and 20 calories per minute, keeping the cyclist lean and healthy and the environment clean and fresh. But aren't there limits to how far you can commute by bike? Jim Pervis doesn't think so. He is an attorney with offices in San Francisco. Each day he commutes by bike from his home in Stinson Beach, 35 miles away. Each morning and each evening he pedals over Mount Tamalpais, where he confronts elevations of 1,500 feet. Spending his days in the tense atmosphere of the courtroom, he looks forward to his bike ride home, claiming that it's the only thing keeping him sane and healthy.

And what about the weather? Unless you're willing to wear bulky raingear to protect you from the rain and heavy coats to protect you from the cold, biking is certainly limited to dry, relatively warm days. But a new generation of bikes called recumbents, with lightweight, aerodynamic fairings covering the rider and machinery, are making their way onto the scene. An article in the *New York Times Magazine* describes the owner of one such machine commuting daily from his Scarsdale apartment to his office in downtown Manhattan, whizzing past stalled cars on the Bronx River Parkway at speeds up to 35 miles per hour—all made possible by the aerodynamic shell, which also protects the rider from the rain.

RACING FOR GLORY

The mushrooming popularity of the bicycle has had a stimulating effect on cycle racing in the United States and Canada. This includes road racing, track racing, and world-record challenges like mine. In 1969 Audrey McElmury returned from Czechoslovakia with America's first gold medal for world-class bicycle racing in 57 years, and, in 1976, the California-born George Mount came within seconds of bringing a gold medal from the Olympics. Today there is hardly a city in the United States and Canada that doesn't have at least one cycle-racing club with aspirants to world records among its membership.

In Europe, bicycle racing causes as much public excitement as baseball in the United States. Each year France hosts the famous Tour de France, a race that lasts 22 days and follows a grueling course up sheer elevations through the Alps and Pyrenees, as well as through scenic rural villages and city streets. The most famous of all bicycle races, it draws athletes from all over the world.

Every country in Europe has its own version of the Tour de France. In recent years Canada and the United States not only have sent athletes to these events, but also have begun sponsoring races that are drawing world-class cyclists to our shores.

The stories of cycle racers like the Belgian Eddy Merckx are legend. At the peak of his racing career Merckx won nearly every major event in Europe, including five titles to the Tour de France. And, with earnings of more than $500,000, he was the highest paid athlete in European history.

Beryl Burton, who in 1967 was named Britain's "Sportswoman of the Year," holds several world records, many of them won in competition against world-class male cyclists. Her daughter, Denise Burton, is also one of Britain's top women cyclists, winning a bronze medal in the 1975 World Pursuit Championship in Belgium.

Whereas Europe continues to dominate the world in organized bicycle competition, cyclists in the United States excel in advancing the technology of the bicycle. Most of this activity is centered on breaking world speed records.

Although most bicyclists ride at an average speed of 10 to 12 miles per hour, the world record is 138.7. This record, held by Allen Abbott, was accomplished on the Bonneville Salt Flats, using a race car to break the wind. The speed record for bikes not assisted by another vehicle is 62.93 miles per hour, accomplished with an aerodynamic bike designed by Al Voight, a California aerospace scientist. In a race on conventional bikes, a well-conditioned athlete will average from 20 to 34 miles per hour, depending on the distance and time of the race.

Many athletes active in other sports consider bicycling an essential part of their training. Ray Cortez, the supervisor of a Richmond (California) chemical plant, took up cycling so that during the summer he could stay in shape for downhill skiing. Bicycling is particularly useful for skiers, building up muscles needed for winter sports, increasing general endurance, and developing balance techniques compatible with both activities. Sandy Beebe, an airline pilot living in Idaho, finds that bicycling enhances running, skiing, and tennis. He enjoys them all and participates with equal vigor in each.

Bicycle riding has always been an integral part of training programs for Olympic skating teams. Indeed, it has not been unusual for skating champions like Eric Heiden and Sheila Young to make excellent showings in both sports. Jim Ochowicz, team leader with the National Speed Skating team in 1980, states that 90 percent of our national speed-skating team use bikes for training.

PEDALING TOWARD SOCIAL CHANGE

The growing popularity of the bike is reflected in social, political, and economic changes. For example, increasing numbers of states are allocating funds for bicycle paths. Resort communities such as Palm Springs and Nantucket draw people from all walks of life, using full-color travel brochures that invite tourists to enjoy their miles of scenic bike paths.

In California, the city of Davis has taken to the bicycle in force. Located on flat terrain, with warm weather the year around, this town is characterized by a dependence on the bike that goes way back. Throughout the 1950s and '60s bicycles actually outnumbered residents. It became a custom in Davis, a college town, that when students left town, they left their bikes behind for the use of their friends. Bikes that weren't locked or licensed were considered community property. If you needed to get somewhere fast you simply looked around for one of these bikes, jumped on and raced off, leaving it at your destination for the next person who might need it. Today, however, bicycles are closely regulated in Davis, and the town has carefully developed a master plan for its bike paths.

In Eugene, Oregon, where rain, snow, and freezing weather would seem likely to deter bicycling, 40,000 pedalers equipped with raingear and cold-weather clothing use the town's excellent bike paths year-round. Bicycles are encouraged through excellent planning by the Eugene Bicycle Committee. The development of Eugene's exemplary bike-path system owes much of its success to Ruth Bascom, who dedicated many years to carefully educating the city council and the public to the advantages of bike paths and bicycle parking facilities. Today, even Eugene's city manager rides his bike to work.

If other communities followed the lead of towns like Eugene, Davis, Nantucket, and Palm Springs, the energy savings could be enormous. The U.S. Department of Transportation estimates that if people living less than ten miles from their jobs would commute by bike three times a week, we would save between 16 and 23 million barrels of oil each year.

Consider the wide range of contemporary problems that can be alleviated by use of the bike: crowded streets, limited parking, the skyrocketing cost of fossil fuels, the rumble and roar of big-city traffic, the escalating costs of repairing and insuring automobiles, the pollution of our air. For some things cars and trucks will always be needed, but I predict that in the years ahead a large proportion of our transportation needs will be met by the bike.

Can there be any doubt that our national love affair with the automobile is fading? I think not. But on the heels of that old love for the car is a new romance—with the bike. Far less expensive to purchase, simpler and cheaper to maintain and repair, and certainly far better for our health, the bicycle has won our hearts by serving our practical needs while also fulfilling our dreams.

A FREEWHEELING HISTORY OF THE BICYCLE

oday's bicycle—the vehicle with which a physically conditioned but otherwise normal person can travel 300 miles in a single day—is a masterpiece of technological innovation. In their exhaustive engineering studies comparing the energy-effectiveness of the bicycle to other means of locomotion, David Gordon Wilson and Frank Rowland White concluded that in its present form the bike is more efficient than walking. Even with the extra weight of the machinery, the rider uses 30 percent less energy to propel body and machine forward than to walk the same distance.

This efficiency has been developed in response to the needs of bicycling enthusiasts over the course of more than a century. In the year 1900, bicyclists numbered half a million in Europe and 150,000 in the United States, as people rushed to embrace the vehicle that provided the very first means of private transportation to the broad public. Over the decades, this enormous market appeal has continually fueled the eager minds of manufacturers with ways of refining and improving their products. Generations of bicycle engineers have labored over the key issues of bike design: pedaling efficiency, bicycle weight, rolling resistance, and wind resistance, resulting in technical innovations that might confound the unsuspecting novice venturing into a bike store. The following telescopic look at how the bicycle evolved into its present form—and where it's going in the future—will reveal the purpose and logic of its design with an eye toward aiding you in sorting out the seemingly limitless choices that will tempt you in purchasing a bike.

IT BEGAN AS A WHEELED BEAST

Historians are not certain when the first bike was invented, but rough sketches by Leonardo da Vinci put it in the 15th century. We do know that the popularization of the bicycle began in 1790, when a Frenchman, M. de Sivrac, appeared in the gardens of the Palais Royal riding a contraption with two wheels mounted on a wooden frame shaped to resemble a horse (see Fig. 2–1). The *vélocifère*, as it was called, couldn't be steered around corners, and it had no pedals. The operator pushed it along with his feet in much the manner of a child pushing a scooter. Etchings from this period depict grown men dressed in top hats and tails, straddling ridiculous-looking vélocifères that sported the heads of horses or lions.

By removing the ornamental animal heads and making other improvements, the machines became lighter in weight, more graceful in appearance, and *steerable*. In 1819 a riding school for the improved vélocifère opened in London. It was called "Denis Johnson's Riding School," and it catered exclusively to "well-bred young men."

In 1860, a Scotsman by the name of Kirkpatrick Macmillan constructed a beautiful and functional machine that was a prophecy of things to come. Built of wood and iron, it was "pedaled" by an ingenious leverage system attached to cranks on the rear wheel. It had a front wheel that could be steered, a brake system operated from the handlebars, a sprung seat to absorb road shock, and even a fender to protect the rider from dirt thrown up by the rear wheel. Thereafter, bicycle technology progressed by leaps and bounds.

By about 1865, bicycling had become a craze that affected France, the United States, and England. The railroads had replaced stagecoach travel between most large cities, and its influence undoubtedly spurred an active interest in developing other mechanical means of travel.

One cyclists' magazine, *The Velocipedist*, published in New York, ran the following editorial in 1869: "The two-wheeled velocipede is the animal which is to supersede everything else. It costs but little to produce, and still

Fig. 2-1   The bicycle's early ancestor, the vélocifère, circa 1800.

less to keep. It does not eat cartloads of hay, and does not wax fat and kick. It is easy to handle. It never rears up. It won't bite. It needs no check of rein or halter, or any unnatural restraint. It is little and light, let alone it will lean lovingly against the nearest support."

The average person living in Europe at that time couldn't afford a horse. Getting out of town for a weekend jaunt in the country, or just getting away for the afternoon, was expensive. The bicycle changed all that. People who couldn't afford to buy and maintain horses could afford bikes. The purchase of a bike offered the adventure and romance of travel to whole classes of people who had never previously ventured past the city limits.

Diaries of this period tell of people traveling distances of 50 or more miles on their bikes. Bikes were not just playthings for the wealthy classes any more. They were the world's first personal vehicles, carrying single riders at distances and speeds that would compete with the horse.

One problem faced by early bicyclists was the condition of the roads, which were rough and full of potholes and ruts that made passage on small-wheeled bikes difficult because the smaller wheel would drop down into the holes. The most important technical advance, therefore, was the large, high-wheeled bicycle, then called the "Ordinary." (See Fig. 2–2.) The large front wheel made high speeds over rough roads possible for the first time, since it simply rode over the potholes.

Fig. 2-2 *The high-wheeled "Ordinary" enabled riders to travel at high speeds over rough terrain.*

Although the high-wheeled Ordinary carried the sport of bicycling a giant step forward, it was not without its drawbacks. With the rider seated near the top of the wheel, his head seven feet above the ground, the machine was not very stable. If the rider ran into an immovable object, or his wheel dropped into an especially large pothole in the road, he was instantly launched over the handlebars into the ditch.

FROM THE SAFETY BICYCLE TO THE TEN-SPEED

As the 1890s approached, inventors put their efforts into developing what came to be called the "safety bicycle." Bike design as we know it today—that is, with two wheels of equal size, pedals driving the rear wheel through a system of chain and sprockets—made its appearance in 1884. The "Rover" (Fig. 2–3), produced in England in 1886, looks very much like today's bikes. And with the advent of these bikes, recreational rides of 50 miles and more became commonplace.

Early bicycle wheels were equipped with hard rubber tires, which transferred road vibration directly to the rider's poor derrière. In 1888, a Scotsman by the name of John Boyd Dunlop invented and patented a pneumatic tire that absorbed road vibration and bumps like magic. By 1892 every bicycle produced was equipped with this new invention.

Although dominated by men, the sport of bicycling had many female enthusiasts, which made an impact on bicycle design. Drawings of cyclists depict women riding bikes as far back as the 1830s. Illustrated history books

Fig. 2-3   The Rover was a variety of "safety bicycle," which heralded the beginning of modern bicycle design.

show pictures of bicycles designed specifically to accommodate women's long skirts. An engraving published in *Le Monde Illustré* in 1868 shows a race at Bordeaux, with four modestly dressed women racing bikes on a dirt track. (See Fig. 2–4.) A huge crowd of men and women applauds and salutes the riders as they race by in perfect form. In 1890, a Frenchwoman by the name of Mlle. Dutrieux gained professional status as a racer for the Simpson Lever Chain Company, competing against men in international racing events.

Around the turn of the century, Sturmey-Archer of England developed the multiple-speed rear hub. Whereas the high-wheeled Ordinary and other bike designs of the period limited the rider to a single gear ratio and pedaling speed, the first multiple-speed hub enabled the cyclist to select three different ratios with a flick of the tiny lever on the handlebars. The bicycle's capacity for touring long distances over hilly terrain was greatly extended, and higher speeds on a bicycle were made possible.

Soon after Sturmey-Archer's invention became popular in the 30s, the derailleur system of shifting gears appeared on bicycles in France and Italy. This was an adaptation of a ratio-varying technique utilized for decades in mill machinery and other devices driven by chains and cogs. Whereas the early Sturmey-Archer hubs were limited to three speeds, the first derailleurs provided five and eventually ten speeds. Because the early derailleurs were expensive and extremely difficult to operate, they were originally used only

Fig. 2-4   Even before the turn of the century, women athletes enthusiastically embraced the challenge of bicycle racing.

by racers. It wasn't until the late 50s that the mechanism had been refined to the point where it began to appear on European touring bikes. It was left to Japanese manufacturers in the 60s to bring the cost down and make the ten-speed available to the general user.

Although bicycles were kept amazingly light in weight (from 30 to 50 pounds) after the appearance of the safety bike, the frames tended to be soft—that is, springy and flexible. Soft, flexible frames provided riding comfort, but they also wasted the rider's energy. In bearing down on the pedals, the cyclist's efforts were absorbed by the frame instead of being transferred cleanly to the rear wheel. The science of metallurgy, with the development of lightweight, extremely strong alloys, made it possible to produce highly efficient frames that were also comfortable for riding long distances. The new, high-quality metals, used only in the frame, increased the efficiency of the average bike as much as 15 percent.

With the bicycle craze sweeping the United States and Europe, hundreds of manufacturers began vying for the market, and competition became fierce. Manufacturers began sponsoring bicycle races to bring their names and their products to public attention.

Mechanics and designers worked on new technological refinements that might give their bicycles even the smallest edge on the racetrack. Some of the innovations to grow out of the race circuit have made a substantial difference in the efficiency of the modern bike.

Lightweight wheels. Engineers discovered that the lighter the wheel, the faster and more responsive the bike. In fact, reducing the weight of the wheels by ten pounds produces the same effect as reducing the frame by 20 pounds. It simply takes less energy to overcome the inertia of a light wheel than to overcome the inertia of a heavy one.

Low-resistance tires. In addition to weight, the resistance of the tires as they move over the ground has a profound effect on bicycle performance. The invention of "sewup" tires, with the tire casing sewn around the tube and then glued to the wheel, made it possible to produce tires that weighed only ounces, and were capable of pressures up to 130 pounds per square inch. The harder tire translates into less rolling resistance—and more of the rider's energy going into the production of forward motion.

Toe clips. Whereas the crankarms of a bicycle go around a full 360 degrees, the rider's legs on bare pedals work only on the downstroke, for 180 degrees. However, the invention of toe clips has made it possible for the rider to lift as well as push on the pedals, producing power throughout the full 360 degrees of the crankarm's motion; this is estimated to give the cyclist as much as a 20-percent advantage.

Handlebar design. The first bicycle makers positioned the handlebars at approximately waist level, following the traditional horseback-riding position. In this upright riding position, the rider's body presented a major source of wind resistance. Having observed this, bicycle racers boosted their perform-ance by bending their handlebars so they could ride in a crouched position to reduce wind drag. The new riding position accomplished two important things: first, it reduced wind resistance by 30 percent; and second, it allowed the rider to exert more pressure on the pedals, since he or she could pull up with the hands to bring more power to the legs. The back, shoulder, torso, and arm muscles, previously passive in cycling, could now be brought into play.

Miscellaneous refinements. Sprockets designed with teeth that minimize friction against the chain; lightweight, smooth-running chains; low-friction bearings in all moving parts; quick-release hubs for fast tire changes; and aluminum alloys used in the production of components—all have grown out of the pressure of bicycling competition. Thanks to these design innovations, even the casual rider can enjoy the pleasure of a responsive machine that pulls efficiently uphill, shifts smoothly from one gear to the next, and delivers the rider invigorated, rather than drained, to distant destinations.

THE NEXT GENERATION

Considering the numerous engineering advances that have contributed to the development of the bike, one cannot help but wonder how much further its refinement can go. Has the bicycle evolved to the upper limits of its potential? The evidence is very clear that it has not. Metallurgists continue to develop lighter and stronger alloys, with properties that promise even more efficient bike frames. Engineers continue to refine sealed bearings for all moving parts, making the bicycle as maintenance-free as anything mechanical can possibly be. And aerodynamics engineers are designing fairings to cut the bicycle's wind drag as much as 50 percent.

The newest frontier of bicycle design is, in fact, centered around the issue of wind resistance. Working together with Fred Wilkie, a Berkeley (Cal-ifornia) bicycle builder, engineer David Gordon Wilson discovered that by redesigning the bicycle frame so that the rider's body is set in a reclining, or recumbent, position (feet stretched out in front to pedal), wind resistance can be reduced by about 20 percent. The recumbent rider sits on a small padded platform much like a lawn chair with a backrest. (See Fig. 2–5.) This position not only provides far greater comfort than the conventional narrow cycling seat, but also enables the rider to deliver more power to the pedals. Instead of counteracting the force exerted on the pedals by pulling on the handlebars or standing up off the seat, as one does on a conventional bike, the recumbent rider simply pushes back into the seat. The result is less backstrain, less fatigue, and greater pedaling efficiency. Furthermore, in the recumbent position more of the cyclist's lung capacity is in use than in the crouched riding position of the conventional ten-speed.

Fig. 2-5   The Avatar is one of the first production recumbents available to the public. (Photo courtesy of Bicycling *magazine.)*

Tests by experienced cyclists indicate that the rider must learn a slightly new set of responses to master the recumbent, but this adjustment period is relatively short and requires no instruction. Reflecting on this in *Bicycling* magazine, John Schubert comments: "After a week or two, I was hooked; I would scorn other bikes in the house to take the Avatar [a recumbent] to the corner store. I found it at least as easy to ride and stable as a conventional bike, and it was much more comfortable. I had no qualms about cruising in traffic with the Sunday *New York Times* under one arm."

Although recumbents are available through specialized outlets, they have not yet made the breakthrough into the general market. In the opinion of David Wilson, this is because of industry conservatism and antagonism to the design among racers.

From the vélocifère to the recumbent, the horizons of pedal power continue to widen spectacularly. The significance of these developments is not limited to racers whose needs can be satisfied only by the state-of-the-art machine. In fact, even the simplest models have benefited enormously from the ingenuity that has gone into advancing bicycle efficiency. And, as the technology progresses, today's state-of-the-art machine can easily become tomorrow's basic model.

Now let's take a look at what is available today.

THREE

THE ADVENTURE OF BUYING YOUR FIRST BIKE

Shopping for a new bike sparks the excitement of even the most seasoned cyclist. Each year, subtle new technological and stylistic refinements attract the discerning cyclist's attention. One year you'll see improved frame designs; the next it will be lighter-weight, smoother-operating components such as derailleurs or cranksets; and in another year you'll find more attractive colors or bold aesthetic innovations. Because of all that's available today, shopping for a bike can be as bewildering as it is exciting. Whether you are looking for a kid's bike, a good, old, reliable one- or three-speed utility bike for running errands, a nostalgic cruiser, a stylish ten-speed, or even a custom-built bike, this chapter is intended to guide you through the maze of choices so that you come out the other side with the bike that best suits your needs. *

Even if you can afford the best and most expensive machine available, it is useful to approach the choice of your first bike as you'd approach the selection of a tool for your trade or profession. The fact that a bike costs $1,000, for example, does not mean that it will suit the job you want it to do. If you want a bike to pick up groceries at the neighborhood supermarket, six blocks away, a $150 bike with wire carrying baskets will do a much better job than an ultra-light ten-speed set up for racing. †

---

*Further information on commuting bikes, touring bikes, and racers will be found in the later chapters dealing with those subjects.

†Any prices quoted here and throughout reflect market values at the time of this writing. They are necessarily approximate and subject to change.

If you're a bicycle tourist, you can easily spend $1,200 for a state-of-the-art touring bike from a company like Singer of France or Jack Taylor of England. The $1,200 bike will, of course, be more comfortable to ride and will make better use of your energy than a bike costing $250. But the differences can be subtle, and for many people those differences just aren't worth the financial sacrifice. Countless tourists have logged thousands of carefree miles on bikes costing from $250 to $350. Indeed, in the chapter on touring we tell about one cyclist who rode around the world on such a bike.

Weigh your needs carefully before you set out to buy your first bike. Don't buy more bike than you need, and don't buy less. Let's consider some examples.

Patty Harrison lives four miles away from the bookstore in which she works. There is only one small hill between her job and home. Wanting to use her car less and get more exercise, she bought a ten-speed bike. After trying it out for two weeks she stopped riding, explaining to a friend that she was just never comfortable with all the gears. The friend offered to trade her one-speed utility bike for Patty's ten-speed. Patty made the trade and has been riding regularly ever since.

At the opposite end of the scale are those who buy too little bike, perhaps heavy three-speed machines they expect to ride ten or fifteen miles the first day. The bike turns out to be too heavy, too hard to pedal, and downright uncomfortable. Not understanding all the reasons for these problems, the new biker becomes discouraged.

Margaret Greers lives in a small town in Minnesota and wanted a bike for weekend jaunts to a recreational area 25 miles from her home. She had been riding an old one-speed bike to her job, which is a mile from her apartment, and had also been using it for shopping. Her fondness for hiking kept her in reasonably good physical condition. She bought a heavy three-speed bike to ride on weekends to the state park, but her first trip turned out to be a sad disappointment. She arrived at her destination exhausted and had to beg a ride home from a friend.

Several weeks later she had the opportunity to borrow a friend's ten-speed, on which she made the same journey. This time her trip to the country was a real pleasure, thanks to lower gearing and a bike that weighed nearly ten pounds less than the three-speed she'd purchased. She sold her three-speed bike for fifteen dollars less than she'd paid for it and bought a ten-speed that better suited her needs.

Experimenting with various bikes can help you find exactly what you want. Borrowed or even rented bikes can fill the bill, and some bike shops will let you try out different models.

If you do buy a bike that turns out to be unsuitable for your needs, don't give up and leave it parked in your garage. Sell it to someone who will use it, and get a bike that is right for you. If this seems uneconomical, consider the relative economics of owning a piece of machinery you never use. Remember, bikes have low depreciation (better bikes even increase in value from year to year), and you can usually sell a used bike in good condition for no more than a 10- to 15-percent loss within the first year after your purchase.

Secondly, look for names associated with the bicycle world: Raleigh, Peugeot, Gitane, Motobecane, Schwinn, Fuji, Dawes, Windsor, Univega, C.C.M., and Nishiki, to name a few. Most bicycles will need minor repairs from time to time. If you get a *name* bike, you can be assured of service at a reputable bike shop.

Before buying a bike, make absolutely certain that the vendor has a full-time service department devoted *only* to bicycle adjustments and repairs. The shop mechanic will, after all, be setting up and adjusting your bike. His or her skill can mean the difference between annoyance and delight with your first bike. Bike adjustments can be very subtle, and rider comfort, ease of operation, and reliability all depend on the assembly and adjustment being done properly. When we questioned the management of a national department store chain, whose local outlet claimed to have a service department for their bikes, we found that the "service department" was in fact one high-school boy who came in twice a week to assemble bicycles ordered by customers.

KIDS' BIKES: START YOUR CHILD OUT WITH A QUALITY MACHINE

As the first major possession in most children's lives, the bicycle makes a big impression. A good machine allows its owner to experience pride and joy, while the owner of a poor-quality machine may experience frustration and disappointment. Too often, the child makes the mistake of believing that it is his or her own inadequacy, rather than a failure of the bike, that makes the machine hard to operate. Moreover, it is important for a child to learn that things can be fixed. Doing without the bike while it's in the repair shop may be difficult, but getting it back "as good as new" is a real pleasure. Good-quality bikes can be repaired by mechanically minded youngsters. A poor-quality machine may not be repairable, leaving the budding child mechanic with the wrong impression about his or her ability to learn new skills.

Bicycles for children come in such a wide variety of shapes and sizes that it's almost impossible to do justice to the whole range. You can buy a bike with 12-inch tires and training wheels for a five-year-old. You can buy a Stingray-style bike, with 20-inch wheels and a "banana" seat, for kids slightly older. You can buy three-speed, five-speed, or ten-speed bikes of the lightweight European type or the balloon-tired "Cruiser" style.

As with adult bikes, try to match the bike to the rider's needs. Where kids are concerned, those needs may be dictated as much by peer pressure as utility. By far the most popular children's bike is the "bicycle motocross" (BMX) style, which has an interesting history. (See Fig. 3–1.)

In the early 1960s, children in the 10-to-15-year-old age group began

Fig. 3-1   With BMX bicycles, children imitate their motorcycle motocross heroes. Buy it readymade or build it up from separately purchased components.

stripping down their 20-inch Stingray-type bikes and using them to ride dirt trails, imitating motorcycle motocross stars. This fad, created by the kids, grew until today it is a highly organized and carefully regulated sport comparable to Little League baseball.* Point standings and safety supervision of BMX races are provided by groups such as the National Bicycle League, the National Bicycle Association, and the American Bicycle Association. Bicycle manufacturers sponsor young riders and put thousands of dollars into engineering and technology every year.

All this activity makes BMX the most glamorous and sought-after bicycle style among children of the 8-to-15 age group. The bicycles themselves can be purchased in two ways: ready-to-ride from the store or as components. The list of component choices includes frames of highest quality tubing and advanced engineering, alloy rims, "mag" wheels, sealed bearing hubs, and lightweight aluminum-alloy cranksets, to name a few.

BMX-style bicycles are not limited to organized racing; they're good on the streets and sidewalks too. In addition, many children are intrigued by the "component" aspect of the sport, which allows them to upgrade their bikes, trade components with friends, and endlessly compare notes and debate about the performance features of one product or another. In this fashion they learn mechanical skills and become discriminating in their choices.

What about three-speed and ten-speed bicycles for the younger set? In general, the same range of quality and price is offered for kids and adults. Even the prestigious European bike builders, with names like Masi and Raleigh and Peugeot, offer bikes in sizes for youngsters.

UTILITY BIKES: EASY FOR ERRANDS

Utility bikes are intended for riding distances of less than five miles at a stretch. They may be used in large industrial plants to get from one section of the factory to another. They may be commercial delivery bikes, such as those used by news carriers and messenger services. They may be used by students to get to school each day. Or they may be nothing more than that rusty old bike with a wire basket on the front that leans against the side of the house, ready for a quick trip to the grocery store.

The basic utility-bike design includes a heavy but sturdy and comfortable frame. (See Fig. 3–2.) In the case of factory or plant bikes, and bikes used for delivery, the frame may have some extra tubes—usually just under the top tube—to reinforce them for carrying heavy loads. The extra frame weight isn't critical because such bikes are ridden at low speeds in relatively flat terrain.

---

*A grownups' version of this sport also exists. See our discussion of the "Cruiser" bicycles.

Fig. 3-2   With the addition of a carrier rack, this balloon-tire utility bike can be the perfect vehicle for neighborhood errands and light shopping.

Utility bikes may come equipped with one-speed, three-speed, five-speed, or even ten-speed hubs. But the most common ones have single-speed coaster brakes or are the style that used to be known as the "English racer." The English racer is not a racer at all, but is a durable, narrow-tired bike with hand brakes, a three-speed hub, and a heavy, soft frame. In the 1940s and 1950s, English racers made by Raleigh were imported to the U.S. in great numbers at a time when most bikes in the States were single-speed coaster-brake models manufactured by companies such as Schwinn, Columbia, and Elgin. Next to our heavy, if luxuriant, single-speed bikes, the Raleigh three-speed did indeed seem like a "racer." It was only in the 60s—when the sleek European and Japanese ten-speeds became popular in the U.S.—that we began to see that the English racer was really a rather slow and ponderous, if comfortable and utilitarian, machine.

The utility bike is designed to be ridden in an upright position, which most people will find comfortable for short-distance riding in relatively flat terrain. However, it becomes less than comfortable and efficient on longer rides or on hills. In city traffic, the upright position makes it easy to see and be seen by drivers of motor vehicles.

Utility bikes often come equipped with 26-inch wheels (rather than 27-inch, as on good ten-speed bicycles), steel rims, and low-pressure (45 to 65 psi) tires. There are three common tire widths: the big balloon tires (2.125 inches wide), middleweight tires (1.75 inches wide), and lightweight tires (1.25 inches wide).

In flat terrain, at low speeds, wheel weight isn't critical; comfort and stability may be more important there. The wider balloon tire makes for a cushy ride and puts a lot of tread on the ground, making the bike relatively stable in gravel or on wet pavement. These balloon tires can be purchased with tractor tread patterns for gravel and dirt or with smoother road tread for the street.

Middleweight tires come in both dirt and road tread patterns. The narrower tread, of course, puts proportionately less rubber on the ground. Lightweight tires come in standard road tread patterns only, and they have slightly less rolling resistance (less friction between tire and road) than their wider counterparts.

Utility bikes have the advantage of being exceptionally simple. A delivery or plant bike, for example, might be equipped with a single-speed coaster brake. A one-piece steel crank, wheel rims and handlebars of steel, and frequently a forged front fork make the bike heavy but durable. The utility bike is relatively maintenance-free compared to a fine ten-speed racing bike.

Pedals are usually of the rubber-block type. Although heavier than steel and alloy pedals, the rubber ones help keep your feet from slipping off in wet weather, and they are more comfortable than steel pedals if you're planning to ride with street shoes or canvas shoes.

Three-speed utility bikes, and English racers, are equipped with enclosed hubs rather than derailleurs. Although they provide a smaller range of gears, enclosed hubs are considerably easier to use than derailleurs. There are also five-speed enclosed hubs available, but more often than not the five-speed models have derailleur systems. The five-speed derailleur is identical to what you'd find on a ten-speed bike except that it has a single shift lever operating a derailleur on the rear only. There is no front derailleur.

Utility bikes usually come equipped with wide, sprung seats. When first sitting down on them, you'll probably feel more comfortable than on the narrower seats found on most ten-speeds. However, a wide seat limits the amount of energy you can exert on the pedals, since it forces you to sit in a position where your legs can't fully extend. Full power can be exerted on the pedals only by standing up. In addition, wide saddles will cause chafing on the insides of your thighs if ridden any great distance. I recommend having the wide saddle replaced by a narrower one if you plan to ride distances of more than three miles at a stretch or to ride in hilly terrain.

Many people get the wrong impression that a utility bike is just an inferior version of the ten-speed. While it may be true that the components on a utility bike are not as refined as you'd expect to find on a $1,000 ten-speed, it is unfair to compare the two. The issue is not one of quality so much as appropriateness. If a single-speed coaster-brake bike suits your purposes, don't get anything else. Ten-speed derailleur systems, hand brakes, drop handlebars, and quick-release hubs may only be in your way.

Many avid ten-speed riders have utility bikes for short trips to the neighborhood store or for just knocking around. For one thing, it is easier to hop on your utility bike and ride off than it is to get out your ten-speed, check the tires, adjust the toe straps, etc. Perhaps part of it is psychological, but if you have a trusty old utility bike leaning up against the side of the house you may find yourself using it more often than you'd use your ten-speed.

Another distinct advantage of having a utility bike is that you usually don't have to worry about someone ripping it off during those few minutes you're in the store. The lower dollar value of the utility bike makes it less attractive to thieves. And even if it does get stolen, your loss is small.

There is certainly something to be said for the utility bike's relative simplicity of operation. On a coaster-brake model you balance, pedal, and go. You stop by backpedaling. All your attention stays on traffic or on having fun.

A three-speed bike requires only slightly more attention to operate than a coaster-brake model. The simplest of three-speeds incorporates a coaster brake for the rear wheel and a hand brake for the front.

THE CRUISER

In the past few years, an updated adult version of the big, balloon-tired machines we knew as kids has made its way onto the scene—identified by names like Cruiser, Klunker, Bomber, Beach Cruiser, and Mountain Bike. (See Fig. 3–3.) Although some of these bikes have been built up around older frames resurrected from the junk heap, most are equipped with the very latest offerings in bicycle technology from Japan, Italy, France, England, and the United States. Alloy rims, sealed-bearing hubs, and custom frames made of the most sophisticated tubing one can buy are much in evidence. Not just nostalgia pieces, these machines open up a whole new range of possibilities to the cyclist, taking their owners into rough terrain, over gravel roads and beaches, and even into the backwoods on fire trails miles from the nearest motor vehicle.

Whereas the original fat-tired bicycles had single-speed coaster brakes, many of the newer models boast five or ten speeds, hand brakes, and sometimes motorcycle-type brake drums. And while the originals often weighed 50 and 60 pounds, some of the new ones weigh about the same as a medium quality ten-speed—that is, in the neighborhood of 30 pounds. Costs vary from about $150 to upwards of ten times that much.

Styling is as individualized as the owner. On the beaches in Southern California you can see Beach Cruisers with artistically painted fenders, horn "tanks," and even whitewall tires. In the Midwest there are Clunkers—plain utilitarian machines made from resurrected frames from the 40s, with alloy rims, knobby tires, and forks, handlebars, and brake levers borrowed from a child's BMX bike.

Fig. 3-3 Complete with whitewall tires, this production-model cruiser sells for about the same as an inexpensive ten-speed.

Organized races and Cruiser bike meets take participants over rugged back-country terrain, where one needn't worry about tangling with cars. Such bikes make perfect camping companions, providing wonderful transportation to places where even three-speeds or ten-speeds can't travel because of their narrow tires. Wide tires make the bikes stable in everything from rocks to wet sand.

How do you get such a bike? Two production models are presently available from Schwinn dealers. Most dealers also know of local bike builders who are building their own versions of this popular machine.

If you have mechanical ability, you can find an old frame and rebuild it, using components available at most bike shops. If you want expert advice, there's an excellent catalog available that lists a wide variety of parts and tells you how they fit together. It's put out by the makers of Trailmaster and Breezer cruiser frames:

The Cove Bike Shop
#1 Blackfield Drive
Tiburon, CA 94920

When you write, ask for the "Trailmaster Catalog."

Fig. 3-4   This ten-speed features high-quality alloy components throughout. The frame is constructed of Reynolds 531 double-butted tubes. This is an excellent bike for the beginning racer or for the more athletic recreational rider.

TEN-SPEED BICYCLES

The ten-speed bicycle comes closer than any other human-powered vehicle to fulfilling the age-old dream of a perfect relationship between the human body and a machine. (See Fig. 3–4.) With its wide range of gear ratios, the ten-speed guarantees you the maximum speed and distance for the energy you expend in cranking the pedals. Riding a ten-speed can be like having the perfect dancing partner; each enhances the best efforts of the other.

There is more variation among ten-speeds than within any other category of bikes. A ten-speed can cost anywhere from $150 to $3,000, depending on the quality of materials and the amount of handwork involved in its construction. Bicycle building is one of the few industries left in the world where the romance of handcrafting is still very much alive, and this fact often figures prominently in the ultimate cost.

In buying a ten-speed it is especially important to remember that bicycles come from the manufacturer only partly assembled and that it is up to the retail dealer to do the final setup and adjustments. Because of the relative complexity of the ten-speed, it is crucial for this work to be performed properly. Check out the action in the repair shop before selecting a dealer. A good mechanic always has a lot of business, and that's what you're looking for.

The discussion that follows will be pointing out the features of top-quality ten-speeds, not to advocate the top of the line for every rider, but to provide

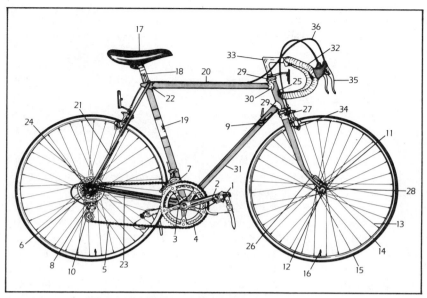

Fig. 3-5   The essential parts of a ten-speed bicycle.

a single standard against which you can measure your needs. The above diagram is intended as a guide to the myriad nuances of lugs, derailleur cages, bottom brackets, cranksets, and all the other perhaps unfamiliar terms that necessarily come up in any thorough discussion of the ten-speed (Fig. 3–5).

Key to Bicycle Parts

1. Pedals: The first part of the leverage system that transfers your energy to the rear wheel of the bike.
2. Cranks or crankarms: The steel or alloy levers that transfer your energy from the pedals to the chain.
3. Bottom bracket: The bearing assembly by which the crankarms are connected to the frame. Contains a ball-bearing system that minimizes friction as the crankarms are turned.
4. Chainwheels or chainrings: The two large sprockets fastened to the crankarm assembly and turned by the pedals.
2–4. These parts together make up the crankset.
5. Chain: The average chain has over a hundred links, each with its own bearing surfaces to deliver energy from your feet to the back wheel of the bike. Different gear ratios are attained by shifting the chain from one size sprocket to another.

6.   Freewheel: A cluster of five small gears attached to the rear wheel hub. The chain turns the freewheel, which in turn rotates the rear wheel. The freewheel includes a ratchet system to allow the bike to coast forward.

7.   Front derailleur: The mechanism that moves the chain from one chainwheel to another. It is controlled by the shift lever (9) on the left side of the bike.

8.   Rear derailleur: The mechanism that moves the chain from one gear to another on the freewheel. It is controlled by the shift lever (9) on the right side of the bike.

9.   Gear-shift levers (usually referred to as *shifters*): Two levers, one on the right, one on the left, by which the rider moves the derailleurs to select different gear ratios.

10.   Tension roller (an integral mechanism in the rear derailleur): A system of two small chain sprockets providing spring tension to keep the chain taut as it shifts from one set of gears to another.

11.   Hubs: This assembly contains the bearings for the wheels. The hub flanges have 36 holes for the spokes.

12.   Quick-release levers: A lever system that replaces nuts for fastening the wheel to the frame. These levers are so named because they allow the cyclist to remove a wheel instantly without the use of tools, for repairing flat tires or making other minor repairs on the road.

13.   Spokes: Each wire spoke has a wire nipple which connects it to the rim. This nipple is threaded, providing a way to tighten or loosen the spoke, adjust the wheel for stiffness, and remove wheel wobble.

14.   Rims: Steel or alloy bands which hold the tires and which connect to the axle and hub assembly through the spokes.

15.   Tires: Two basic types are available—clinchers for touring and recreation and sewups for racing and high-performance cycling. Sewup and clincher tires require different kinds of rims.

16.   Tire valves: Devices for inflating the tires.

17.   Saddle: The purpose of the saddle, in addition to supporting you, is to place your body in its most efficient position in relation to the pedals and handlebars.

18.   Seat post: A steel or alloy tube that connects the saddle to the bike frame and allows it to be adjusted for height.

19.   Seat tube: The frame member that runs from the seat to the bottom bracket.

20.   Top tube: The frame component that runs from the seat to the head tube.

21.   Seat stays: Frame tubes that run from behind the seat to the rear axle of the bike.

22.   Seat lug: A pressed-steel reinforcement that connects the top tube,

seat tube, and seat stays to the frame. The seat lug also has a clamping device which provides a way to tighten the seat post into the frame.

23. Chain stays: The frame tubes that run from the bottom bracket to the rear wheel of the bike.

24. Rear dropout: A lug brazed to the ends of the chain stays, providing a junction for the chain stays and seat stays and a surface for attaching the rear wheel to the frame. The dropout on the right side often has a built-in bracket for fastening the rear derailleur to the frame.

25. Head tube: A frame member that joins with the top tube and down tube of the bike. A bearing insert called a headset allows the fork to be attached to the head tube.

26. Front fork: The assembly that holds the front wheel, connecting it with the frame through a system of bearings mounted in the head tube. The handlebars connect to the fork at the top of the head tube.

27. Fork crown: The metal assembly that joins the two fork tubes to the steering tube.

28. Front dropouts (also called fork tips): Lugs brazed to the front fork tubes that provide a solid metal surface for attaching the front wheel axle to the frame.

29. Headset: A ball-bearing assembly, including one bearing at the top and one at the bottom of the head tube/fork assembly. This bearing system allows the front wheel to be turned while holding the fork in the frame. Good-quality headsets are important because they must absorb road shock transmitted from the road through the front wheel while also allowing the bike to be smoothly steered.

30. Lugs: These metal reinforcements are used wherever one or more frame tubes come together. The shaping and finishing of the lugs is often the trademark of custom frame-builders, distinguishing their product from others.

31. Down tube: The frame member that runs from the head tube to the bottom bracket.

32. Handlebars: In addition to steering the bike, the handlebars are an integral part of the leverage system by which the bike is powered forward; pulling up on the handlebars increases the force exerted on the pedals.

33. Handlebar stem: The metal clamp assembly fastening the handlebars to the front fork. These come in different sizes, making the distance between the handlebars and the seat longer or shorter to accommodate individual rider differences.

34. Caliper brake: Either side-pull or center-pull brakes, shaped like calipers, that press the brake pads against the wheel rim, allowing the rider to stop the bike.

35.   Brake lever: The hand lever—mounted to the handlebars—that allows
        the rider to control the brakes.
36.   Brake cable: A thin wire cable that runs from the brake lever to the
        calipers, controlling the brakes.

Frame Features

Before you look at anything else on the bike, look at the frame. The tubes in
a quality bike frame will be made of high-carbon steel called chrome molyb-
denum. Bikers shorten this to "chrome moly" (pronounced "molly"). This
steel, developed for the European racing circuit, provides extraordinary qualities: strength, lightness, and a lively feel. Chrome-moly tubing absorbs road
shock while preventing or minimizing frame "flex" or "whip."

Whip—twisting that happens when you stress the tubes by pedaling—is
the mark of a low-quality frame. Even a biker of medium strength can twist
the frame of an inexpensive bike enough to make the chain rub against the
derailleurs, causing the latter to malfunction. Not only is this whipping action
annoying, but it also means that the metal is flexing, causing fatigue in joints
and in the tubing itself.

A high-quality frame requires significantly less human energy to pedal
than does a low-quality frame, mainly because the rider's efforts are going
directly into turning the rear wheel rather than bending the metal. The high-
quality frame feels good to ride: lively, comfortable, and efficient. What's
more, everything stays adjusted on a good frame: derailleurs, brakes, and
wheel alignment. On a low-quality frame, tube alignment is in a constant
state of flux, and consequently nothing stays adjusted for long.

The finest quality bicycle tubing is "double-butted." Look for a seal with
names like Reynolds 531 (see Fig. 3–6), Vitus, Tange, Columbus, and Ishi-
wata on the frame. Double-butted frame tubes are thick at the points where
they join together and thinner between the joints. (See Fig. 3–7.) The extra
thickness provides strength and surface for joining the tubes, while the thinness
reduces the overall weight. Because each tube must be individually manufactured, double-butting adds considerably to the cost of the tubing. A good-
quality straight-gauge tubing, which is thick throughout its length, adds a few
pounds—usually between three and five—to the total weight of the bike while
reducing the cost of the bike between 15 and 20 percent over a double-butted
frame.

The manner in which the tubes are jointed together also affects the
bicycle's performance. On the best frames, the ends of each tube are filed or
mitered until they form a tight, perfect joint where they are to be connected.
This mitering requires skilled handwork comparable to that of a fine jeweler.

On a finely crafted frame, tubes are jointed with a reinforcement device
known as a lug. (See Fig. 3–8.) All the frame parts are clamped into a jig and
then skillfully brazed—or, in the case of the best frames, silver-soldered—

Fig. 3-6 Look for a label identifying the kinds of tubing used to construct better quality bikes.

together. The process of brazing or soldering requires the use of very high temperatures, which can weaken the metal if not carefully controlled. Silver-soldering requires lower temperatures than brazing and therefore presents less potential for damaging the integrity of the metal. Well-crafted joints, whether executed by brazing or silver-soldering, can make the difference between a long-lasting, responsive bicycle frame and a whippy one that might even break

Straight-gauge tubing.

Fig. 3-7 Double-butted tubing.

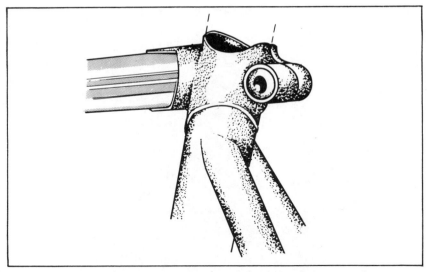

Fig. 3-8   Lugs reinforce frame tube joints, providing extra frame strength.

when you really pour on the power. Among the things you pay for in a top-quality bicycle are the extra skill and knowledge of the man or woman who puts the frame together.

The fork tips and dropouts of a good frame will usually be forged—that is, cast of high-quality metals—and have a smooth, sculptured look about them. Here again you'll find highly skilled soldering or brazing, and the frame builder may even stylize the joints in these areas.

Quality framebuilders take a great deal of pride in their paint, just as the makers of the world's best cars do. A good paint job is unmistakable: smooth and evenly colored. Fads come and go in detailing, but most of the classic bicycle frames have a clean, uncluttered appearance. Sometimes you'll find tasteful, reserved striping around the lugs, but most paint jobs will be under-stated, as if to say that the frame speaks for itself and needs no embellishment. Good frames have few if any decals or stickers, the exception being a discreet seal identifying the tubing that went into the frame's construction.

Sometimes frame and fork tips are chrome-plated. Chrome stands up a little better than paint where the wheels are being removed and replaced frequently to change tires, put the bike into a car, etc. But there are frame builders who refuse to chrome-plate any part of a frame because they say it changes the temper of the tubes.

After a couple of hours looking at good frames, you'll begin to appreciate the handcrafting that goes into them and justifies their cost. There are a great many casual bicyclists who buy their bikes as much for aesthetics as utility. Albert Eisentraut, a California framebuilder, was a sculptor before he started building frames, and, even though he now sells hundreds of frames each year, his products continue to reflect his fine-arts background. Similarly, custom-built bicycles have sold in boutiques for prices up to $3,000 each. Art collectors with no intention of ever riding them have purchased bicycles to hang on their walls.

Wheels and Tires

During my 1980 transcontinental ride, I experimented with different wheel designs and concluded that the wheels are the most important parts of any bike.

The first thing to note about a wheel is weight. The rim—that is, the circular strip of metal to which the tire attaches—can be made of either steel or aluminum. Steel rims can add as much as ten pounds to the total weight of the bike. Dr. David Gordon Wilson, of the Massachusetts Institute of Technology, states that ten extra pounds of weight in the wheels is equivalent to twenty additional pounds in the frame. This is dictated by the laws of physics: i.e., it requires more energy to turn the wheel itself than it requires to move the load carried by that wheel. The only reason to use steel rims is that they cost less than aluminum ones. Steel rims are not stronger.

Next look at the spoke pattern of the wheel. Bicyclists use terms like "three-cross" and "radial spoking" to describe the way a wheel is spoked. (See Fig. 3–9.) Radial spoking means simply that the spokes radiate straight out from the hub to the rim, in the fashion of a wagon wheel.

Three-cross spoking is a bit harder to explain. In 1876 James Starley showed that a strong yet resilient wheel could be built with wire instead of wooden spokes if the spokes came from the hub at an angle rather than radiating directly out from it. One must visualize this difference to fully un-

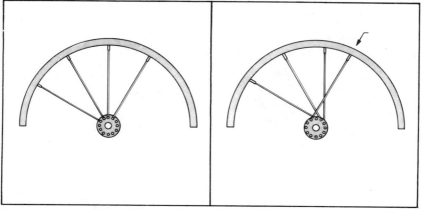

Fig. 3-9   Radial spoking. Spokes radiate directly from the center of the hub to the rim.

Three-cross spoking. The spoke indicated by the arrow crosses over three other spokes between the hub and the rim.

derstand it. By crossing the spokes, Starley created a wheel that made excellent use of the muscular force exerted by the rider and absorbed road shock and vibration better than any other wheel design. Starley's innovation quickly caught on and has been used ever since.

Three- and four-cross spoking patterns are the most popular designs used in wheel building today. Because the distance the spoke must span is greater in four-cross than in three-cross, a longer spoke is required. The longer spoke is more elastic than a short one, so a four-cross wheel will be softer—that is, more resilient—than a three-cross, two-cross, or radially spoked wheel.

The third element of the wheel to consider is the hub. Except in the least expensive bikes, these are cast of aluminum. The axles fasten to the frame with either nuts or quick-release levers. The latter are highly preferable, since they greatly simplify wheel removal for repairing tires or transporting the bike in the trunk of a car.

Look for smooth-running bearings in the hubs. A good bearing will turn easily as you spin the wheel and will be as smooth as those you'd expect to find in the most precise industrial machine.

There are both high- and low-flange hubs. This refers to the size of the side flanges (or edges of the circular discs that form the sides of the hub) from which the spokes radiate. Because the spokes must be longer to span the distance between the low-flange hub and the rim, a low flange produces a softer, more resilient wheel. For that reason, some tourers prefer it to the high-flange design.

Finally look at the tires. The best tires will carry from 85 to 130 pounds of pressure per square inch (psi). The higher pressure reduces rolling resistance significantly. There are two styles of tire construction: clincher tires, which hold onto the rim in much the same way an automobile wheel does, and sewup tires, which are glued to the rim. (See Fig. 3–10.)

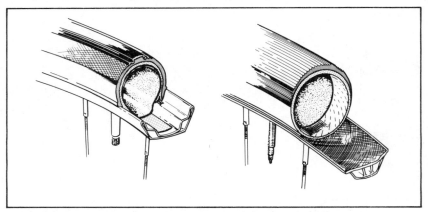

Fig. 3-10   Clincher tire.   *Sewup tire.*

Sewup tires are preferred by racers. With tire and tube constructed as a single unit, the racer can carry a spare in a neat package under the seat. In the event of a puncture, an experienced rider can strip off the old tire and put on the spare in a matter of three or four minutes. Patching the sewup is another matter altogether. The seam that holds the tire and tube together as a unit must be cut open to get at the tube. Then after the tube is patched the tire must be reassembled, requiring a skillful hand at sewing and care at gluing back into place a fabric liner that protects the stitching. For an inexperienced person, sewup tires take as much as an hour—and a great deal of patience— to patch. For this reason, many cyclists end up throwing punctured sewup tires away, even though there may still be hundreds of miles of tread left on the casings. At a cost of $18 to $50 apiece, sewup tires can become an expensive proposition. If you are a competitive cyclist for whom winning the race is the ultimate turn-on, sewups will probably be worth the price, since they'll allow you to change tires quickly and get on with the race.

In contrast to the sewup tire, clincher tires can be patched in a matter of minutes. But because the tube and tire are two separate units they take a little longer to change on the road. Most clinchers will require the use of lightweight tire irons to remove them from the rims, whereas sewup tires can be removed without the use of tools. Several companies sell spare clincher tires that fold up into a neat package and can be carried on your bike like a sewup tire. But having the spare doesn't shorten the changing time on the road. It simply provides you with a spare casing—handy on long tours—for those rare cases when the tire itself is slit by glass or sharp stones. Recreational riders and tourists prefer clinchers because they can be easily patched on the road and are relatively inexpensive to maintain. A high-quality clincher tire will sell for $20, on the average. A tube for the clincher will sell for around $4. Both can be used over and over again, and they require very little skill to patch.

Today's tire technology has provided us with clincher tires that perform as well as sewups. They are as narrow (1⅛ inch) as a sewup and can carry as much pressure (up to 110 psi), so they have about the same rolling resistance (friction or resistance at the point where the tread meets the pavement) as the sewup. With these recent technological developments, even racers are turning to clincher tires for their training rides.

Cranksets

Now turn your attention to the crankset. This is the assembly that includes the crankarms, to which the pedals are attached; the two large chain sprockets, called chainwheels or chainrings, which are turned by the crankarms; and the bearings which hold the whole unit in the frame. (See Fig. 3–11.) A high-quality crankset will be made of aluminum alloy except for the bearings,

Fig. 3-11   High-quality cranksets are fabricated of aluminum alloys and are metallurgical masterpieces.

which are steel. It will be cast and finished as smoothly and precisely as a part you'd expect to find in a fine watch. Each tooth of the chainwheel will be carefully shaped and machined to minimize friction as it turns the chain. The bolts that hold the various parts together are jewels of shining perfection.

But beauty alone is not what distinguishes a high-quality crankset. On the best, the hardness of the metal has been carefully formulated to minimize distortion (or bending) of the crankarms and chainrings.

Chainrings on good-quality cranksets can be easily changed. There are two advantages to this: First, worn chainrings can be replaced without replacing the entire crankset; second, larger or smaller chainrings can be bolted on to provide another set of gear ratios. Selecting larger or smaller chainrings can be important if you ride in hilly terrain, if you plan to be carrying heavy loads, or if you're planning to go on an extended tour. A person who rides a fast road bike for athletic challenge may require a completely different set of gears when he or she loads up the bike for a weekend tour.

Handlebars

Handlebars serve several important functions. First, the handlebars carry a fair amount of your body weight. Second, when you are pedaling hard uphill, or pedaling fast, you can pull against the bars for extra leverage and power.

Inexpensive bikes frequently come equipped with steel handlebars. Although good-quality steel bars are sturdy enough, they transmit every vibration and bump in the road to your hands. Over a number of miles this can irritate nerves in your hands and cause soreness, numbing, or even temporary inability to move your fingers. Good-quality alloy bars have a "softer" feel to them. The alloy absorbs road shock better than steel while being of equal or superior strength.

Derailleurs

The word "derailleur" comes from the French, meaning literally "to derail." When you move the shift lever on a ten-speed bike, a cable activates the derailleur cage, moving it to the left or right, depending on which way you moved the lever. As the derailleur cage moves, it pushes the chain off one gear sprocket (derails it) and lines it up with another gear sprocket. In the front there are two gear sprockets, technically known as chainwheels; in the rear you will find a freewheel with five gear sprockets which transmit the power you exert on the pedals to the rear wheel. (See Fig. 3–12.)

What is the reason for all these gears? With the choice of a wide range of gear ratios, you can select the way you will use your energy. A low gear lets you repeat the pedaling action more times per mile than with a higher gear. The principle of repetition is the same in pedaling a bike as in lifting a given amount of weight. A very strong person might easily lift a 200-pound weight

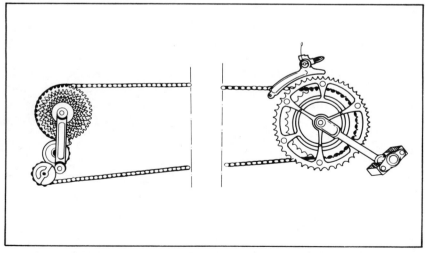

Fig. 3-12   Modern derailleur design provides smooth shifting at moderate cost.

in a single motion. A weaker person can lift the same 200 pounds, but must do it by repetition—that is, by lifting 50 pounds four separate times.

Climbing hills on a bike is similar to lifting a heavy weight, in that the steeper the hill the more energy is required to "lift yourself" from the bottom to the top. You accomplish the hill-climbing task by cranking more revolutions per mile than you would crank to travel the same distance in flat terrain, and this is accomplished by changing to the low gear range of your bike.

To keep the difference between low gears and high gears straight, remember that you spin the pedals more revolutions per mile in low gears than you do in high gears. Going into a lower gear means increasing the number of times you will *repeat* the action of pedaling.

Now back to the basic mechanics. Examine the front and rear derailleurs and the shift levers used to control them. Like all other aluminum-alloy components of a fine bicycle, these will be precision-molded and beautifully finished. Excellent derailleurs come from Japan as well as Europe, but the Italian-made Campagnolo still maintains first position with bicycle aficionados.

Brakes

Ten-speed bikes come equipped with one of two kinds of brakes: center-pulls or side-pulls. (See Fig. 3–13.) When constructed of high-quality alloys, the side-pull design gives more exacting control and better braking power than center-pulls and is preferred by professional racers. Because of its engineering peculiarities, the manufacturer must use extremely high-quality, costly alloys in its construction. A good set of side-pull brakes (front and rear complete) will cost from $70 to $175.

Center-pull brakes can provide excellent service even though constructed of only medium quality alloys. This design is the choice of cyclists wanting good performance at a reasonable price ($30 to $45). The center-pull, therefore, is standard equipment on bicycles ranging in price from $150 to $500.

Some three-speeds and low-quality ten-speeds come equipped with low-quality side-pull brakes. These are suitable only for light duty. Since they are made of low-quality alloys, the metal parts tend to flex, and even bend permanently, making for a brake that can be trusted only at lower speeds on relatively flat terrain, carrying light loads.

The Best Bike for Your Money: A Comparison

Bottom-of-the-line ten-speeds, costing (at this writing) between $130 and $225, come equipped with heavy frames made with straight-gauge tubing. The wheels have heavy steel rims and low-pressure tires. Derailleurs, handlebars, and cranks are of steel rather than alloy. Weight is from 35 to 39 pounds.

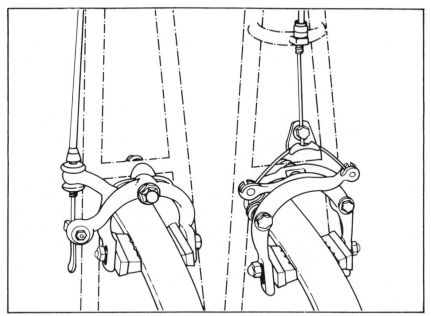

Fig. 3-13   Center-pull brakes, right, *are the best buy for high performance at moderate cost. High-quality side-pull brakes,* left, *give more positive braking than center-pulls at considerable extra cost.*

Bikes in this group, from any of the major bike manufacturers, are fine for commuting short distances (under ten miles each way) and for light recreation, but because of their weight they are not recommended for cycle training, commuting long distances, racing, or touring.

Middle-of-the-line bikes—$225 to $350—come equipped with frames that are reasonably light, efficient, and comfortable. Often the three main tubes are double-butted, while all the other tubing is straight-gauge. Wheels have alloy rims and are equipped with high-pressure clincher tires of medium quality. Derailleurs, cranksets, and handlebars are made of alloy and are of good quality, though not necessarily beautiful in their finish. Weight is from 25 to 32 pounds. Bikes in this group are excellent for commuting, recreation, cycle training, and touring. Frames are, as a general rule, on the soft side compared to top-of-the-line racing bikes, so they are not recommended for serious competition.

Top-of-the-line production bikes start at $350 and can run as high as $3,000. They come with all-double-butted frames. Wheels have alloy rims with a choice of sewup tires or narrow, high-performance clinchers for competition or wider clinchers for touring. Components such as cranksets, derailleurs, and handlebars are either top-of-the-line Japanese products or a combination of Japanese and European. Weight is from 21 to 26 pounds. With these better bikes, one should be specific about how it is to be used; racing bikes have short, stiff frames, and tourers have longer, softer frames with brackets for attaching touring racks.

MADE-TO-ORDER MODELS

Custom bikes are built up by bike shops according to your own specifications. You choose the frame and components yourself. You can even have special wheels built with your choice of hubs, spokes, rims, and tires. Before having a bike built, you should know exactly how you want to use it. A bike that will be ridden in the hills should be different from one to be ridden on the flats. Touring bikes will be significantly different from racing bikes. Your strength and experience as a rider will determine the kind of gearing the mechanic will build in. If you are not an experienced rider and aren't certain about the kind of riding you'll be doing, buy a production bike, ride it for several months, become fully acquainted with your biking needs, and then consider ordering a custom-made bike. Otherwise, the choice of components will all be guess-work.

The custom bike begins with a good frame, as described in the previous section, and that's where you start when money is no object and you want the best bicycle available. After purchasing a frame you pick out your own components, from Weinmann center-pull brakes at $30 a set to Campagnolo side-pulls as $150 a set; from SR handlebars at $7.00 to Cinnelli bars at $30; from a molded plastic saddle for $10 to an Ideal 90, with titanium frame, at $75; from a Suntour derailleur set at $30 to a Campagnolo at $150; and, finally, wheels from $75 a set to more than $300. Beginning with a high-quality, bare frame at $300, your finished bike can have a final price tag of anything between $600 and $1,500. What do you get for your money? You get efficiency, speed, excellent handling characteristics, components that operate like clockwork, aesthetic appeal, and the opportunity to hand-pick every piece of equipment that goes on the frame.

Now, before you jump in the saddle and hit the road, there's one last crucial step involved in ensuring your riding satisfaction. Read on.

FOUR

THE PERSONAL TOUCHES THAT ADD UP TO A PERFECT FIT

Selecting the right bike is the first step toward getting on the road. But your enjoyment of the ride depends on getting the proper fit—that is, paying close attention to the small adjustments that will make your bike truly yours. Beginning riders are often amazed to discover the magic of bicycle adjustment: Raising or lowering the seat less than an inch can increase a rider's pedaling efficiency immeasurably, and a new sense of self-confidence often comes with that. A different tilt to the handlebars makes the brake levers easy to reach and instantly causes the rider to feel more secure. A new handlebar height alleviates sore hands, and the rider is relieved to find that this discomfort isn't "just part of being a bicycle rider."

When I first started riding seriously, I had problems with my knees and shoulders. I went to Paul Cornish (who held the world's record for the transcontinental ride before my 1978 ride). Paul helped me make adjustments on my bike—sometimes it was a matter of changing something just a 16th of an inch—and those adjustments completely solved my problems. So now, when people say they don't like riding a bicycle because they get aches and pains all over their bodies, I tell them, "It's because your bicycle isn't adjusted correctly, and you're not positioned right while you're riding."

Proper bicycle adjustment includes the obvious matters of choosing the right size for the frame and adjusting the seat and handlebars. But it doesn't stop there. It also includes making those refinements in your equipment (adding toe clips and handlebar padding, exchanging your saddle for a better one, etc.) that will give you the lasting pleasure that comes from knowing your bicycle is perfectly tailored to suit your individual needs.

BASIC ADJUSTMENTS

Sizing Up Your Frame

Bicycle frames come in many sizes, usually 19, 21, 22, 23, 24, and 25 inches. (Three-speed and utility bikes come in a more limited selection of sizes.) A few manufacturers build 27-inch frames, but usually these must be special-ordered. Frame size always refers to the distance between the seat lug and the center of the bottom bracket.

Don't make the mistake of thinking that if your frame is a little too small for you, you can adjust it simply by raising the seat. Standard seatposts can safely be raised only about 3½ to 4 inches above the frame. (A minimum of 2½ inches must protrude into the frame for safety.) If you go higher than that most seatposts will flex, and some may even bend under the rider's weight and strength. If the frame is too small, you won't be able to set the handlebars at a comfortable height. Finally, the seat tube and the top tube are proportionately cut—that is, the longer the seat tube, the longer the top tube. Thus a 25-inch frame will not only be taller than a 23-inch frame, it will also be longer. This will affect your "reach," or the distance you sit from the handlebars.

A frame that is too large for you can pose a real danger in mounting and dismounting from the bike. This is the main source of groin injuries to bike riders. Parents often make the mistake of buying bikes that are too large for their children, with the idea that they will "grow into" them. This practice can, and too often does, lead to serious injuries to the genitals.

Determining Frame Fit

There is a rule of thumb among bikers that the bike frame should be nine to ten inches less than your inseam measurement—the distance between your crotch and the floor while you are standing in your bare feet. As a general rule, this works out pretty well. But because of certain other variables—notably, bottom-bracket and tire-size variations—it may prove less than a perfect formula.

Before you go out to buy a bike, take the time to determine your inseam measurement. Then, at the store, straddle a model of the bike you intend to buy that is theoretically your right fit. With both feet flat on the floor (shoes removed), the top tube of the frame should be from ¾ inch to 1 inch below your crotch.

Seat Height

To adjust the saddle height, sit on your bike in a normal riding position with your hands on the handlebars and your bare feet flat on the pedals. Have a friend adjust the saddle up or down to accommodate you. The crank arms should be in the position shown in Figure 4–1, and your heel should be centered on the pedal. Your leg should be fully extended and your pelvis should be level on the seat—that is, not tipped either to the left or to the right.

After establishing the correct height of the seat, adjust it so it's approximately level across the top from front to back. Some people will find that the saddle is more comfortable with the front tipped slightly down, while others will prefer it slightly up. Experimentation after a number of miles of riding will reveal what's best for you.

The saddle may also be adjusted forward or back. The rule here is that the nose of the saddle should be 2 to 2½ inches behind a centerline drawn perpendicular to the bottom bracket.

When everything is lined up, get on the bike and see how it feels. If you're an experienced rider, you will know as soon as you get on whether or not the adjustments are right for you; as little as a 16th of an inch off will be

Fig. 4-1   Adjust the saddle with your leg fully extended and your heel on the pedal.

obvious. And most experienced riders will be able to tell exactly which way the saddle should go to make it perfect.

If you haven't been riding on a regular basis, the proper seat adjustment may not immediately be apparent. Your body will go through a number of subtle changes as you ride, and in a short period of time the saddle adjustment will feel right and will give you the greatest cycling efficiency. So go by the book until you've clocked a hundred miles or more on your new bike. At that point, your body will be fairly well adapted, and you may benefit from fine adjustment.

Saddling Up

Never underestimate the importance of a good saddle. When I graduated from college I decided to ride my bicycle from San Diego to Los Angeles—a distance of 120 miles, which seemed like a long way at the time. I got my old ten-speed out of the garage and started to fix it up. It needed a seat, so I went to the Thrifty store nearby and bought a molded plastic one for about $3. By the time I got to L.A., I was in horrible shape; I had open sores on my rear end. I called a friend to come and pick me up, and I couldn't sit for three days afterward.

Most bicycles in the low-to-medium price ranges come with the kinds of molded plastic saddles that caused my problems on that ride to Los Angeles. Sometimes these saddles are padded and have a vinyl cover. Some bikes may even come equipped with inexpensive cushioned saddles with coil springs that are supposed to make the ride more comfortable.

Cushioned saddles usually feel more comfortable than narrow leather racing saddles when you sit on them in the store, but that comfort may not extend to a ride beyond three miles. The narrow racing saddle may look uncomfortable and may even feel that way when you first try it out, but this design has evolved through several decades of bicycling history, and it does work better than anything else in the long run.

A bicycle saddle must do much more than just support your weight as a stool would do. The difference is that a stool supports you in a relatively static position, while a saddle must support you during vigorous exercise— specifically, scissoring your legs up and down to pedal your bike. Obviously, a seat that is too wide will restrict this activity or cause chafing around your buttocks and upper thighs.

The narrow traditional bicycle saddle supports your pelvis while allowing your legs to move freely. With the seat and handlebars properly adjusted, your body weight rests on both the handlebars and the seat—not just the seat. In addition, much of your weight is distributed to the pedals when you are pedaling, so your comfort will come not merely from the *softness* of the saddle but also from the way in which the complete bike accommodates your body while you're cycling.

In recent years, bicycle saddles have undergone significant improvement. The two most successful designs are the hard leather saddles, such as those made by Brooks and Ideal, and the molded plastic saddles with leather covers and special padding designed to conform to your body, such as those made by Avocet and Selle Milano.

The so-called hard leather saddles conform to the rider's body after a hundred miles or so, and, as in breaking in a pair of new boots, one must endure a certain amount of discomfort in the process. The leather does soften in time, and it does become compatible with your rear end. The crucial feature of leather is that it breathes, preventing sores caused by perspiration that wouldn't be able to escape with a plastic saddle. On my transcontinental tour, I discovered that plastic saddles—even those equipped with leather coverings—radiate heat much more than traditional all-leather models.

Leather saddles require simple maintenance and a breaking-in period. Before installing the saddle on your bike, lay it upside down in the sun and swab the underside with neatsfoot oil for several days in a row. Insofar as possible, avoid getting oil on the face of the saddle—that is, the part you'll be sitting on. After several days of the sun-and-neatsfoot-oil treatment, take the saddle inside and work the outer surface with saddle soap. A few evenings spent squeezing the leather with your fingers, kneading the edges, and working in saddle soap, will be that many hours you won't have to work the leather with your posterior.

Padded, plastic-based saddles require little or no break-in period. The best of the padded saddles have a thin layer of foam material that will shape to your body. Never ride very far with a plastic-covered saddle. The plastic won't breathe, and the extra moisture and heat it causes in your crotch will cause rashes, blisters, and even fungal infections.

Top-quality padded saddles are designed for either wide or narrow pelvises. Studies by orthopedists have shown that for women the wide design is usually more comfortable than the narrow one, while the narrow design usually accommodates a man's bone structure better than the wide one.

You should expect to pay between $20 and $65 for a good- to excellent-quality saddle. The more miles you ride, the more important your saddle becomes, so take the plunge if you are planning to make riding an important part of your life. The agony of spending a few extra dollars will be forgotten long before the ongoing agony of trying to ride on a cheap saddle.

Finally, do yourself a favor and break in your new saddle gradually. Just as you wouldn't start out on a ten-mile backpacking trip with a brand new pair of hiking boots, don't start out on a hundred-mile bicycle ride before your saddle and your rear end have gotten acquainted with each other. Making this acquaintance is a vital part of getting accustomed to a new bike, just as a vital part of breaking in new boots is getting your feet toughened up to the unique configurations of strange leather. Give yourself time to toughen up your bottom while softening up your saddle.

Handlebar Adjustments to Improve Your Pleasure

Handlebars can be adjusted to suit not only the size of your body, but your riding style as well. For example, a track racer may set the bars six to eight inches lower than the seat, putting the rider in a streamlined, crouched position that also provides the potential for the tremendous amounts of leverage necessary for short, fast sprints. A recreational rider, on the other hand, may want to set the handlebars level with the saddle to afford better visibility in traffic and greater comfort in the long haul.

There are two adjustments to consider here: height and reach (see Fig. 4–2). Height is established by raising or lowering the stem. But bear in mind when you're doing this that you must keep about 2½ inches of stem in the frame. If you have less than that, a number of problems may occur, from a wobbling, squeaking stem to a broken one. Start out with the bars an inch below the saddle. Ride the bike a mile or more and see how it feels. Then, if you feel that the bars should be higher or lower, make your adjustments accordingly. Don't be afraid to experiment.

Most bicycles come equipped with a stem that provides the average rider with a comfortable reach. If this stem-reach average doesn't suit you, it can be changed. To measure for this adjustment, place your elbow against the nose of the saddle and reach out toward the handlebars. The tips of your

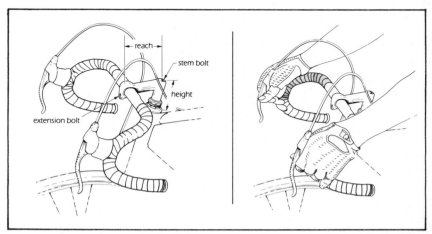

Fig. 4-2   Adjust the handlebar stem for   Fig. 4-3   Riding on the levers.
both reach and height.

fingers should be somewhere between just brushing the edge of the bars and ending about an inch away.

Stems may be purchased in different *extension* or *reach* sizes. For example, if you have a long torso and long arms, you may want a longer-than-average stem. Similarly, if you have a short torso or arms, you may require a shorter stem on your bike.

Riders' physical differences are only part of the story, however. If you want your bike for touring, riding around town, or commuting to work, you will probably prefer a more upright riding position, which can be acquired by installing a shorter stem and raising the handlebars to their maximum, that is, leaving at least 2½ inches in the head tube. The racer, on the other hand, may want a stem with a long extension so that he or she stretches out over the bike to establish a lower center of gravity and a more aerodynamically efficient position.

When you're buying a new bike, most dealers will adjust the handlebars for you and will even exchange stems, if necessary, at a nominal extra charge.

Next, consider the tilt of the handlebars. Have someone hold the bike as you sit on it in a normal riding position. If your bike is equipped with dropped handlebars, place your hands on the hooks, or lower part of the bars. The bars should feel comfortable when you grasp them tightly. To adjust them to the right angle, loosen the bolt on the stem extension (Fig. 4–2) and turn the bars up or down until they fit your hand comfortably. Your arms should have a slight bend at the elbow when grasping the handles. This prevents sore elbows caused by road shock and vibration. Although there is no hard-and-fast rule about handlebar tilt, I have found that tilting the bars so that their ends are aimed like an arrow at the rear axle provides the greatest comfort.

Don't be hesitant about changing the adjustment of your handlebar tilt from time to time. On my transcontinental rides I'm constantly making small changes in this adjustment. It is easy to do and can make a big difference in the way you feel on a longer ride. Eddy Merckx, the great Belgian bicycle racer, always carried a wrench for making adjustments during a race. He became very adept at making even complex seat adjustments while riding along in the pack.

Adjusting the Brake Levers

The hoods of the brake levers are used by most riders as extensions of the handlebars. Indeed, *riding on the levers* is one of the more common riding positions among experienced bikers. (See Fig. 4–3.) With your hands on the brake hoods, your fingers actually touch the brake levers—a feature you'll fully appreciate if you have to make a sudden stop. When the brake levers are properly adjusted you will find this position comfortable, easy, and efficient.

To adjust the brake hoods, sit on your bike and place your hands on the hoods. You should now be able to wrap your fingers around the levers, just as the rider in the illustration is doing. If you can't, you'll want to adjust the position of the hoods on the handlebars.

In most cases, you'll probably have to peel off and replace the tape on the handlebars. Good fabric tape will tolerate this process two or three times before it loses its adhesive qualities. Besides, new tape is inexpensive and is available in all good bike shops. Chapter 15 provides instructions for rewrapping handlebars.

After removing the tape you'll be able to see that the brake hood is clamped to the handlebar by a thin metal band. The band must be loosened to move the brake. This is accomplished by means of a screw inside the hood. (See Fig. 4–4.) If you can't do it that way, turn to Chapter 15, which gives more complete details for adjusting and replacing brake levers.

When you've loosened the adjustment screw for the metal band that holds the lever to the bar, you'll be able to slip the lever up or down the bar until you find the right position. Then tighten the adjustment screw and see how it feels. Does the hood feel good in your hand? Can you reach the brake lever with your fingers? If the answer to both these questions is affirmative, your adjustment is complete. Rewrap your handlebars with the tape and you're ready to go.

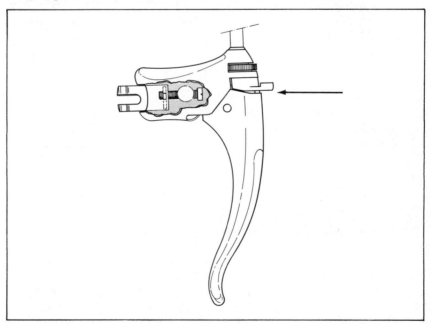

Fig. 4-4 The adjustment nut for moving the hand brake levers is located under the brake hood.

UPGRADING YOUR BIKE

For the avid cyclist, adjustment of the bike doesn't stop with changing the heights of the handlebars and saddle, buying a better saddle, or altering the positions of the brake levers. As you log more and more miles, and your strength and riding techniques improve, you will demand more of the bike. Whereas the beginning rider must improve his or her body to meet the demands of the bike, eventually there comes a time when the bike must be improved to meet the new demands of the rider.

Growing stronger, you find yourself taking longer rides in hillier terrains and at higher speeds. To enjoy these new dimensions of your cycling experience, you may want to add pedals with toe clips and smoother bearings to make better use of your energy. You exchange your original, wide, low-pressure tires for narrow, high-pressure ones. Instantly your bike feels, and is, more responsive to your physical efforts. Later, you discover that the crankset that came with your bike flexes every time you bear down on the pedals. You didn't notice the limitation of the crankset before because your leg muscles weren't yet strong enough. To adjust the bike to match your new capacities, you install a new crankset, one made of a better-quality alloy that doesn't flex when you push to your limits.

Most riders upgrade their bikes gradually over a period of months or even years. You recognize the need for better equipment only as your riding abilities improve, and this is a gradual process. Sometimes you upgrade when it becomes necessary to repair something that has broken down. Tires wear out and you replace the original low-pressure tires with high-performance ones. Or a pedal bearing wears out, and instead of having it repaired you install new, high-quality racing pedals with toe clips.

In general, upgrading is easy to do and relatively inexpensive. For less than the price of a tuneup on your car, you can have the world's best crankset or a set of high-performance wheels installed on your bike. Upgrading presents a good case for buying a bike with a good frame. Relatively inexpensive bikes can be found with Reynolds or similar-quality tubing used in the three main tubes of the frame. A poor-quality frame just doesn't justify the investment you might make in upgraded components.

The following paragraphs describe some of the most common component changes that cyclists make as they gain riding experience and demand more of their machines.

Handlebar Helpers: Tape and Sleeves

If your bike has dropped handlebars wrapped with plastic covering, you might want to exchange the original for fabric tape, which provides a better gripping surface than plastic and doesn't get cold in the winter. In addition, fabric tape absorbs perspiration, keeping your hands dry, while plastic becomes slippery when your hands sweat. For extra insulation against vibration and road shock, try double-taping your handlebars—that is, wrapping one row of tape over another.

Several manufacturers now offer rubber sleeves that fit over the bars and provide softer padding than any other handlebar covering previously available. A growing number of cyclists now use these sleeves instead of the traditional tape.

Fabric tape and handlebar sleeves come in colors as well as black. Although colors are attractive at first, they don't stay that way for long. Change a tire on the road, or replace a chain that has slipped off the sprockets, and you'll quickly discover how the convention of black handlebar tape evolved. Like most sales incentives, the value of colored handlebar tape doesn't extend past the showroom window.

Handlebar Designs

For ten-speed bicycles there are two basic styles of handlebars: flat and dropped. Though the new rider often finds the dropped-style handlebars uncomfortable at first, they actually aid riding comfort by providing a variety of hand positions. Each position changes your riding posture, which keeps you from getting stiff. The lowest portion of the bars, sometimes referred to as "the hooks," offers extra leverage for climbing hills and a more streamlined posture for racing or bucking a headwind.

Some riders prefer flat bars for commuting. The flat riding position puts your head up higher, making you more visible to motorists and pedestrians. The flat position also makes it a little easier to look around in traffic.

Bars come in two materials: steel and aluminum alloy. The alloy is much lighter and absorbs road shock better than the steel bars. The only advantage of steel bars is that they cost about a third less than alloy.

It is time-consuming but not difficult to change handlebars on your bike. You'll have to remove the tape and the handbrakes, unbolt the clamp that holds them to the stem, and reassemble. Incidentally, steel and alloy bars have different diameters, requiring you to change the stem if you change to different bars. Brake levers are not transferable from dropped bars to flat or vice versa. You'll have to purchase new levers designed for the style of bar you've installed. (Check with your bicycle shop to make sure that the new parts will be compatible.)

Pedals for Efficient Foot Action

Pedals come in a variety of designs, ranging from the rubber-block type found on children's bikes, which sell for five or six dollars a pair, to alloy racing pedals found on track bikes, selling for a hundred dollars a pair.

The reason for upgrading the pedals on your bike is this: In normal riding you turn the pedals at an average of 60 to 90 revolutions per minute. This translates to 3,600 to 5,400 revolutions for every hour you ride. Thus even a small amount of friction, multiplied by the above factors, can make a tremendous difference in the amount of energy you must exert to ride for an hour or more.

All bearings have *some* friction and therefore waste some *energy*. In a high-quality pedal, bearing surfaces made of high-temper metals are precisely machined. When assembled, they are carefully adjusted for minimal friction. A less expensive pedal will have stamped metal bearings—a fabrication method that produces only a mediocre bearing surface. A good-quality pedal can last a lifetime and will waste only a minute amount of energy. An inexpensive pedal may last only a few hundred miles before its bearings begin to break down and eat up energy that should be going to the back wheel. Good-quality pedals priced from $12 to $35 are made by Lyotard, Atom, and KKT.

Toe Clips: A Small Change That Really Matters

Toe clips (Fig. 4–5) add both safety and efficiency to your ride. As a safety factor, they prevent your feet from slipping off the pedals and causing you to lose control of the bike. And, they allow you to exert pressure on the pedals on both the downstroke and the upstroke, increasing your efficiency by 30 to 50 percent, depending on your strength and riding skill.

Beginning bike riders often see toe clips as a hazard. Having one's feet strapped in the pedals does indeed sound treacherous at first. However, unless you are wearing special cycling shoes (see Chapter 14), you can remove your feet nearly as quickly from toe clips as from bare pedals.

The straps on toe clips have quick-release buckles that come loose with a flick of your thumb. However, you can ride toe clips with their straps adjusted loosely around your feet, gaining pedaling efficiency while still allowing you to remove your feet from the pedals quickly, easily, and, after a few tries, automatically.

You can add toe clips—to metal pedals only—with two small bolts. A strap then weaves through the pedal and up over the top of your foot, where it feeds through a metal loop in the toe clip. The end of the strap joins the buckle on the outside of your foot, where you can easily reach it for adjustment or release.

Toe clips come in small, medium, and large sizes. Just as with all other bicycle adjustments, getting the right toe-clip size is important. Clips of the wrong size, especially if they are on the short side, can cause a variety of leg and back complaints. To get the right fit for you, wear the shoes you intend to wear when you ride. At the bike shop, place your foot on the pedal with the ball of your foot directly over the pedal axle. Then hold the toe clip in

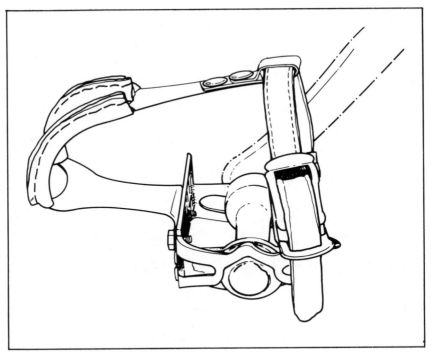

Fig. 4-5 Toe clips can increase your pedaling efficiency by 30 to 50 percent.

place against the pedal. (You'll need someone to assist you.) The toe clip should not rub against your toe, as this could cause chafing—either ruining your shoes or irritating your toes. If you must make a choice between clips that are slightly too small and clips that are slightly too large, go with the slightly larger size.

Tires: Treading Lightly

Many bikes selling for less than $500 come equipped with tires that are wide, carry relatively low pressures, and are comparatively heavy. Beginning riders sometimes prefer these tires because they're comfortable and give the bike a solid, predictable feeling. That feeling is eventually recognized by the rider as sluggishness as he or she gains riding experience.

The heavy original tires that come with many bikes have a large amount of rolling resistance. According to David Gordon Wilson, the amount of energy it takes to pedal a bike can be reduced as much as 50 percent by using narrow, high-pressure tires rather than wide, low-pressure ones.

When you change to high-performance tires, you'll immediately notice how much more responsive your bike feels. This is not an illusion. Equipped with these tires, the bike requires less energy to pedal, will go faster, and actually is more stable, even though it may not feel that way at first. Converting to high-performance tires is one of the most rewarding changes you can make for a small amount of money. A pair of good tires, with tubes, will run between $20 and $40.

Bicycle-tire technology is a sophisticated science. If you are touring, for example, you may require a different tire than you will if you're racing. So check with your bicycle shop before you buy new tires. A salesperson should be able to match the tires to your needs.

Derailleurs: Shifting with Ease

Most ten-speed bikes come equipped with adequate derailleurs made by Sun Tour or Shimano of Japan or by European manufacturers such as Simplex and Huret. But derailleurs do wear out. The plastic wheels that maintain tension on the chain are the first to go. Or the cages that enclose the chain on the front and rear derailleurs bend or wear, inhibiting smooth shifting.

The Italian Campagnolo ("Campy") derailleurs continue to be the choice of racers. The present cost for a set of Campy derailleurs (front and rear, with cables and shift levers) starts at approximately $150. Campy equipment shifts faster than most others, lasts longer, and has small parts that can be replaced, which can't be done with many other companies' products.

The Japanese and French companies make top-of-the-line derailleurs that perform nearly as well as Campagnolos for about half to two-thirds the price. Except for hard competition, these will do the job.

Costly and Common Cranksets Compared

Cranksets are generally durable and long lasting. Those components most vulnerable to wear are the bearings that hold the axle of the crankset inside the bike frame and the teeth in the chainwheels, which sometimes wear such that they no longer fit the chain. The latter can cause hard shifting, excessive chain wear or both.

Cranksets are made of different materials, ranging from steel to the most advanced aluminum alloys. Surprisingly, the difference in material can dramatically affect your ride. An inexpensive, soft steel or alloy crankset may flex as much as three-quarters of an inch as you pedal. As a beginning rider, you may notice nothing in simply pedaling around town, but as you get stronger you'll find that the chainrings and crankarms twist when you really bear down on the pedals. This not only wastes energy, but can also cause the chainwheels to rub against the front derailleur, causing faulty shifting and excessive derailleur wear.

People sometimes change lower-quality cranksets to get a different gear ratio. But with better-quality cranksets you can simply change the chainwheels without replacing the whole assembly. The most popular chainring setup on production bikes is a 52-tooth chainwheel on the outside of the crankset (for the high gear range), with a 40-tooth chainwheel inside (for the low gear range). But if you are riding in hilly terrain you may want to change to a 38-tooth inner ring, with a 48-tooth outer ring, since that would give you lower gear ranges to match your terrain.

Special touring sets are also available. A French company, TA, is the unchallenged world specialist in manufacturing cranksets with three instead of two chainrings, making it possible to shift to a super-low gear for climbing mountains with a load of camping gear. TA also offers a larger selection of chainring sizes than any other company, with 28 to 60 teeth available. See the gear chart, Table 5–1 (in Chapter 5), to figure out the gear ratios you'd like to have.

Favorite Freewheel Ratios

The freewheel is the five-geared assembly attached to the rear wheel hub. The main reason to replace the freewheel is to change the gear ratios available on your bike. The most common freewheel setups on production bikes have gears with 14, 17, 19, 22, and 26 teeth. But freewheels are available with as many as 34 teeth in the largest gear—called an "Alpine" gear for extremely hilly terrain. Racers prefer what is called a "close-ratio cluster," a freewheel with only small difference between gears: 13, 15, 17, 19, and 21 teeth. (Again, see the gear chart, Table 5–1, for the gear ratio that best suits your needs.)

Freewheel gears, or sprockets, can be changed individually rather than replacing the whole unit. Consult your local bicycle shop for exact details on how to do this, since each manufacturer has a slightly different design. A good bicycle shop will be set up to change sprocket sizes for you at a nominal fee.

Wheels: Rolling True and Light

When properly maintained—spokes tightened and "trued," bearings repacked and adjusted yearly—wheels will last for many years. Occasionally rims get dented as a result of hitting a curb or riding over a deep pothole, requiring that the rim be straightened out or replaced. Spokes sometimes break, but this usually necessitates only replacement of the broken spokes, plus a "trueing" of the wheel if it wobbles as a result.

If your bike is presently equipped with steel rims, you might consider upgrading it by having a wheelbuilder replace the steel rims with alloy. This is done by removing the old spokes and rim and "lacing" a new rim onto your hub, usually at a cost of around $30 per wheel. The alloy rim, equipped with a top-quality tire, will vastly improve your bike's performance, making it faster, more comfortable, more responsive, and easier to pedal.

Professional wheelbuilders have their own theories about wheel construction, so you'll want to discuss the new wheels in detail with your wheelbuilder. For example, if you're looking for a comfortable touring wheel, you may want low-flange hubs with a resilient three-cross spoke pattern and wide rims. For competition you might want stiffer wheels with high-flange hubs, a three-cross pattern, and rims made for sewup tires. The following chart will provide you with general guidelines, but reserve your final decisions until after you've consulted your wheelbuilder.

Table 4–1   Custom Wheel Selections

Type of Use	Style of Hubs		Spoke Patterns		Style of Rims		
	High-Flange	Low-Flange	Three-Cross	Four-Cross	Narrow Clincher	Wide Clincher	Sewups
General recreation	X			X		X	
Commuting	X			X	X		
Cycle training	X		X		X		
Light touring		X		X	X		
Heavy touring		X		X		X	
Competition	X		X				X

Brakes: Stopping Power at Your Fingertips

As with cranksets, the quality of alloy used in the construction of brakes will determine how well they work. Softer alloys cause the arms that press the brake pads against the rims to twist, making braking uneven, requiring more pressure on the hand levers, and causing excessive brake-pad wear.

The pads on the brakes—that is, the composition rubber portions that rub against the wheel rims—wear out at about the same rate as tires. (Replace the pads at least every time you replace the tires.) If you have inexpensive brakes, you'll discover that they can be vastly improved by exchanging the original pads for pads made by Campagnolo or by a company called Scott Mathauser, which specializes in brake pads. Not all brake-pad assemblies are interchangeable from one company to another, so it's best to check this out with your bike mechanic to make certain that the components are compatible.

Let's say your bike is equipped with Weinmann or Dia-Compe center-pull brakes. You can remove the brake pads that came with them and replace them with a super-gripping set made by Mathauser of a special high-tech composition for about $20. The braking power at your fingertips will increase from 10 to 15 percent, while the pads will last three to four times longer than the originals.

Excellent side-pull brakes are made by Campy, Dura Ace, Universal, Gran-Compe, Weinmann, Zeus, and others. Prices for top-quality brakes range from $65 for Grand-Compe to about $275 for Campy's best. These prices include hand levers, cables, and the braking mechanism itself.

The Pleasure of Perfect Adjustment

Many changes, whether in adjustments or in the installation of higher-quality components, make only subtle differences in your comfort or riding efficiency. You may not notice the differences in the first couple of miles, although they are important, but after several miles your body will begin to signal its response to the changes by manifesting comfort and ease. Keep this in mind whenever you work on your bike. Unless the change you make definitely feels wrong the first time you try it, give your body a chance to feel the effects of the change and respond to them. Your patience and attention to detail will reward you many times over with riding pleasure you might otherwise find difficult to imagine.

FIVE

THE CYCLIST'S GUIDE TO BASIC RIDING KNOW-HOW

One of the major reasons for the bicycle's wide appeal is that anyone—with or without athletic ability—can become proficient enough to really enjoy the sport. There are no unusual skills to learn such as forehands, backhands, free throws, wedge shots, knuckle balls, jump shots . . . just ordinary movements we all use every day in the course of walking down the street, climbing stairs, or running. Moreover, the bicycle is its own athletic coach, since the frame itself guides you through the movements for proper form and peak efficiency.

No doubt many readers will have gotten down the basics of bicycle riding in childhood. These skills are quickly refreshed in adulthood, even when you haven't ridden for years. If you haven't ridden before, ask a knowledgeable friend to assist you. Using a one- or three-speed model, practice on empty parking lots or paved areas around playgrounds and parks where bikes are allowed. Try to find an area with a slight downslope so that you can practice balancing as you roll downhill without having to pedal.

For the person who already knows the basics, there are subtleties of pedaling, braking, shifting, and riding position that can dramatically improve your efficiency and bicycling pleasure. And there's also the often-neglected aspect of *training*, or tuning up your motor—your muscles and cardiovascular system—so that you can fully enjoy bicycling whatever distances you choose to travel.

MAXIMIZING YOUR PEDALING POWER

Regardless of the type of bike you're riding, the way you actually work the pedals will affect the quality of your ride. Most people carry over from childhood a bad pedaling habit called "pumping." If you watch a child riding up a hill, you'll see that he or she stands up and applies weight and power to the pedals about one-third to half of the way down to the bottom of the stroke. (See Fig. 5–1.) This produces a characteristically short, choppy, pumping rhythm that is extremely inefficient.

An experienced cyclist learns to extend the power stroke to a full 180 degrees. If you ride without toe clips, concentrate on the way your muscles feel when your foot reaches the top of the stroke, or just slightly beyond the 12-o'clock position. Think of this as the trigger point—the signal for you to pour on the power and push the pedal to the bottom of its stroke.

When you start riding with toe clips, you acquire a second trigger point. When your foot is in the 6-o'clock position you pull up on the pedal, using

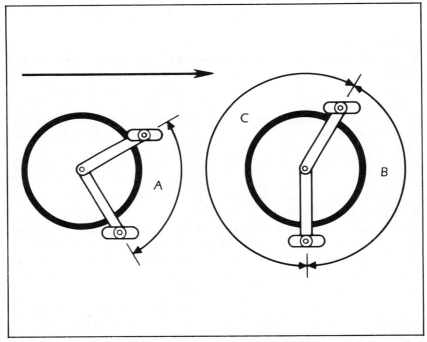

Fig. 5-1 *Beginning riders tend to push the pedals only within the quadrant marked "A," producing a characteristic pumping action. Such pedaling greatly limits the amount of power transmitted to the rear wheel. The experienced cyclist learns to push the pedals through the "B" arc. With toe clips, the rider can apply power, by pulling up on the pedals, through the "C" arc as well, greatly increasing pedaling efficiency and power. Such pedaling produces a characteristic spinning action.*

the toe clip to lift the pedal to the 12-o'clock position. Using your imagination, learn to visualize your feet spinning around in powerful, efficient circles. Actually form a picture of this in your mind. You'll be surprised to discover that this exercise of imagination really does influence your physical performance, since it programs your nervous system to send specific signals to your muscles. As every accomplished athlete knows, the mind plays a major role in perfecting every physical technique.

HANDLING THE BRAKES

Coaster brakes such as those found on many children's bikes hardly need a word of instruction. By simply reversing the direction of your pedals, you make your bike slow down or come to a stop. If you are riding a three-speed or a ten-speed bike, you'll be using handbrakes to stop.

As surprising as it may seem, all too many cyclists never take the time to learn which lever controls which brake. They simply squeeze the levers indiscriminately whenever they want to slow down. This practice can be dangerous, especially when you need to stop quickly, because each brake actually requires slightly different handling. Here's why.

In all braking situations, the front wheel—not the rear—has the most weight on it and thus has the best traction. Watch the way a car or a motorcycle dips down in front when it's braking, and you'll see this principle in action. Because of the traction on the front wheel, the front brake is more effective and requires more pressure than the rear brake. Conversely, with reduced traction on the rear wheel, applying too much brake pressure can stop the wheel from turning altogether, even though the bike continues to move forward, causing it to go into a skid. Thus it's worth your while, before you take your next ride, to ascertain which lever controls which brake.

Once you've got these principles in mind, you will be able to stop smoothly and safely in all circumstances. Just remember to apply gradual, even pressure rather than intermittent or grabbing pressure. You'll quickly develop a sensitivity to the effects of your hand pressure on the brakes and make adjustments automatically to control your stop.

GETTING THE MOST OUT OF YOUR RIDING POSITION

If your bike is equipped with dropped handlebars, your upper body gets to play an active role in maximizing pedaling effectiveness. Your arms, back, and stomach muscles make corrections for balance; they also flex to provide leverage for your leg muscles when you're climbing a hill or pouring on the speed. There are three basic hand positions provided by dropped-style handlebars, each with its aerodynamic as well as muscular advantages. (See Fig. 5–2.)

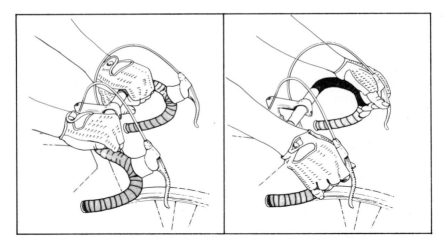

In the lowest riding position, with your hands on the "hooks," you are crouched over to minimize wind resistance. This position also enables your arms, back muscles, stomach muscles, and legs to work together to bring maximum power to the pedals. This is the most effective position for pulling uphill and for attaining high speeds.

For leisurely pedaling in flat terrain, you can place your hands on the top of the handlebars. In this position—although you increase the wind resistance against your body—you gain visibility, which is useful when you need to watch the traffic or want to enjoy the passing scenery.

The compromise between these two positions is what cyclists call "riding the brakes"—that is, resting your hands on the padded brake hoods as you ride. In this position your body is relatively aerodynamic while you retain good visibility; you have good leverage for pedaling power; and you can easily reach the brake levers. For these reasons, this is the most common and comfortable riding position for the experienced cyclist.

Experiment with each position in a variety of riding circumstances. Changing positions frequently as you ride minimizes sore hands and aching muscles.

THE SECRETS OF EFFECTIVE SHIFTING

What is the reason for having multiple gears on a bike? Because of the way our bodies are made, we are able to produce maximum pedaling power and efficiency only while pedaling in the range of 60 to 100 revolutions per minute.* Pedaling slower than 60 rpm strains muscles and can cause sore or

*Professional bike racers train to pedal at speeds up to 120 rpm for short bursts.

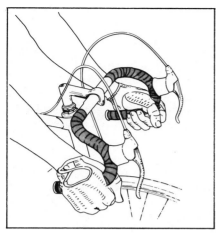

Fig. 5-2   The ten-speed-style handlebar is an amazingly versatile tool that has evolved from practical experience in racing and touring. These dropped-style bars offer three basic hand positions, as shown above. Each position offers different pedaling and comfort advantages.

injured joints and tendonitis. Pedaling faster than 100 rpm just isn't physically possible for most people.

Bicycle gearing is designed so that you can maintain your optimal pedaling speeds regardless of the terrain. A low gear lets you pedal at 60 to 100 rpm even though you're climbing a steep hill at five miles per hour. A high gear lets you pedal at 60 to 100 rpm even though you're traveling along a flat, open road at 20 or 25 miles per hour. Without a wide selection of gearing you'd find yourself pedaling at, let's say, 20 rpm to climb a hill (hard on the knees!) and 210 rpm (a physical impossibility) to make that same bike travel along the open road at 20-25 mph.

If you're a three-speed rider, shifting your bike is a cinch. You simply flick the gearshift lever while you are coasting or standing still. Do not attempt to shift while you are pedaling your bike. (As you will see, exactly the opposite is true for shifting a ten-speed.) With most three-speed bikes, the low range is 33⅓ percent lower than the middle-range gear, and the high gear is the same percent higher than the middle-range gear. Knowing which gear range to choose becomes obvious very quickly—usually within the first half-hour of riding.

Shifting a ten-speed, derailleur-equipped bike is considerably more complicated, not only because you have two shift levers and ten gear speeds to deal with, but also because—unlike the three-speed—the sequence of positions of the shift levers does not reflect the actual sequence of gears. But more about that in a moment. Let's begin with the practical aspects of operating the shifters and save the theory of gearing for later.

The best way we know of to demystify the derailleur mechanism is to play around with it and examine its workings before you get on the road. Bear in mind that the *derailleurs can only be shifted while the cranks are in motion.*

This is very important. You can easily jam and damage your gears by attempting to shift when you are not pedaling.

For practice before you actually get on and ride, we suggest that you suspend your bike by ropes from a tree branch or the garage rafters so you can turn the cranks by hand while freely manipulating the shift levers. It's best to position yourself on the right-hand side of your bike, using your left hand to crank the pedals (at about 30 rpm) and your right to shift the gear levers. Don't hesitate to be aggressive in your experiments, and watch what happens to the chain as you shift.

STEP 1.   Start by putting the bike in its lowest gear (see Fig. 5–3), with the chain on the biggest sprocket in the rear and the smallest sprocket in the front. This is the gear you'd use for climbing a hill. Notice how it feels to crank the pedals, and notice the positions of the shift levers.

STEP 2.   Put the bike in its highest gear, with the chain on the smallest sprocket in the rear and the largest sprocket in the front. You'd

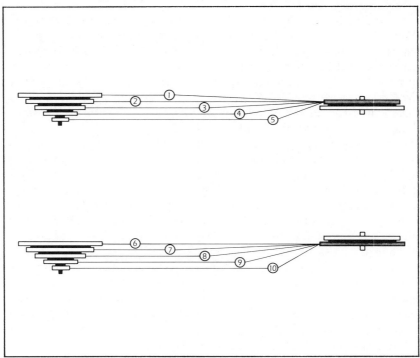

Fig. 5-3   *Low gears are for pulling hills, while high gears are for speed. Notice that gears 5 and 6 require extreme crossovers of the chain. On most bikes this causes excessive wear in chain, sprockets, chainwheels, and derailleurs and should be avoided.*

use this gear on flat, open road. Notice how it feels to crank the pedals, and notice the positions of the shift levers.

STEP 3.   Set your gears in a mid-range position: chain on the large gear in front and the middle, or third, gear in the rear.

Continue to experiment with your gears until you feel comfortable about the process of shifting. Then set your bike in its mid-range gear and remove the ropes so you can ride. Ride for 10 or 15 minutes in the mid-range gear so you'll become familiar with the way it feels. Shift into the low range and see how that feels. Then shift into high range and see how that feels.

Practice shifting from high to mid-range to low range, and then back again, as you ride. Repeat these patterns again and again, riding in a leisurely manner as you do so, until you feel comfortable.

After you've mastered these three gears, the rest will come easily and naturally. When the pedaling gets too hard, select the next lower gear. When it gets too easy and your pedals are spinning without making headway, shift to the next higher gear. As you progress you'll learn how to shift one gear at a time and to anticipate the terrain ahead so you can get your bike in the right gear when it's needed. But all these are techniques that the bicycle will dictate to you as you ride, so don't worry about trying to understand them verbally. As everyone learns in the end, the bicycle is its own best teacher.

TIPS FOR SHIFTING DERAILLEURS

1.   Anticipate the terrain. Think about the gear you'll want to be in when you get to the beginning of a long hill, for example. When you're bearing down on the pedals on a steep hill, the derailleur usually won't carry the chain to a lower gear. So get into that lower gear before you find yourself on a hill, sweating and cursing because you're in a gear that's too high and you can't get shifted into a lower one.

2.   Shift into lower gears when approaching stop streets or signal lights. Remember, you can't shift gears standing still, and you'll want that low gear when you start out again. Think ahead and drop into the lower gear by shifting a few yards before you stop.

3.   Learn to recognize and adjust for the sounds made by the chain rubbing against the derailleur cage or improperly aligned on a sprocket. The chain should move noiselessly on the sprockets. If it makes a noise, move the shift lever—front or rear—in small increments until the sound goes away. With experience, you'll be able to tell from the sound which derailleur needs adjustment.

4.   If your chain slips off either the front or rear sprocket, your derailleur needs adjustment. Check Chapter 15 to learn how to do it yourself (it's not hard), or take it to your bike shop, where they'll charge you a small amount to correct the problem.

5.   If your bike slips out of gear, your shift levers probably need adjustment. Shift levers have an adjustment screw on the end of the axle shafts that hold the levers themselves. Better levers have wire loops, wing nuts, or knurled knobs so that the rider can easily make this adjustment while riding. However, a few brands of levers have a screw that requires a dime or a screwdriver to tighten it. Experiment with this adjustment and get into the habit of checking it routinely.

UNDERSTANDING THE INNER WORKINGS OF GEARING

Most people become quite proficient at shifting gears through the trial-and-error method described above. As you progress in your riding abilities, you may want a deeper understanding of gearing systems so you can select exactly the gear you want without relying exclusively on trial and error. One of the most useful mental tools you can have for understanding gears is a gear table, which reveals how the positions of the chain on the chainwheel and freewheel affect the distance you travel with each turn of the cranks. Here is an example: Look at Table 5–1, the gear table, right now. Read across the table for the ratio you'll get with the chain of your bike lined up on the 40-tooth chainwheel and a 12-tooth rear freewheel sprocket. The ratio achieved with this gear selection is 90.0.

An experienced rider will refer to this as a "90-inch gear," but what does that mean? All the ratios on the gear tables in use today are based on the old-fashioned high-wheelers, or "Ordinaries." A 90-inch gear is the equivalent, on a 10-speed bike, of riding an Ordinary with a wheel 90 inches in diameter. Basic physics will demonstrate that the larger the wheel the greater the distance you'll travel with each turn of the crank. The smaller the wheel the shorter the distance. Thus a small wheel—say, 30 inches in diameter—will be better for climbing steep hills, whereas a large wheel—say, 90 inches in diameter—will allow the rider to achieve high speeds on flat terrain.

A question that many people ask is, "How far do I travel with each turn of the cranks?" To calculate this, you have to know the *circumference* of the wheel, which you get by multiplying its diameter by pi—that is, 3.1416. Thus, with a 30-inch wheel you'll travel 94.248 inches (30 × 3.1416 = 94.248), or 7.85 feet. With a 90-inch gear you'll travel 282.74 inches (90 × 3.1416 = 282.74), or 23.56 feet.

The truth is that few cyclists concern themselves with what the ratios really mean except to note in their minds that a 30-inch gear is good for climbing hills, while a 90-inch gear is good for higher speeds in flat terrain. The numbers are used only for comparison of one gear to another—a sort of kinetic code that begins to have meaning only as your body becomes accustomed to the way it feels to ride in one gear or another.

Table 5–1   Gear Table for 27-Inch (Standard 10-Speed) Wheels

Rear Sprocket Size (Rear Derailleur)	Chainwheel Size (Front Derailleur)												
	26	28	30	32	34	36	38	39	40	42	43	44	45
12	58.5	63.0	67.5	72.0	76.5	81.0	85.5	87.2	90.0	94.5	96.7	00.0	101.2
13	54.0	58.1	62.3	66.5	70.6	74.8	78.9	81.1	83.1	87.2	89.3	91.4	93.4
14	50.1	54.0	57.8	61.7	65.6	69.4	73.3	75.2	77.1	81.0	82.9	84.9	86.8
15	46.8	50.4	54.0	57.6	61.2	64.8	68.4	70.2	72.0	75.6	77.4	79.2	81.0
16	43.9	47.2	50.6	54.0	57.4	60.7	64.1	65.2	67.5	70.9	72.5	74.3	75.9
17	41.3	44.4	47.6	50.8	54.0	57.1	60.3	61.9	63.5	66.7	68.3	69.9	71.5
18	39.0	42.0	45.0	48.0	51.0	54.0	57.0	58.5	60.0	63.0	64.5	66.0	67.5
19	36.9	39.7	42.6	45.5	48.3	51.1	54.0	55.4	56.8	59.7	61.0	62.5	64.0
20	35.1	37.8	40.5	43.2	45.9	48.6	51.3	53.0	54.0	56.7	58.1	59.4	60.7
21	33.4	36.0	38.5	41.1	43.7	46.2	48.9	50.3	51.4	54.0	55.2	56.6	57.8
22	31.9	34.3	36.8	39.3	41.7	44.2	46.6	47.0	49.1	51.5	52.7	54.0	55.2
23	30.5	32.8	35.2	37.6	39.9	42.2	44.6	45.8	47.0	49.3	50.4	51.6	52.8
24	29.2	31.5	33.7	36.0	38.2	40.5	41.8	43.4	45.0	47.3	48.3	49.5	50.6
25	28.1	30.2	32.4	34.6	36.7	38.8	41.0	42.1	43.2	45.4	46.4	47.5	48.6
26	27.0	20.0	31.2	33.2	35.3	37.4	39.5	40.5	41.5	43.6	44.6	45.7	46.7
27	26.0	28.0	30.0	32.0	34.0	36.0	38.0	39.0	40.0	42.0	43.0	44.0	45.0
28	25.0	27.0	28.9	30.8	32.8	34.7	36.6	37.6	38.6	40.5	41.4	42.4	43.4
29	24.2	26.0	27.9	29.8	31.6	33.5	35.4	36.3	37.2	39.1	40.0	41.0	41.9
30	23.4	25.2	27.0	28.8	30.6	32.4	34.2	35.1	36.0	37.8	38.7	39.6	40.5
31	22.6	24.3	26.1	27.8	29.6	31.3	33.0	33.9	34.8	36.5	37.4	38.3	39.1
32	22.0	23.6	25.3	27.0	28.7	30.3	32.1	32.9	33.8	35.5	36.3	37.1	37.9
33	20.7	22.2	23.8	25.4	27.0	28.6	30.1	31.0	31.8	33.3	34.1	34.9	35.7
34	19.5	21.0	22.5	24.0	25.5	27.0	28.5	29.2	30.0	31.5	32.2	33.0	33.8

Table 5–1 (continued)

Rear Sprocket Size (Rear Derailleur)	Chainwheel Size (Front Derailleur)												
	46	47	48	49	50	51	52	53	54	55	56	57	58
12	103.5	105.7	108.0	110.2	112.5	114.7	117.0	119.3	121.5	123.7	126.0	128.2	130.5
13	95.5	97.6	99.7	101.8	103.9	105.9	108.0	110.0	112.1	114.2	116.3	118.3	120.4
14	87.7	90.6	92.6	94.5	96.4	98.3	100.3	102.2	104.1	106.2	108.0	109.9	111.9
15	82.8	84.6	86.4	88.2	90.0	91.8	93.6	95.4	97.2	99.0	100.8	102.6	104.4
16	77.6	79.3	81.0	82.7	84.4	86.0	87.8	89.4	91.1	92.8	94.5	96.1	97.9
17	73.1	74.6	76.2	77.8	79.4	81.0	82.6	84.1	85.7	87.3	88.9	90.5	92.1
18	69.0	70.5	72.0	73.5	75.0	76.5	78.0	79.5	81.0	82.5	84.0	85.5	87.0
19	65.4	66.8	68.2	69.6	71.1	72.4	73.9	75.3	76.7	78.1	79.5	81.0	82.4
20	62.1	63.4	64.8	66.2	67.5	68.5	70.2	71.5	72.9	74.5	75.6	76.9	78.3
21	59.1	60.4	61.7	63.0	64.3	65.5	66.9	68.1	69.4	70.7	72.0	73.3	74.6
22	56.5	56.7	58.9	60.1	61.4	62.5	63.8	65.0	66.2	67.5	68.7	69.9	71.2
23	54.0	55.2	56.3	57.5	58.7	59.8	61.0	62.2	63.4	64.5	65.7	66.9	68.0
24	51.8	52.9	54.0	55.1	56.3	57.3	58.5	59.6	60.7	61.8	63.0	64.1	65.3
25	49.7	50.8	51.8	52.9	54.0	55.1	56.2	57.2	58.3	59.4	60.4	61.6	62.7
26	47.8	48.8	49.9	50.9	51.9	53.0	54.0	55.0	56.1	57.1	58.1	59.2	60.2
27	46.0	47.0	48.0	49.0	50.0	51.0	52.0	53.0	54.0	55.0	56.0	57.0	58.0
28	44.4	45.3	46.3	47.2	48.2	49.1	50.1	51.1	52.0	53.0	54.0	54.9	55.9
29	42.8	43.7	44.7	45.6	46.5	47.5	48.4	49.4	50.3	51.2	52.1	53.1	54.0
30	41.4	42.3	43.2	44.1	45.0	45.9	46.8	47.7	48.6	49.5	50.4	51.3	52.2
31	40.0	40.8	41.8	42.6	43.5	44.4	45.3	46.2	47.0	47.9	48.7	49.6	50.5
32	38.8	39.7	40.5	41.3	42.2	43.0	43.9	44.7	45.6	46.4	47.2	48.0	49.0
34	36.6	37.3	38.1	38.9	39.7	40.5	41.3	42.0	42.8	43.7	44.5	45.2	46.0
36	34.5	35.2	36.0	36.7	37.5	38.8	39.0	39.7	40.5	41.3	42.0	42.7	43.5

There has been talk among some cyclists about revising gear tables so that they tell the cyclist something more concrete than they do now. But we are as slow to change in this as we are in changing to the metric system of weights and measures. To perhaps speed the transition to gear charts that are more meaningful to the general rider, and to provide you with a better perspective about what each gear means in everyday terms, we've prepared a gear chart that tells the actual distances one travels with each turn of the crank. To keep it simple, I based this new kind of table on one of the most common gearing setups for production ten-speeds—that is, a bicycle with 40- and 52-tooth chainwheels and a freewheel cluster with 14-, 17-, 20-, 24-, and 28-tooth cogs.

Table 5–2   Gear Table of Distances Traveled

For 27-inch (Standard Ten-Speed) Wheels

Rear Sprocket Size (rear derailleur)	Chainwheel Size (front derailleur)	
	40	52
14	20.0 ft.	26.1 ft.
17	16.5	21.4
20	14.1	18.0
24	11.8	15.2
28	10.0	12.9

The figures in the body of this table refer to distances traveled (in feet) with each full revolution of the crank.

If you look at the table closely, you'll see that the ratios (distances traveled) do not proceed consecutively from the first to the tenth gear. Rather, they skip back and forth from left to right on the table—in actual practice calling for some very tricky shifting.

On my transcontinental rides, it is important to be able to quickly select the next ratio up or down. To do this sometimes requires shifting the positions of both front and rear derailleurs simultaneously. In order to take full advantage of every ounce of my energy, I've learned to think of the sequence of my gears in terms of actual ratios (distances traveled) rather than derailleur positions, as we've described them up to this point.

TRAINING ROUTES FOR EASY RIDING

With practice and experience, all the riding techniques described in this chapter will become second-nature reflexes requiring no thought at all. To hasten this eventuality, it's a good idea to begin with an ideal training course—a route with light traffic, easy terrain, and no dogs—so you can concentrate on developing your riding skills.

Plot out a route that you will enjoy traveling three or four times a week. Depending on the terrain and your own physical capacities of the moment, this route should be somewhere between five and seven miles long. Such distances can be covered in half an hour, riding at 5–14 mph.

For the first dozen rides, always repeat the same route. This allows you to experience the ways in which higher or lower gears can improve your performance over the same terrain. Try it in a high gear one day and a low gear the next, and compare the differences in the way you feel at the end of the ride. Knowing what's coming up, you can anticipate grades and get into the right gear when you need it.

Finally, set aside a certain time of day for your rides. For some, the best time of day will be early in the morning; for others, the evening hours. Seek ways to make those training rides enjoyable and stimulating: ride with a friend, route your rides through areas you enjoy seeing, or reward yourself at the end of the ride. You'll be surprised at how quickly the ride itself will become its own reward—a source of pleasure to which you can look forward every day.

TIPS FOR IMPROVING YOUR RIDE

The more you ride, the more you'll become aware of ways to improve your cycling form. You may feel that you're working too hard for the distance you travel. Or you may feel that certain parts of your body are more uncomfortable than they have to be. Or you may feel insecure in traffic. Here are five important tips to help you solve these and other problems:

1. STAY IN LOWER GEARS. Beginning and intermediate riders have a tendency to pedal their bikes in gears that are too high. This can cause knee pain because of the pressure exerted on joints and ligaments each time the rider bears down on the pedals. Faster pedaling speeds reduce this pressure by distributing the same power output over more revolutions. Thus these faster pedaling rates use energy more effectively. Try to keep up a regular cadence of 60 to 75 revolutions per minute. You can gauge your rate by counting the number of times your right knee comes up while the second hand of your watch indicates one minute.

2. PEDAL IN CIRCLES. As you pedal, try to visualize your feet making the full circle of the cranks through the complete pedaling stroke. This will have the effect of automatically sending a message to your muscles to do just that. The visualization trick will not work instantly, but the more you remember to practice it, the more efficient your pedaling will become. If your bike is equipped with toe clips, you will in fact be able to apply pressure on the pedals through the full circle of the cranks.

3.   CHANGE HAND POSITIONS FREQUENTLY. Riding (or doing any-thing else) in one position for too long will cause your back and arm muscles to stiffen up. Change positions often as you ride, giving your muscles an opportunity to stretch and flex. This is the best prescription there is for preventing the kinds of stiffness characteristic of cycling.

4.   PAY ATTENTION TO THE WAY YOU FEEL. As you ride, remind yourself to be aware of any discomforts you may be feeling. Are your hands numb or tingling? Do your shoulders feel tight? Is your rear end getting sore? While riding, make small changes in your posture to relieve pressure on the parts of your body that hurt. Change handholds on the bars. Slide a bit forward or back on your seat. Arch your back in a slightly—very slightly—different way. Nod your head gently or rotate it from side to side to relieve stiffness. When specific discomforts persist, consider the equipment itself: Is your seat properly adjusted? Are your handlebars too high or too low? Would handlebar padding make your hands more comfortable? Would a different saddle ease that pain in your rear end? Are your toe clips the right size? Keep exploring new ways to bring pleasure to your ride. When you feel pain or discomfort, assume that these sensations are signals to change something either in your bike or in your riding style.

5.   GET OFF AND PUSH WHEN PEDALING GETS TOO HARD. False pride causes more sore knees, strained muscles, and other health problems than any other single factor in biking. This happens for one of two reasons: You overestimate your present physical capacities and bully the bike up a hill that's too steep, or you neglect to shift into a lower gear in time for a hill. When you find yourself in either of these situations, stop, get off, swallow your pride if necessary, and walk your bike up the hill. Remember, you want to finish your ride with good associations about the experience. In a strange way your body does remember the last ride you took, and even though you may tell yourself it was satisfying to pedal up that impossible hill, your body knows better. Next time you want to go for a ride and you find yourself harboring a vague resistance to the idea, think back to your last ride. That resistance may be your body remembering what you did to it last time on that long, steep hill that your false pride forced it to climb.

A LAST WORD ON TUNING UP YOUR MOTOR

Now that you've got the techniques for riding down pat, don't be surprised if your body registers complaints in the form of aches, vague pains, and general stiffness after an afternoon on your bike. Although your bicycle is a vehicle, it's not like a car. You can't just get in and go without preparation. Your energy and your physical efforts are the bike's only sources of power.

"I try to explain the importance of getting your body in shape for riding to everyone who buys a bike from me. I consider that the most important part of my job." The speaker is Trudy Douglas, a bicycle saleswoman in Minneapolis. "I tell them to ride as much as they can every day, gradually increasing their mileage over a couple of months. Everyone has their own timetables. But you do have to ride to get good on a bike, and for a while it may not be as much fun as you might like. You're going to experience some aches and pains, but that's okay. That's what's supposed to be happening. It doesn't take long, and then bicycling really opens up to you. I mean it *really* opens up. You can do anything with a bike, go anywhere. But getting in shape to ride it well takes time, and it takes patience, and that is the difficult thing you have to communicate to your customers!"

In speaking to a number of bicycle salespeople, I found Trudy's thoughts not at all unusual. Everyone I talked to expressed a concern for telling new riders about the changes their bodies will go through on the way to full enjoyment of the sport. Eventually, every aspect of your life will benefit from your increased lung capacity, your improved muscle strength and tone, and the miles of new capillaries you'll grow to carry oxygen to your muscle tissue. But it takes time and patience for your body to respond to the new demands you're making on it. Our advice is to keep pushing yourself so that your body's capacities grow, but not beyond the point where riding ceases to be a pleasure. If you take it slow and easy at first, tuning up your body over time, you may soon find yourself relishing the greater rigors of commuting or even cycle training.

THE COMPLETE BICYCLE COMMUTER

A friend of mine was in Washington, D.C., attending a national conference addressed to solving transportation problems in the inner city. As he walked through Lafayette Park on his way to one of the meetings, he was passed by a man on a bicycle with a briefcase strapped to a rack over the rear wheel. My friend took particular notice because the cyclist was wearing a shirt with the slogan "Bike to Work" emblazoned across the back. When he arrived at the meeting, my friend was surprised to see the same man who'd passed him on the bike taking his place at the podium to address the conference. It turned out to be none other than Neil Goldschmidt, who at that time was our nation's Secretary of Transportation.

That the bicycle has become recognized as a viable alternative to the automobile for meeting many of America's transportation needs is nowhere better reflected than in the Federal Highway Act of 1973. This act provides funds for developing bicycle routes in all cities in the United States. Under Section 141 of the Surface Transportation Act, $20 million per year is allocated nationwide for the development of bicycle facilities.

Responding to obvious needs at the grass-roots level as well as the federal government's efforts to encourage bicycle commuters, many state and local governments have appointed bicycle transportation coordinators as regular members of their staffs. As early as 1973, the District of Columbia, New Jersey, and North Carolina were busily at work on master plans to solve bicycle transportation problems. One outcome of these efforts was the North Carolina Bicycle and Bikeways Act of 1974, which called for a State Department of Bicycle Transportation to develop and construct a state bikeway system and to promote bicycling and bicycle safety. The North Carolina Act serves as a model for other government bodies that want to develop effective bike routes and facilities.

The rising cost of operating a car has had a major impact on the growing interest in bicycle commuting. The American Automobile Association estimates that in the early 1980s the total cost to drive a car—including depreciation, gasoline, licenses, insurance, maintenance, parking fees, tolls and accessories—will be from 28 to 30 cents per mile. If, like most automobile owners, you drive 10,000 miles each year, you are paying from $2,800 to $3,000 annually for this privilege. Compare these figures to the expense of owning a bicycle. The initial cost of a high-quality ten-speed suitable for comfortable commuting is from $175 to $250. Total maintenance costs are under $50 per year.

How reasonable is it to look to the bike as a substitute for the car? Two studies, one by the Chicago Area Transportation Study and the other by the Transportation Planning Program of Minneapolis/St. Paul, showed that the average person commutes 6.9 miles to work in a car at an average speed of 22 miles per hour. Thus, the car commuter takes 18.8 minutes to drive to work, *not* including the time spent getting into the car, starting the engine, warming it up, finding a parking place at the destination, getting out of the car, locking up, and walking to the workplace.

Now let's take a look at the bike. First, the average commuting distance of 6.9 miles is well within the physical capacities of even a beginning cyclist. Traveling at a reasonable average speed of 12 miles per hour, the cyclist arrives at work in 34.5 minutes, conveniently parking the vehicle at the doorstep. The bicycle commuter wastes no time warming up an engine, finding a parking place, and walking to work from the parking lot. Thus, even though the time it takes to cover the 6.9 miles to work may be 15.7 minutes longer on the bike, the actual door-to-door time for the bicycle commuter turns out to be quite comparable to door-to-door commuting time by car.

According to Peter Rich, owner of one of the most active bicycle shops in the San Francisco Bay Area, the rising cost of gasoline in 1980 has pressed bicycle sales to a new high. Rich says there just aren't enough bikes available to keep up with the demand. Although European, American, and Japanese bicycle makers are working at full capacity, bike retailers are unable to fill all the orders they get. By far the greatest numbers of bikes are being sold to people who want an alternative to the high cost of driving their cars. The same cyclists see their machines as an aid to health and a fine form of recreation, but commuting by bike to save money is the major motivation for new bike purchases.

In response to the growing trend toward commuting to work by bike, many employers nationwide are encouraging their employees by providing safe bicycle parking on the job. Some are offering the cycle commuters lockers and even showers so that those commuting longer distances can freshen up after their arrival. An electronics manufacturer in Kalamazoo, Michigan, has indoor parking facilities for its cycle commuters, and the employees' credit union offers special low-interest loans for people wanting to buy bikes to get to work.

Sometimes, because of the terrain or other geographic obstacles, the commute to work by bike must be aided by mass transit. In the San Francisco area, the A.C. Transit Company, Bay Area Rapid Transit, and the ferryboat system that ordinarily provide transportation between the cities around San Francisco Bay allow you to take your bike along with you. Similar arrangements for bike commuters are available in Portland, Seattle, Chicago, Denver, and Minneapolis, to name just a few. In addition, there are few cities in the U.S. today which don't have marked bike routes and a bicycle transportation coordinator to provide maps and other route information.

CHOOSING THE RIGHT COMMUTING BIKE

To get off to the right start, select a bike that's suitable for the distance and terrain you'll be traveling, giving consideration to the amount of traffic you'll encounter along your route and the parking facilities you'll have available at work. Let's look at some concrete examples:

Tom Barrett is an automobile mechanic in Denver who lives six miles from his job. There are no major hills between his home and his workplace. There are only limited facilities for him to park his bike during working hours, and he hasn't ridden a bike since he was a kid.

For Tom a quality three-speed bike is ideal, and not simply because it is less expensive than a ten-speed. On the contrary, the three-speed actually has some advantages over a ten-speed in Tom's case.

First, he can easily cover five or six miles of flat terrain in 20 to 30 minutes on a three-speed bike. If Tom is in good physical condition and doesn't have to stop for too many traffic signals, he can cover his five or six miles in 15 minutes.

In city traffic, the standard three-speed with flat handlebars will place Tom up high so he can easily see and be seen by motorists. On such a bike his head will actually be higher than most of the cars being manufactured these days. Being able to look around in city traffic is important, and Tom would probably find that doing so is more restricted on a ten-speed with dropped handlebars than on a three-speed with flat bars. Moreover, because the three-speed bike can be shifted while standing still or coasting, he can take his mind off the gears and keep his attention focused on the road.

The three-speed bike is significantly less enticing to thieves than a ten-speed. With the limited bicycle parking facilities where he works, Tom can leave the bike chained to a lamp pole on the street and feel fairly certain that it will still be there when he returns.

Finally, though Tom Barrett's cycling experience is limited, he can learn to operate the three-speed safely and smoothly in an hour or so. Having mastered the operation of the bike itself, he can then keep his attention on navigating through heavy traffic during the commuting hours.

By contrast, let's take the case of Joanne Thompson, who manages a small travel bureau in a suburban shopping center in New Jersey. Having bicycle-toured in Europe as well as the United States and Canada, she is a strong and skilled rider. Although she must commute to work through 15 miles of moderately hilly terrain, her business hours allow her to ride to and from work during times when automobile traffic is light. A large storage room in the back of her shop provides a safe place for her bike during the day.

In Joanne's case, a ten-speed bike makes more sense than a three-speed machine. The distance she travels, in combination with the hilly terrain, almost requires a ten-speed. Since she will be riding during light traffic hours, the factors that Tom has to consider—visibility and shifting gears—are not relevant.

These two cases represent two very different sets of commuter needs. Still another example is Donald Mack, who has purchased a folding, or collapsible, bike. He takes it with him on the commuter train, quickly assembles it upon his arrival, and then cycles three miles across town to his office.

One final example will complete the picture. Jack Fraser teaches at a small community college. He rides nine miles to work each day, four miles through traffic and five through a lightly rolling rural setting. Although he is not a fast rider, he has built up stamina and enjoys his daily bicycle commute. To match his particular needs, he bought a good-quality ten-speed bike and had the derailleur system replaced by a three-speed hub. (See Fig. 6–1.)

The range of gears on Jack's bike is adequate for the kind of riding he does, and the comfort and light weight of the ten-speed frame make his daily ride easy and enjoyable. Preferring the upright riding position, he removed the original dropped handlebars and replaced them with flat tourister-type bars. A sturdy carrying rack over the rear wheel allows him to carry his briefcase back and forth from college. While he is at work he is able to keep his bike behind the desk in his office.

The following chart will help you identify your requirements in a commuter bike.

CONDITIONING FOR COMMUTERS

Once you have the right bike, the next step is to let your body know what you've got in store for it. If you just jump on your bike and go riding off to your job six miles away, your body will extract its due in the form of aching muscles, exhaustion, and a dampened spirit. The next time you want to ride

Table 6–1   Match the Bike to Your Commuting Needs

Type of Commute	Bicycle Specifications			
	Weight	Handlebars	Gears	Misc. Equipment
2–5 miles City traffic Flat terrain Average rider	Not critical	Flat	Single-speed or three-speed	Carrying rack Lights
5–7 miles City and suburban traffic Gradual grades Average rider	35 pounds or less	Flat or dropped	Three-speed or ten-speed	Carrying rack Lights
7–10 miles City and suburban traffic Varied terrain Experienced rider	30 pounds or less	Dropped	Three-speed or ten-speed	Carrying rack Lights Toe clips Tool kit
10 or more miles Varied traffic Varied terrain Experienced rider	28 pounds or less	Dropped	Ten-speed	Carrying rack Lights Toe clips Tool kit
Must carry bike aboard commuter train 3–5 miles bike commute from train	Not critical	Flat	Single-speed or three-speed	Folding bike Carrying rack Lights Tool kit

Fig. 6-1 Variations of this super-three-speed commuter bike have been around for many years—usually custom-built by local bike shops, which start with a ten-speed frame. This bike was built by Hal Bennett for his own in-town use. The three-speed coaster brake is safe and convenient in city traffic. Note the safety equipment, such as lights and a loud bell on the handlebar stem. (Photo by Linda Bennett.)

you'll have to battle with a nagging inner voice that remembers the last time you rode and doesn't want to repeat the experience.

Even if you plan to commute only three or four miles each way to work, you should expect to go through a conditioning period. Your body will adjust to the bike and its physical demands on you. We recommend that instead of starting your commute by bike immediately, you take from two to four weeks to signal your body of your intentions and let it make the physiological changes necessary to meet those demands.

After work, and on weekends, start riding the distance you intend to commute. Take it slowly at first. Make your rides as enjoyable as you can. If you feel sore the next day after a ride, skip your training ride for that day. Give your body a chance to recuperate and grow. However, don't let too much time elapse between rides. Ride *at least* three days every week.

During the conditioning period, expect a certain amount of discomfort. Your lungs, heart, and muscles are, after all, working a little harder than they normally do. Of course, heed the warning all coaches give their trainees: If you have pain that is accompanied by worry, or is persistent, or seems in any way unusual to you, consult your physician.

Your seat will toughen up to the saddle, assuming you're riding on a saddle that's of reasonably good quality and is adjusted right. But the toughening-up process can take time. Have faith and understand that the discomfort you're experiencing will pass.

When your conditioning rides begin to feel more comfortable and pleasurable, make a few trial runs over the same route you'll be taking to work. Do these runs on the weekend, if you wish, so you won't be under the pressure of heavy traffic and time constraints. Do take along your watch, though, and time yourself to see how long the trip takes you.

MAPPING OUT THE ROUTE

Federal laws now require that a certain percentage of all highway taxes goes into developing bikeways. Check with your City Hall or with bike clubs in your area to get more information. Most bicycle shops have the addresses of bike clubs that can help you. Joining a club, even as a non-active member, keeps you in touch with bicycle happenings where you live—everything from race schedules to legislative changes that might affect you as a commuter. As a member of a bike club, you become part of a political entity; most clubs are politically active in lobbying for bikepaths or bike parking facilities.

If you can't get the route information you need through City Hall or a bike club, you can easily map out your route on your own. Go out on your bike, or even in the car, and explore the distance between your home and your job. Look for marked bikepaths first. If you do find them, look the paths over with a critical eye. Don't automatically assume that because they're marked as such they are reasonable routes for you. The bikepaths may be a form of tokenism, put in by politicians who've never ridden bikes, in order to comply with state or federal laws.

Choose your terrain to whatever extent you can. If you don't like hills, and you can find a way to avoid them, do so. But the more you ride, the less the hills will bother you. In time you may even prefer a hill or two to provide you with an early-morning physical challenge.

Next, consider the flow of traffic on your route. Will you be encountering cross-traffic, and, if so, is this cross-traffic controlled by stop signs or traffic lights? Unmarked intersections should be avoided if at all possible. But if you can't avoid them, minimize the risk by stopping even though you're not required to do so.

When you can, plan your route so as to avoid left turns across heavy oncoming traffic. Sometimes this is a matter of mapping out the route to avoid such hazards, and sometimes it's a matter of exercising safety precautions that apply only to bike travel. (See Chapter 11 for further safety precautions.)

Look for broken glass on your route to work. Avoid areas where there appears to be little or no street cleaning.

University professor uses a bike to commute to class. (Photo courtesy of the Archives, California Institute of Technology.)

Residential areas can be more aesthetically pleasing to ride through than industrial areas, but they do pose some bicycle problems of their own. Consider, for example, that you will probably be encountering children darting out into the streets in family neighborhoods and dogs exercising their egos by giving you chase. Neither of these problems need to discourage you. The children may actually give you a boost in the mornings. As for the dogs, very few cyclists are actually injured by dogs. Usually the worst that happens is that you arrive at your destination a little more quickly than you planned. If there are dogs in a residential area that are particular pests, ask the kids you meet in that neighborhood who the obnoxious cur belongs to; kids know these things. Then write a letter threatening to sue the owner if you are again bothered by their pet. This tactic seldom fails. Most pet owners really aren't aware of their animal's offensive activities, and most would rather invest in a chain or fence than see an innocent passerby injured.

Finally, remember that if you're scouting out your commuting route on a weekend, traffic patterns may change during the week. A quiet street on Saturday or Sunday may become a raging river of cars and trucks during commuting hours. Make adjustments in your route accordingly.

AFTER YOU'VE ARRIVED AT WORK

After you get to work, what do you do with your bike? Theft is a major problem for the bicyclist. Although you can lock the frame and wheels to a lamp post, this doesn't protect you from thieves who specialize in ripping off components. All too many cyclists have returned to their bikes after work only to find seat, handlebars, derailleurs, and crankset gone, while the frame and wheels remain securely locked to the post.

The more expensive the bike, the more attractive it is to the bicycle thief. Quick-release levers on wheels make them an easy target. High-quality components can be easily fenced, since they don't usually have identification numbers as frames do.

There are many solutions, or partial solutions, to the problem of bike theft. One biker we know took a can of black spray paint to his new $500 bike. He sprayed the frame and bright metal parts indiscriminately. When he was done, the bike looked like a refugee from the Salvation Army "As-Is" department—hardly worth a second glance from any self-respecting thief. It was sickening to see. When asked if painting his brand-new bike in this way didn't bother him, the spray-can maniac replied, "Not half as much as having it stolen."

Another solution, however, is to find a place at work where you can keep your bike inside. A storage room, a closet, even a space behind your desk will do. If there are other bikers where you work, get together and ask the powers-that-be for permission to establish a safe bicycle parking space in a warehouse, storeroom, or empty office. Michael Osterholm, who is a claims supervisor for an insurance agency in Florida, installed bike hooks (available from any bike shop or hardware store) in a storage room, providing daytime parking for five bikes in a three-by-eight-foot space. Since they hung from the wall by their front wheels, the parked bikes still left plenty of room for storage.

If you must park your bike on the street, be sure to lock it securely with a heavy padlock and chain or with one of the new U-shaped "thru-hardened alloy" bike locks. Choose a place where the bike can be observed during the day, either by you or by a friendly shopkeeper. The more out-in-the-open the bike is, the less likely it is to get ripped off.

Although it seems almost too obvious to mention, many bicycles are stolen after being locked to a short post or parking meter, allowing the thief to lift bike lock and chain right over the top. Always lock your bike to a tall post or one that has a sign on top that will make it impossible to lift over. The same goes for small trees. Police reports show that bicycle thieves think nothing of cutting down small trees to make a score.

The bigger the chain and lock the better. Worried about carrying the extra pounds to and from your job? Some people keep several chains locked to posts near shops, friends' houses, and workplaces they frequent, so they need never carry around a bulky lock and chain.

Case-hardened or thru-tempered chains, together with locks of the same indestructibility, are a must. Thieves often carry heavy-duty bolt cutters that can swiftly cut through less sturdy metals.

WHAT TO WEAR

If you're commuting more than a few miles, you'll probably want one set of clothes for riding and another set for the job. That, of course, may require your changing clothes upon your arrival and again when leaving work. Some cycle commuters keep a flight bag at work, in which they keep an extra change of clothes and personal toilet articles.

Casual wear, such as jeans and cords with simple blouses, shirts, or sweaters, is acceptable in many jobs these days—even in some management positions. That, of course, greatly simplifies the problem of what to wear. In most cases, the same clothes you wear on the job can be worn for riding.

Wear soft, loose-fitting pants to prevent chafing when you ride. Loose shirts or stretchy sweaters also make your ride more comfortable than tight, tailored shirts that restrict your movements. A brightly colored bicycle jersey is ideal for the trip to and from the job, and this can be easily slipped off so you can change into a shirt, blouse, or sweater after arriving.

In wet weather, a Gore-Tex™ parka and pants offer protection from the rain. Gore-Tex™ is the high-tech fabric that keeps rain out while letting your body breathe. With a good rain suit you can arrive at work dry and comfort-

A commuter bicycles to work in his business suit. (Photo courtesy of Bicycling maga-zine.)

able, even after cycling through a driving rain. What's more, this miracle fabric comes in bright colors that make you more visible to motorists. Regular nylon fabrics don't breathe as Gore-Tex™ does. After you've worked up a good sweat, body moisture is held inside. Riding more than five miles wearing these fabrics can be a truly suffocating and damp experience—a little like lifting weights while in a sauna.

Your shoes will get soaked in wet weather, of course. The solution is to wear canvas shoes, remove them at work, and have a dry pair waiting for you in your locker. By the time you're ready to go home your wet shoes will be dry.

In very cold weather, the chill factor of the air moving past you is important to consider. At 15 miles per hour, 50° temperatures will cool your body the same as 40° would do if you were standing still. Add the wind to that, and 50° weather can have a freezing effect on your body. Your Gore-Tex™ rainsuit will cut the wind and will reduce the chill factor somewhat, but you'll still need a down vest or layered clothing underneath.

No matter how avid a cyclist you are, rain and snow will sometimes force you to seek other ways to get to work. Snow and ice make cycling almost impossible. Yet every winter we hear about cyclists who equip their bikes with self-made tire chains so their riding won't be interrupted by such mundane considerations.

Cycling, like other sports, has evolved its own style of clothing. Cycling jerseys, shorts, shoes, gloves, and helmets may be incorporated into your commuting uniform in whole or in part. For example, although you may ride to and from work in your business suit, you may wear cycling shoes, gloves, and helmet as well, from which you later change into something more acceptable for everyday wear. Or you may wear the full cycling regalia during your commute, which you change upon your arrival at work.

If you want to learn more about specialized cycling clothes, turn to Chapter 13, "The Well-Dressed Cyclist."

POLLUTION AND THE CYCLIST

In 1977, the Department of Transportation published the results of its test on bicyclists commuting in Washington, D.C. Compared to motorists following the same routes, the cyclists showed lower levels of carbon monoxide and other pollutants in their blood.

One might think that cyclists, being out in the open, would have higher levels of carbon monoxide in their blood than the more protected motorists. Although the report provided no explanations, Dr. John Samson, who compiled the data, suggests that the more active lungs of the cyclist may expel pollutants more effectively than the sedentary lungs of the motorist. Our

New York City rush-hour commuters. (Photo courtesy of Bicycling *magazine.)*

respiratory passages are, after all, equipped with mechanisms for preventing pollutants from entering our lungs, and it is known that these mechanisms work better during exercise than in less active states.

Bicyclists did complain of eye and throat irritation more than motorists did. The researchers in the Washington, D.C., tests suggest that this may have been due to the fact that the cyclists were instructed to breathe only through their mouths during the test. Furthermore, the tests were conducted during smog-alert days, when chemical pollutants that cause irritation of mucous membranes would have been inordinately high. Most of the cyclists tested reported that their irritation disappeared in a matter of 20 to 30 minutes after they stopped riding.

CYCLE COMMUTING INTO THE FUTURE

Whatever your motives for commuting by bike, you should know that you are joining one of the fastest growing cycling groups in the United States. Although born of necessity in many cases, bicycling to work becomes something more than that for most people. The daily ride to and from work becomes a time to get in touch with bodily sensations numbed by the rigors of a demanding workday. And, as Drs. Paul Dudley White and Clifford L. Graves—long-time bike advocates—have been telling us for years, there are few sports in the world that equal biking as a way to reduce mental stress.

As a bicycle commuter you are doing much to reduce pollution in our cities, and at the same time you are reducing the effects of pollution on your own body. As for economizing on our use of fossil fuels, a projection of figures published by the U.S. Department of Transportation indicates that by 1985 we will be saving between 16 and 23 million barrels of oil a year by riding our bikes to and from our jobs.

As you grow to enjoy your daily commute by bicycle more and more, you'll probably find yourself thinking of ways to expand your bicycling experience. Who knows, that three-mile commute to work each day may ultimately encourage you to get ready for a long, exciting tour of Europe with a group of close friends or your family.

SEVEN

THE ADVENTURE OF HIGH-LEVEL CYCLE TRAINING

Growing numbers of people are dedicating at least a part of their lives to what I call high-level fitness—that is, a level of physical conditioning that goes far beyond what is needed for a leisurely ride on a weekend or even for commuting 10 or 20 miles to and from work each day. There are literally thousands of runners training for highly publicized events such as the Boston Marathon, the New York Marathon, or San Francisco's annual Bay-to-Breakers race. And while these numbers are impressive, there are also thousands of cyclists quietly training for "centuries" and "double centures" (100- and 200-mile rides) held in nearly every major city in the U.S.—races that receive very little attention in the media. High-level fitness, and the challenge of a marathon or century ride, satisfies something in the human spirit that cannot be satisfied within one's profession or family life. It touches something deep and personal in one's being, providing a source of self-expression, pride, and a power that reaches beyond the bounds of everyday existence.

There is a qualitative difference between the effects of commuting 5, 10, or even 20 miles to work each day, at a leisurely pace, and committing yourself to the adventure of high-level cycle training. Training to achieve optimal physical performance requires months of hard work—stressing your body time after time, demanding the most from it, battling with temporary defeats and coming back stronger than before, learning to have faith that the discomfort you feel today will pay off tomorrow in new levels of confidence and pleasure in your body. To me there is real beauty in having fully strengthened and integrated your body and mind to match the challenge of a century or a longer ride.

AEROBICS: THE KEY TO HIGH-LEVEL FITNESS

To understand high-level fitness, we need to take a look at the work of Dr. Kenneth Cooper, who in the late 1960s introduced the term "aerobics." As explained in his book *The New Aerobics*, the term refers to exercise that is continued for a sufficient intensity and duration, such that it produces changes in the various systems and organs of the body. This, of course, is what we call being fit or being in condition. Cooper says that unless you are exercising aerobically, you cannot receive the benefits of this conditioning. In his own words, aerobic exercise does the following:

1. It strengthens the muscles of respiration and tends to reduce the resistance to air flow, ultimately facilitating the rapid flow of air in and out of the lungs.
2. It improves the strength and pumping efficiency of the heart, enabling more blood to be pumped with each stroke. This improves the ability to more rapidly transport life-sustaining oxygen from the lungs to the heart and ultimately to all parts of the body.
3. It tones up muscles throughout the body, thereby improving the general circulation, at times lowering blood pressure and reducing the work of the heart.
4. It causes an increase in the total amount of blood circulating through the body and increases the number of red blood cells and the amount of hemoglobin, making the blood a more efficient oxygen carrier.

All of Dr. Cooper's work is based on medical research measuring the effects of various kinds of physical exercise with the use of highly sophisticated tests and medical technology.

Many changes must take place in your body before you can feel the benefits of aerobics or comfortably ride a bicycle 50, 100, or more miles per day. And only at the point at which those changes have occurred can you expect to experience high-level physical training as a source of pride and self-expression. Maybe the fact that our bodies are capable of growing complex new networks of blood vessels to nourish the heart, leg, and back muscles is part of the mystery that intrigues us when we set out to achieve these higher levels of physical performance. Not that you are ever fully conscious of these changes occurring, any more than you are conscious of lungs and chest expanding, or hormonal constitutions altering, or volumes of blood in the cardiovascular system increasing, or the production of blood cells speeding up, or the capacities of muscle cells to absorb nutrients and oxygen improving. You are conscious that your physical abilities are broadening, that you can do a lot more with less effort than before, and that physical challenges that once exhausted and distressed you are now highly invigorating. But these inner changes happen silently and, for the most part, are invisible to the naked eye.

So how do you develop the levels of fitness that become a source of such deep pleasure for so many people? If you are a beginning or intermediate rider who has been cycling for a year or more, you will be able to look back a year and recall that in the beginning cycling was much harder then than it is now. Only one thing made it get better and easier—the act of bicycling itself. The more you rode, the better you got at it and the more you enjoyed yourself. The next level of training is just more of the same, except that if you are already riding regularly you will have achieved a level of physical fitness that will let you benefit greatly from training techniques used by competitive athletes. One of the first things you'll need to develop is a way of judging how much exercise you should be getting and how hard you should be working at it.

How Much and How Often?

The intensity, duration, and frequency of your workouts must all be taken into account when designing or evaluating a training program.

Intensity. In *The New Aerobics,* Dr. Cooper tells us that you must exercise at between 60 and 90 percent of your maximum heart rate (based on age) before you can enjoy aerobic benefits—that is, exercise resulting in the healthy growth of your cardio-vascular and oxygen-collecting systems.

To determine your maximum heart rate, subtract your age from the base number of 220. For example, let's say you are 40 years old. Subtract that from the base number to get 180, and 60 to 90 percent of that gives you the figures 108 and 162. In simple terms, that means you should exercise intensely enough to keep your heart working at between 108 and 162 beats per minute.

Counting your pulse beats while riding your bike isn't easy. Here's how it's done: Hold the handlebars with the same hand on which you wear your wrist watch. With the first two fingers of your other hand, feel the pulse in your carotid artery, located about two inches to the right or left of your Adam's apple. (See Fig. 7–1.) Count the beats for 10 seconds. Multiply that number by 6, and you've found the rate at which your heart is presently beating. This number should fall within the range you've previously calculated as your maximum-heart-rate range. If you are working below that rate, you need to bicycle harder. If you are working over that level, slow down.

Duration. Try to get between 15 and 60 minutes of continuous aerobic exercise each time you ride. Duration and intensity are interrelated. That is, using the example of the 40-year-old rider again, he or she would derive the same aerobic benefits riding 60 minutes at 106 beats per minute as riding 15 minutes at 162 beats per minute. You can adjust duration and intensity as you wish, as long as you maintain at least the lower end of your maximum heart rate.

Frequency. Plan to exercise between three and five days each week. Few

Fig. 7-1 The carotid artery is located about 2 inches to the left of the windpipe.

training benefits can accrue unless you exercise a minimum of three days per week, and, interestingly enough, there is little or no measurable physiological benefit derived from riding more than five days per week.

LSD and POT Are Essential Training Ingredients

There are two basic styles of riding through which you can achieve the levels of training we're discussing here. These are represented by the acronyms LSD and POT—terms coined by Joe Henderson in his book *Long Slow Distance Training*. No, we are not advocating drugs for boosting your performance. LSD stands for "long, slow distance," while POT stands for "plenty of tempo." Let's explore these one at a time.

LSD, though not Dr. Cooper's term, was derived from his work showing that aerobic benefits are best achieved not by sporadic, heroic efforts, but by regularly sustaining a rather moderate output over a minimum duration of 20 to 30 minutes.

The basic principle of long, slow distance is that your body will adjust and grow, reaping the benefits of physical exercise best when you establish a program where you are exercising for relatively long periods of time, covering distances of sufficient length, even if your pace is fairly slow. You must, even with LSD, work hard enough to give your heart and lungs a good workout, but you need not be heroic in your efforts.

The form of training Henderson calls POT is based on the principle that after you have achieved a certain level of conditioning, you can expand your capacities past that point only through *stress*. In this case, stress means putting new, higher demands on your body for short periods of time until your heart, lungs, and vascular system grow up to the capacity you desire.

Let's say, for example, that you're riding three days a week, 10 miles each day, at an average speed of 15 miles per hour. You feel comfortable doing this, but you want to double your output in preparation for a week-long bicycle tour you are planning with friends. The POT advocate would tell you to keep doing your usual routine of 10 miles a day at 15 miles per hour, but with short POT (plenty-of-tempo) sessions added to those rides. What would this mean exactly?

At the end of your ride, you might add another two miles over flat terrain. In this additional two-mile stretch you'd push yourself all out. Instead of riding at your regular rate of speed, covering the extra distance in about 8½ minutes, you'd double your output, covering the same distance in 4¼ minutes.

The extra push at the end of your ride presents your body with a new level of stress. Your heart and lung capacities will grow to meet that new challenge.

From time to time, popular sports magazines carry articles arguing the advantages of LSD over POT, or vice versa. But making a choice between the two training styles misses the point. We have found that LSD allows you to *maintain* a particular level of conditioning, while POT provides you with an effective tool for *increasing* that level to a new plateau. Our bicycle training program, which follows, integrates the two philosophies.

Before committing yourself to this or any other strenuous physical training program, however, we suggest that you discuss your plans with your doctor. Many physicians now have equipment available for testing your cardio-vascular system under stress—that is, while you work out on a treadmill or stationary bike. Also, an increasing number of sports clinics around the country are making this service available. By measuring your present capacities in this way, you can get a clear picture of the way you should begin training—how much, how soon?—and the speed at which you can progress. This is especially important if you're over 40, if you haven't been exercising for a number of years, or if you're known to have heart disease, diabetes, or any other condition affecting your heart, lungs, and vascular system.

YOUR CYCLE TRAINING PROGRAM

Choosing a Good Bike

A fast, responsive, highly tuned bike will aid and encourage you in attaining your goals for high-level physical training. Look for a lightweight bike (under 27 pounds) with high-speed precision bearings, lightweight wheels, and low-resistance tires. (See Fig. 7–2.) Such bikes generally cost $500 and up. Less expensive recreational bikes ultimately cannot do the job because they are designed for comfort rather than high performance. You can no more expect to train your reflexes for this kind of program on a recreational bike than you can condition yourself for driving the Indianapolis 500 in Aunt Sarah's Edsel. You can get started with a lesser bike, but you'll soon find yourself looking for

Fig. 7-2   A lightweight ten-speed featuring top-quality aluminum alloy parts will provide a welcome boost to your cycle training performance.

something faster, leaner, and more responsive to match the performance of your body.

Bike shops catering to racers will generally carry a larger selection of good training bikes than shops catering primarily to recreational riders.

Setting Performance Goals

Goal-setting is essential to any fitness training program. It is only through continually achieving and surpassing your goals that growth takes place. Your first goal should be to attain an aerobic training level—that is, to attain your maximum heart rate and sustain it over the desired period of time.

To achieve this basic goal, you will have to give some thought to your training route. If you live in the flats of Kansas, you may be able to maintain your maximum heart rate by traveling a 20-mile course in an hour, while a person living in hilly terrain might achieve the same effect by pedaling a strenuous 12-mile course in an hour. You will have to determine your course by trial and error, trying out different routes until you find one that works for you. If traffic is a problem, causing you to lose intensity by stopping and starting too often, try riding early in the morning when traffic is light.

Once you have achieved and maintained your aerobic level for a period of time, you will find that your heart rate begins to drop as your body's strength and endurance grow. As your heart rate drops, you will have to keep adding new challenges—increasing your miles, cutting down the time you take to complete your course, or taking on a new and difficult grade—in order to maintain your maximum rate.

Goal-setting gives you a target, a point toward which you can direct your mental and physical energies. Set these goals consciously, writing them down with dates in a notebook. For example, "June 15. Rode canyon loop in three hours. Goal: to cut time to 2½ hours." Later you can look back and see that you accomplished your goal as you said you would. That is one of the most powerful incentives to keep you working at your program.

Warming Up

Before you throw yourself into an all-out workout, warming up can help get your blood flowing at a rate at which it can liberally supply your muscle cells with the oxygen and nutrients they need. As Dr. Arthur Guyton points out in his book *Medical Physiology*, for every one-degree rise in your body temperature achieved during the warmup period, your metabolism—your ability to produce energy—is raised about 13 percent. At higher temperatures, oxygen is transmitted from your blood to your muscle cells at a higher rate, causing chemical reactions that result in a release of energy within your muscles. In addition, nerve responses are quickened, and the force and speed at which a muscle cell can respond is vastly improved. Warmups are especially important for middle-aged and older people, who, according to studies conducted by Dr. Paul Fardy, otherwise do not generally have sufficient coronary circulation for strenuous exercise.

Finally, as James Fixx points out in *The Complete Book of Running*, warmups are one of the best ways to prevent athletic injuries. When a person starts out cold, muscle strain, tears of muscle tissue or ligaments, or simple muscular stiffness or soreness are much more likely to occur than when you warm up first.

One of the advantages of bicycling is that the warmup can take place during the first 15 minutes of your ride. Choose a comfortable gear and ease into your pedaling without attempting to achieve your training level of output. Warmups should be intense but not fatiguing. When you begin to perspire, that's the sign that your body temperature has risen sufficiently to start your workout. Usually a 15-minute warmup is sufficient.

Some people prefer to begin with warmup exercises. In the following pages are some stretching exercises we recommend because they warm up and limber your muscles gently and effectively while stretching the muscles beyond their normal range. Stretch each muscle group to the point where you just begin to feel the pull; then go a little further and hold the position for 30 seconds. Avoid sudden bouncing, violent stretching, or rigorous calisthenic routines; these can create muscular contractions and accomplish just the opposite effect from the one you want.

After doing the stretching routine, do leisurely situps or run in place until you begin to feel yourself heat up. At that point you're ready to ride.

Fig. 7-3 Position One   *1. Sit with your knees bent and the soles of your feet pressed together. Draw your heels as close to your body as you can. Hold the position for 10 seconds. Relax. Repeat several times, at your own rate, for two minutes.*

   Stretches inner thigh and groin muscles.

Position Two   *2. Sit up and bend one leg directly behind you, as shown. Lean back slowly to gradually stretch the front of your thigh. Hold the position for 30 seconds. Do the exercise twice for each leg.*

   Stretches thigh and pelvic muscles.

Position Three   *3. While lying on your back, pull one leg toward your chest. Keep your back and head on the floor. Hold this position for 30 seconds. Do the exercise twice for each leg.*

   Stretches lower back, buttocks, and backs of thighs.

Position Four   4. *Lie on your back. Lift your feet and roll your hips over your head. Keep your legs straight. Touch the floor with your toes. Hold the position for 30 seconds. Relax. Repeat three times.*

   Benefits lower back, buttocks, and backs of legs.

Position Five   5. *Sit with both your legs straight out in front of you. Bend forward as though to touch your toes. Reach as far as you can, either to your ankles or to your toes. Hold for 30 seconds. Repeat three times.*

   Stretches lower back, legs, and hamstrings.

Position Six   6. *Lie on your back. Bend your knees. Put the soles of your feet together. Lower your knees toward the floor as far as you can. Hold the position for 30 seconds. Relax.*

   Stretches lower back and groin muscles.

Position Seven 7. *Lie on the floor near a wall. Press your seat against the wall with your legs straight out in front of you. Hold the position for three to five minutes.*

Benefits circulation in legs.

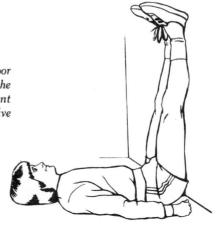

Position Eight 8. *Stand up for a moment. Let your body relax. Lean over as though to touch your toes. Let your body just hang there in a passive position for about half a minute.*

Stretches lower back and hamstrings.

Position Nine 9. *Place your hands against the wall at shoulder height. Walk backwards three or four feet, keeping your feet a foot apart. Straighten and stretch your arms, back muscles, and shoulders. Hold the position for 30 to 60 seconds.*

Stretches and relaxes upper back and shoulders.

Position Ten 10. *Place one foot a few inches from the wall. Place the other three to four feet from it. Slowly move your hips forward and down until you feel the calf in your straight leg stretching. Hold the position for 30 seconds for each leg.*

Stretches calf muscles and Achilles tendons.

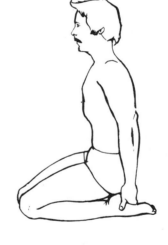

Position Eleven 11. *Sit on your legs with your toes and ankles stretched backwards. Hold your feet straight—that is, turned neither in nor out. Hold the position for 30–60 seconds.*

Stretches and loosens muscles in front of feet, ankles, knees, and thighs.

Position Twelve 12. *Sit on the floor with both legs straight out in front of you. Place your left leg over your right knee. Turn your upper body to the left, placing your right hand against your left buttock. Hold the position for 30 seconds. Do the same on the other side of your body.*

Stretches and relaxes back, hip, pelvic girdle, and shoulder muscles.

The Ride

Start each ride slowly. Take several deep breaths and relax, letting your body and mind come to terms with the bike. Enjoy these early moments of the ride and the sensation of the air on your skin. Feel the strength of your body as you propel the bike forward.

At some point within the first five or ten minutes you'll begin to feel fully focused on the activity of riding. This is what we call "centering." You and the bike are now working together as a unit.

Look for a clear space of a block or more in the road. Take your pulse using the method we described. If your pulse rate is too low according to the maximum-heart-rate schedule you worked out, speed up your pace. Take your pulse at different exercise levels until you become familiar with what your output must be to achieve the training level you want.

Once you know how it feels to exercise at an aerobically beneficial level, it is a simple matter to sustain that intensity for the duration you wish. But go slowly at first. Work at rates that are comfortable and enjoyable. If you learn to associate pleasure with each ride, you'll find yourself highly motivated to do it again the next day.

To give you a concrete idea of what a training ride is like, Hal Bennett—using a micro-cassette recorder—has provided the following record of one of his typical rides. This particular ride is a 23-mile loop with total elevation differences of about 1,800 feet. It starts with a climb of 387 feet from Bennett's home in the Berkeley (California) hills to Tilden Park, a mile away. From the park, the route descends 300 or 400 feet to San Pablo Dam Road, then gradually climbs again for about six miles. After a long descent comes a series of smaller, gradual uphills, then finally a hard one-mile climb of about 300 feet to his home.

Hal's bicycle is equipped with a Pacer 2000—a device that provides an accurate measurement of distances, times, and speeds. Bennett celebrated his 44th birthday three days prior to the ride. He considers himself an intermediate rider. The maximum heart rate at which he was aiming on this ride was 140. The following is transcribed directly from a tape Bennett dictated during his ride:

> Departure time: 11:05. Date: Sept. 26, 1980. Temperature: hot.
>
> Going through Tilden Park. Pedal speed about 85 rpm. Feeling good. Sweat forming on my brow. The sweat on my shirt is cooling me, though the temperature must be about 85 or 90 degrees through here.
>
> Just passing the first three-mile mark. I feel my body beginning to warm up, my muscles beginning to respond to the exercise. Leg muscles feel limber, strong, spinning smoothly, everything evening out.

Just passed Inspiration Point—five-mile mark. Not stopping for my
usual drink of water. It's about 105 degrees up here. Rather
be moving, letting the air cool me off as it rushes past me.

A long downhill into a hard headwind. Pacer says I'm only going
22 mph, though it feels faster pushing against the wind. Pedaling hard in highest gear. Breaking into a sweat, though heat
and wind are evaporating it quickly.

Passing the stables halfway down the hill. Feeling great. Cadences
higher than usual today: 80s on lesser grades, 90 and 110 on
the flats. No trouble maintaining those levels. Remembering
a conversation with John [Marino] about how hot weather can
help us metabolize faster and more efficiently. Is that what's
going on today? Last time over this route it was foggy, with a
temperature of 55 degrees.

Cars whizzing past me like a speedway. I've gotten used to them,
automatically tune them out. Odometer reads 9.23 miles.
Cadence in high 70s. Speed on a slight uphill about 16 to 18
mph. Not bad. Earlier this year I was doing pretty well to
maintain 12 mph.

Exactly noon. Eleven and a half miles. Checking pulse rate after
about a half-mile steep climb: 145 bpm.

I pass the reservoir. Water looks inviting. I drop down on the hooks
to streamline myself pedaling into the wind on a long downhill.
Speeds up to 38 mph. Sheer ecstasy.

Now approaching downtown El Sobrante. A lot of traffic. Shoulder
here is full of glass, sand, parked cars, and bumpy pavement.
What a drag. Averaging 21 mph just the same.

A long, gradual climb out of El Sobrante. Lots of traffic. Hot.
Exhaust fumes from the diesels. I drop to my lowest gear and
just spin along at about 75 to 80 rpm. Going about 10 mph.
Taking it easy, giving myself a little break in the smog and
heat.

Back to the land of stop streets every other block. About four more
miles 'til I'm home. Hard to make the transition to this from
those long, uninterrupted miles behind me.

Home at last. 12:45. Pacer says I did the ride in one hour and 46
minutes; 22.87 miles. Average speed 13 mph.

I walk my bike up the driveway to cool off. Check my heart rate.
It's 115 three minutes after getting off the bike. Five minutes
later, it's down to 100.

I check my pulse rate 30 minutes after my ride. It's down to 75.
An hour later it's down to 60. I feel great.

I check over my log book to see how I did the last time on this

route, four days ago. Elapsed time was one hour and 56 minutes. Average speed 12 mph. Shows an improvement this time.
It's 2:00 p.m. About two hours after the ride, I feel deeply relaxed,
yet full of energy. Content with myself. Proud of my performance.

It's just as important to cool down after the ride as it is to warm up before.
This prevents muscular stiffness and also gives your heart and lungs a chance
to come gradually and naturally back to at-rest heart and respiration rates.

Use the last five minutes of your ride to cool down. During this five-
minute period, lower your output to a leisurely pace. Drop to a lower gear,
where you can pedal at a fast but not strenuous rate.

After you get off your bike, run through some or all of the warmup
exercises described earlier in this chapter in a leisurely fashion. Cooling-down
exercises help clear your system of toxic by-products, which are normal in all
forms of exercise. Taking time to include a cooling-down period in your
training schedule will reduce your chances of having aching muscles the next
day. It helps in these cases to know what is causing your discomfort and how
to minimize its effects on you. Understanding the discomfort is an important
part of any training program, since your reactions to it can mean the difference
between success and failure.

Interpreting Pain

The most painful part of any exercise program is the first two or three weeks.
The activity itself may seem uncomfortable—an odious task at best—during
that early period. Muscles ache or are stiff each morning after you exercise.
You may even feel aggravated with your training program and annoyed with
yourself for not being able to do something that's seemingly so simple and
from which so many other people seem to derive boundless pleasure. Maybe
you want to drop the whole thing after the first week, convinced that you're
the kind of person who just doesn't get along well with physical exercise.

It may surprise you to learn that this is a normal course of events for most
people when they start on a demanding exercise program, or when they start
over after laying off for the winter. The discomfort, annoyance, and sheer
aggravation of the first weeks of training often seem, to the reasonable person,
to be clear signals to stop. But if you go on beyond this point, you'll discover
quite another set of new experiences. The discomfort passes and is replaced
by pleasure in one's body and deep self-satisfaction in the physical accomplishment. Contrary to what most nonathletic people may think, it is this
pleasure period—not the uncomfortable period preceding it—that people seek
in exercise.

When one begins an exercise program, muscles need to stretch, strengthen, and become more resilient. Capillaries need to grow, both to carry the increased supplies of nutrients your body demands and to cleanse away waste products from muscle cells that are metabolizing at a more rapid rate than before you started exercising. In the beginning your heart and lungs must work doubly hard to supply blood to your muscle cells through an inadequate network of blood vessels. After the new capillaries grow, as indeed they will, the blood supply reaches the muscle cells with far less effort.

And what about the aching muscles and stiffness after exercise during the first weeks of the program? Most of this stiffness is caused by a buildup of lactic acids and waste products around muscle cells. These buildups are uncomfortable, even painful, and they occur because not enough oxygen (carried by the blood through your capillaries) is reaching the muscle cells you're asking to do this new work.

Lactic acids are part of a chain of chemical events that take place when cells are asked to produce energy in the absence of adequate oxygen supplies. Discomfort resulting from lactic-acid buildup will disappear as you grow more numerous capillaries and increase your ability to take in oxygen and feed it to your cells. Once your cells are receiving adequate oxygen supplies through your bloodstream, stiffness and pain will disappear. Exercise then literally fills you with energy.

When you're aware of the changes one's body goes through to be comfortable and invigorated by exercise, you can design a program to get into top physical condition with a minimum of discomfort. The secret lies in starting slowly and gradually increasing the amount of exercise as your body grows to meet each new demand.

A major cause of discomfort is breaking your training schedule—that is, laying off for a week or two and then expecting to go back to the same training level you left without gradually building back up to it.

Keep Exercising Regularly

It is important to understand that fitness is maintained only by exercising regularly. High-level fitness deteriorates after you've laid off for two weeks or more. You'll lose half the improvement you've gained through the kind of program we're describing if you suspend it for 4 to 12 weeks. And, if you're like most people who develop a high level of fitness, you'll fall back to your fitness level prior to starting your exercise program, if you go without exercise for eight months or more. So, unless you want to start all over again, make high-level cycling a way of life. Stick with it.

Too often, as doctors know only too well, people who exercise *occasionally* try to make up for lost time on weekends or during vacations. Because they've been exercising a little during the week (though usually not as much as they think they have), they overestimate their capacities and push themselves past safe physiological limits. The consequences of this error of judgment can be as serious as heart attacks and as benign as simple lethargy or depression the day after.

If you're ill for a couple of weeks, even with nothing more than a cold, it's important to build back up to your previous training level gradually. Many people make the mistake of trying to pick up exactly where they left off, which can prove to be both too strenuous and discouraging.

Interruptions of any kind cause your aerobic capacities to backslide, especially if you're over 30. In addition, infections—even minor ones, like colds, or immunizations given by your physician—take energy from the muscles you use for cycling and divert it to organs needed for healing or producing antibodies. Switching back to vigorous exercise after an infection takes time.

How do you catch up after you've been away from your training schedule? First of all, everyone has a slightly different rate for catching up. And if you're just getting over a cold, or you've been under unusual emotional stress, your rate of catching up will be different than if you've been relaxed and well since you last exercised. Thus you need some personal guidelines to follow, and these can be found in signals from your own body—signals which I call the "symptoms of overexertion."

Recognizing the Symptoms of Overexertion

Our bodies and minds have ways of telling us when to slow down, when we're pushing ourselves too hard. Learn to recognize and heed the signals summarized below.

Physical symptoms. Stop exercising and rest if you feel: lightheadedness, severe breathlessness, chest pain, nausea, dizziness, or loss of muscle control.

Heart recovery rate. Take your pulse five minutes after you've finished a workout. If it's over 120, you've pushed yourself too hard for your present capacities. Take your pulse again ten minutes after exercise. If it's not below 100, ease up on your exercise program and build up more gradually.

Breathing recovery rate. Do you find yourself still short of breath ten minutes after you've exercised? Normal breathing rates are from 12 to 16 breaths per minute. If it's more than that, it's a good sign you need to ease up a bit and start building up more gradually.

Emotions after exercising. Although this factor varies a great deal from person to person, most people feel self-satisfied and even elated in the first hour or so after a good workout. If you feel agitated, anxious, restless, or discouraged after a ride, that's a good sign that you should cut back and build up more gradually.

Let these signs be your guides, both in your initial training period and during any period of catching up after a layoff.

A TOOL KIT FOR ENHANCING PERFORMANCE

As you can tell from Hal's log (a few pages back), training rides provide an excellent means for getting to know your body and its capacities. You'll find out more about the impact of diet, rest, climate, weather, and other factors on your body when you are giving it a challenging workout than when you are just going about the rest of your daily routine. The effects of those French fries or last night's carousing will not be nearly as apparent when you are just sitting at a desk as when you are sweating and puffing your way up that hill that seemed so easy just the other day.

Keeping a log book of your rides will enable you to record and measure your progress and its effects. Some riders log in only their times, mileages, and pulse rates. We recommend keeping more extensive notations, including thoughts that occur to you along the way about how you can improve your performance or your bike; feelings you have before, during, and after the ride; information on your diet, the kinds of warmups you are doing, or anything you notice that particularly improves or handicaps your ride. You can jot your ideas down right after your ride or, like Hal, record as you ride on a micro-cassette recorder.

The more you ride and the higher your level of training, the more you'll want to have all your powers working for you. In the following section I describe a group of techniques that I've found particularly valuable in my training for transcontinental rides. Look on these as tools for refining your ride and for increasing your pleasure in the experience of high-level cycle training. The tools fall into three categories: diet, breathing, and motivation. Although each of these categories is important, I have put diet first because in some ways what you eat has more dramatic effects on your performance than the other two categories combined.

Eating Your Way to High-Level Fitness

Nothing is more controversial among athletes and their trainers than the subject of diet. But if there is agreement on any one point, it is that the good old American meat-and-potatoes diet is not conducive to optimal fitness. Dr. John W. Farquhar makes no bones about it, stating unequivocally, "The average American diet is, in fact, decidedly hazardous to your health."

The more you exercise, the more your body dictates certain dietary changes. The folly of eating large quantities of anything at all just before or during a long ride, for example, quickly becomes apparent to the cyclist through such symptoms as cramps, stomach ache, nausea, diarrhea, head-ache, a sudden, unexpected drop in energy, and even anxiety and depression. You'll also notice that too much meat in your diet makes you feel listless during a ride, that a high sugar content in your diet causes uneven energy cycles—with extreme highs and lows—and that too much salt in your diet increases your heart rate in an unhealthy way and causes your body to retain more water than it needs.

Bicycling taught me an important lesson about the effects of food on physical performance. When I first started bicycling I was on a long ride with a group of other cyclists who were more experienced than I was. Most of them were health food nuts. At that time I believed you could eat just about anything you wanted, as long as you were exercising. We stopped at a restaurant, and my friends ordered salads and fruits. I had a hot roast-beef sandwich with gravy and potatoes. My friends were warning me not to eat like that—especially not to eat meat, because it would drag me down. They argued that after eating like that all my blood would be going to my stomach for digestion, and nothing would be left over for cycling. Sure enough, I got on my bike a while later and I just couldn't move. I felt as though I had some kind of chemical depressant in my system.

In recent years serious athletes have discovered that they can perform best on vegetarian diets—in some cases fully vegetarian, and in other cases augmented with small quantities of meat, especially fish and fowl. In her book *Women's Running*, Dr. Joan Ullyot observes: "Looking at the blood chemistries of more than a thousand healthy people in my research, I've noticed incidentally that the most ideal pattern (in my mind) is shown by vegetarian runners. Second best are the sedentary vegetarians, followed by the non-vegetarian runners. All are better, in terms of blood fat and cholesterol levels, than the average, healthy American, who seems well on the way to overweight and heart disease."

The subject of diet among any group of people, athletes or not, is an emotional one. However, athletic people find themselves in a unique position. The activity in which they're engaged can be made miserable or be delightfully enhanced by what they eat, and, in order to increase their pleasure and improve their performance, they're willing to put aside their biases and take a closer look at diet. One of the first revelations that comes to such people is that they have been bombarded by false information about diet most of their lives. Many of their own biases and habits have been shaped by food packagers—by cereal companies, large commercial bakeries, the milk lobby, the meat producers, the fast-food chains, etc. As Dr. John W. Farquhar points out: "We have received much nutritional misinformation about our true need for protein and calcium, and we are surrounded by a culture that encourages us to consume far more calories, sugar, fat, and cholesterol than is healthy."

Writing in *Food for Fitness*, Dr. George Sheehan directs our attention to common food intolerances—foods that are known to cause digestive and metabolic problems in humans. Dr. Sheehan suggests that everyone involved in athletic training programs should understand these intolerances and the ways in which they can affect performance. If you have this information at your fingertips, you may be able to make a connection between a food you're now eating and a symptom that's affecting your cycling performance. Simply eliminating that food may increase your performance and enjoyment of your activity tremendously.

Milk. Many people, especially those from the Mediterranean, the Middle East, and Africa, are particularly intolerant of milk. In addition, about 8 percent of all Caucasians have milk allergies. Digestive problems such as gas, bloating, and stomach pains can occur after eating foods that had even a small amount of milk used in their preparation. If you simply don't care for milk, don't drink it. In fact, you should avoid it. Your body is telling you something—that it just doesn't get along well with milk. No one requires milk after the first decade of life in any case.

Grain. Dr. Sheehan tells of a runner who experienced diarrhea and blood in his stool whenever he ate bread before a race. The cause of this was traced to wheat, the culprit in which is gluten—a protein found in all grains except corn and rice. It can even be the cause of a disease known as "sprue," or chronic diarrhea. According to Dr. Sheehan, many athletes develop this disease and/or intolerance to gluten when placed under stress. To avoid gluten, keep the following out of your diet: bread and all baked goods, cereals, gravies, sauces, and soups that may contain flour or gluten as a thickener. In addition, avoid mayonnaise, ice cream, ale, and beer, which can all contain gluten and gluten derivatives.

Coffee. Coffee and caffeine-containing tea and cola drinks frequently cause hyperacidity of the stomach, stomach spasms, and spasms of the colon in people who are sensitive to caffeine. It also stimulates bowel action and acts as a diuretic.

Excessive Roughage. Athletes with irritable, sensitive, or spastic colons may experience pain, gas, bloating, and thin, pencil-shaped stools after eating large quantities of raw fruit, raw vegetables, baked beans, cabbage, nuts, or corn.

Hyperallergenic Foods. Foods known to cause allergic reactions—such as minor rash, headaches, nasal congestion, itching, bloating, diarrhea, and hives—include shellfish, chocolate, melons, nuts, citrus fruits, strawberries, egg white, and pork.

In addition, there are a number of food additives that can affect your performance: MSG (monosodium glutamate), often used in restaurant sauces, especially for Chinese and Italian foods, can cause headache, itching, or burning sensations throughout your body, even a general sense of disorientation. Refined sugar can leach B-vitamins from your system. Citral, a lemon flavoring, and other artificial flavorings and colorings can make it impossible for your body to use vitamin C. Nitrites, implicated as carcinogenic, are sodium and, at the very least, can cause your body to retain fluids. Alcohol leaches B-vitamins as well as electrolyte minerals (magnesium, potassium, calcium, and sodium) from your system, disrupting natural controls on fluid exchange between cells, impeding metabolic processes within muscle cells, and interfering with the transmission of electrochemical impulses in nerve cells.

You'll find few packaged foods available that aren't filled with chemical additives, including the ones above as well as literally hundreds of others that we don't have the space to list here. Hal Bennett has a way of simplifying the whole issue of chemicals in our foods: "If you can't pronounce it, don't eat it."

Now that you know what you shouldn't eat, what about what *is* good for you? Let's turn to some general guidelines for a training diet.

The human body's fuel system is indeed complex. In an article published in *Bicycling* magazine, Tracy DeCrosta points out that your muscle cells get energy from three basic sources:

1. ATP (adenosine triphosphate): Stored in muscle cells and immediately available for short, strenuous bursts of activity, these energy sources are quickly used up.
2. CP (creatine-phosphate): Also stored in muscle cells, this substance regenerates ATP as it is used up.
3. Glycogen: Stored in muscle tissue and in the liver, it is processed by our bodies to produce more ATP and CP.

Glycogen is made in your body, mainly through the digestion of carbohydrates. Its production, storage, and utilization are very efficient. Fats from meats are also used as fuel, but their conversion to energy for the muscle cells is quite inefficient. As DeCrosta tells us, the waste products of meat and high-protein foods " . . . are processed through the kidneys, and that extra digestive stress during an activity like cycling can be a hindrance."

According to Arthur Guyton, a conditioned athlete can store up to 70,000 calories of fat in his or her body. In *Eating Your Way to Health*, Ruth Kunz-Bircher explains that this storage of fat need not be supplemented by large quantities of meat. The fact is that we can satisfy all our needs for fat from vegetable sources and from small quantities of oils used in food preparation.

So what kinds of foods are best for athletes in training? The answer is simple, natural carbohydrates. Here's why: Otto Brucker explains that even though our bodies convert carbohydrates to glycogen very efficiently (glycogen being rapidly converted to energy in our muscle cells), our bodies can store only 2,000 to 3,000 calories' worth of carbohydrates. Because of this high utilization and low storage ratio, John Farquhar and Joan Ullyot recommend that at least 55 percent of a person's diet consist of carbohydrates.

When I am in training, my diet consists almost wholly of vegetables and fruits. I came to this nutritional regimen by trial and error and by taking the advice of numerous coaches and nutritionists until I found what worked best for me. This diet can act as a guideline for others interested in high-level cycle training. Consider the following four principles:

Eat foods with "life" in them: raw fruits and vegetables, or vegetables that have been cooked only for short periods of time.

Eat dried legumes (lentils, beans, etc.) for your main protein source. Instead of large quantities of beef or pork, eat small quantities of fish or fowl.

Eat whole grain rather than refined grain products: whole-wheat bread, brown rice, granola breakfast cereals, etc.

Eat small quantities of food frequently rather than large quantities less frequently. Never stuff yourself, especially prior to or during a ride.

I don't recommend suddenly changing your diet. Both body and mind will rebel if you do. Rather, set goals for yourself and work into new nutritional habits gradually. Here are some goals that I recommend to other cyclists who want to improve their training diets. Try one goal at a time, advancing to the next goal only when you feel satisfied with achieving the previous one:

1. When you feel a craving for a sugary snack, grab an apple or other fruit instead.
2. When you feel the need for a cup of coffee, a beer, or a cola drink, reach instead for an herbal tea drink (hot or iced) or a glass of fruit juice. Most stores now carry a stock of individual, chilled bottles of fruit juice, which you can drink down as you would a bottle of pop.
3. For your lunches, try vegetarian sandwiches such as avocado and tomato; tomatoes, sprouts, and lettuce; or peanut butter with grated carrots and apple slices—always made with whole-wheat bread or pita bread.
4. Buy a vegetable steamer and wok, and experiment with cooking fresh vegetables instead of canned or frozen ones.
5. Instead of eating ham and eggs for breakfast, have a bowl of fresh, whole-grain granola or "Familia" with slices of fresh fruit on top.
6. Eat meat for only one meal a day. Avoid red meat. Fish or poultry is easier on your digestion.
7. Replace beef, pork, or lamb in your diet with fish or fowl (skinned to reduce fat).
8. Look in recipe books for vegetarian main courses, and have these in place of meat-centered dinners at least twice a week.
9. Try out meat substitutes such as falafel and soy-burgers, which are available at health-food stores; let them replace meat in your diet two or three times a week.

10.   Replace snack foods such as ice cream with yogurt and fresh fruit;
       replace cakes or candies with oatmeal cookies (made from any recipe,
       but with sugar reduced and raisins or dried fruits added).

Improved nutrition will reward you not only in higher athletic performance, but in better overall health as well. The American Heart Association
tells us that cutting down on our intake of meats, dairy foods, and eggs will
reduce our risk of heart disease. In addition, the higher bulk content of foods
such as fresh vegetables, fruits, and whole grains reduces one's risk of a long
list of digestive diseases, ranging from chronic indigestion and heartburn to
colonic cancer. And, in his book *Mental and Elemental Nutrients*, Dr. Carl
Pfeiffer indicates that proper diet stabilizes our energy levels, freeing us from
the extreme highs and lows in mood and motivation that are caused by eating
high-calorie, low-nutrition foods.

Breathing for Increased Performance

While food is essential in producing the stuff that allows us to use our muscles,
without oxygen our bodies would be unable to convert the things we eat into
energy. For this reason it is important to develop our lungs' capacities to their
fullest.
       Most people breathe shallowly, never fully inflating their lungs. In the
following exercise, the objective is to increase your lung capacity by concen-
trating on your lower abdominal area.

1.   Sit cross-legged, either on the floor or on a wide couch. Loosen your
      belt and pants. Let your hands relax on your knees. Take a deep breath.
      Hold it. Let it out. Do this a second and third time to loosen up your
      chest and abdominal muscles.
2.   Take a deep breath. Deeper! Expand your abdominal muscles. Let
      your belly balloon out. Breathe in still more air, expanding your chest.
      Slowly raise your shoulders, keeping your hands on your knees. This
      complete inhalation should take about seven seconds. When your
      lungs are filled, hold that breath for a moment.
3.   Exhale for seven seconds, lowering your shoulders while your chest
      and abdominal muscles are relaxing.

Do this complete exercise several times over for about ten minutes at a
time. Practice it two or three times a day, whenever the opportunity arises—
while waiting for an appointment, while stopped in heavy commuter traffic,
or even while working at your desk. It's an excellent exercise to combine with
watching television or listening to music.

Creating Your Own Motivational Programs

Although many books on exercise include some advice on diet and even breathing, I know of none that talk about motivation. For most people motivation is a mysterious force, something that comes and goes with no rhyme or reason. The popular conception is that some days you feel motivated and some days you don't; the muse is either there or it's not. However, unlike "Fickle Fortune" or "Lady Luck," we really can do something about motivation. We can learn how to turn it on, and we can learn how to plan and direct it to fulfill our goals. Without this ability, I know I would never have made it through that first year of cycle training.

A man by the name of Gordon Smith taught me many of the motivational techniques that helped me attain my goals. Smith is a remarkable man. While in the Marines, he set the intermilitary Marine Corps record for the most pushups in 1½ hours: 2,010 pushups. He is a concert pianist, speaks several languages (he learns each one in an average of four to six weeks), and went through the UCLA undergraduate program with a grade point average of 4.0. There is no doubt that Smith has a touch of genius, but he attributes his success to a positive mental attitude and a motivational technique he calls "auto-generational acquisition theory."

According to this system, thoughts range on a continuum from positive to negative. A positive mental attitude Smith labels as "attitudinal expectancy," or AE. Negative attitudes are known as "attitudinal deprivation," or AD.

When an individual sets out to do something, Smith contends, he should always expect success. Think success and expect results. This is attitudinal expectancy. Setbacks will occur, of course, but these should be looked upon as learning experiences. For instance, going the wrong route in a maze is not necessarily a mistake; it shows which way *not* to go in the future. The individual never has to go in that direction again.

Smith outlines several methods for increasing AE and decreasing AD. He teaches his students to make "alpha" tapes. These are motivational tapes to remind you that you can accomplish anything—that you *can* complete your goal. Smith recommends making these tapes yourself. Record your thoughts as you train.

I tried this method when I trained for my first transcontinental trip. One night I strapped a tape recorder to my back, with the microphone attached to my shirt, and recorded what I felt as I rode around a one-mile course. I rode around and around until fatigue set in. The more fatigued I became, the more often I repeated, "I can do it, I can do it!" I recorded whatever came out. I tried to visualize New York City Hall and kept telling myself that I could make it. I got so emotional that I almost started crying right there on the bike!

I extend this principle into all areas of my life. I consider my tape recorder an absolute necessity for all activities. I think that whenever you feel good, you should sit down and record all the great things you do and have done in your life. That way, whenever you get "down," you have only to play the tapes back; they can really motivate you to great heights.

In addition to alpha tapes, Smith suggests that you develop a "pseudo-environment." This should be an actual room or other physical area where you can surround yourself with artifacts reminding you of specific goals you have set. For instance, if a century ride (100 miles) is your goal, put up signs that say "100 miles," "I *can* ride 100 miles," etc., to spur you on. Put up posters showing heroes who have accomplished great tasks. If you have trophies and awards, display them to recall what you yourself have achieved. In short, the pseudo-environment is a place where you can go to concentrate on your goals and focus on accomplishing them.

Sometimes motivation comes in the form of daydreams—visions of yourself succeeding that pop up in your mind when you least expect them. I feel that instead of just letting these daydreams pass, you should take advantage of them, enjoy them, and play with them. Let them mingle in your mind and join your growing warehouse of motivating material. Positive attitudes toward your own abilities really do provide you with extra power to succeed.

DEEP PERSONAL REWARDS

High levels of physical training need not involve world-record challenges or heroic efforts to compete against the best. On the contrary, for most of us, achieving a high level of physical training and proficiency as a cyclist is a quiet and personal thing. Still, there is a part of each of us that shares the feelings of victory that the greatest of athletes experience each time they complete a particularly fine performance. For me, the greatest feeling of victory came at the conclusion of my 1980 ride. I remember when the red ribbon marking my finish line came into view. I broke through it and was instantly mobbed by my crew. They raised me on their shoulders, cheered, and hugged me; together we wept with joy and relief at our joint accomplishment. I was the happiest man in the world. There are no words that will ever explain how I felt. The thrill of being able to cover distances with the energies of one's own body that most people would consider covering only in a motor vehicle sparks something deep and basic in everyone who has ever done it. While the exact source of the unparalleled excitement of this experience remains an elusive and seductive mystery, most cyclists who have acquired high levels of fitness understand that they've touched and expressed parts of themselves which perhaps lie sleeping in everyone and may be as essential and universal as friendship and love.

EIGHT

STATIONARY BICYCLING

According to the *American Bicycling Federation Rule Book*, Bruce Hall, of San Diego, California, holds the world's record for pedaling the longest "distance" on a stationary cycle in 24 hours. He established that record in January 1977 by riding the equivalent of 792.7 miles in a single day on a bike mounted on bike rollers—a form of stationary bike. Although people aren't exactly lining up to challenge Hall's record, the stationary bike is fast becoming one of the more popular forms of indoor exercise.

One of the reasons for the stationary bike's growing popularity is its usefulness for prescriptive exercise therapy. This includes both disease prevention and rehabilitation for many forms of cardiovascular disease. If you're following an exercise program, you can use a timer, odometer, and speedometer on a stationary bike and be assured that you're working within safe limits previously measured by your personal physician. The stationary bike enables you to get your workout in the safety and comfort of your home. If you experience any discomfort or other problems while working out, your bed, medication, and a phone call to your doctor are readily at hand.

Another reason people are turning to stationary bikes is that they provide a way for joggers, skiers, swimmers, cyclists, and other athletes who ordinarily work out on the road to keep in training the year round, even when the weather is bad. Furthermore, because indoor bicycling puts a minimal amount of stress on knee and ankle joints, the stationary bike is often used by athletes to stay in shape while they recuperate from an injury associated with another sport. Dr. Donald A. Chu of the Ather Sports Injury Clinic in Dublin, California, has called the stationary bike "an excellent tool for cardiovascular and knee/ankle rehabilitation."

Finally, the stationary bike can provide you with the same opportunity for aerobic exercise as outdoor cycling. Modern stationary bikes can be adjusted for various workloads, approximating the challenge of a steep hill or a flat stretch of open highway. The speedometer and odometer which come as standard equipment on a good stationary bike enable you to design an exercise program comparable to your outdoor cycle training route. Some stationary bikes even have a second hand on the timer so that you can easily measure your pulse to determine whether you are working at your maximum heart rate.

If I'm beginning to sound like a stationary-bike booster, it's because I am. Exercise on a stationary bike has been an invaluable part of my training, and I want to convey my enthusiasm to you. On those days when I can't put in road time on my regular bike because the weather is bad or there's a smog alert or I just don't have enough time, I just jump on my stationary bike. I feel that in an hour's time I get a workout equivalent to two hours on the road.

WHEEL AWAY DISEASE ON A STATIONARY BIKE

Of course, any form of exercise can strengthen and benefit your cardio-vascular system. The advantage of the stationary bicycle—and, as we mentioned earlier, the reason why physicians have become so keen on it—is that its timer, odometer, and speedometer enable you to attain a very specific, controlled workout. There's no other form of exercise that can be measured so accurately.

Now let's look at some of the specific prevention and rehabilitation benefits you'll get from your stationary bicycle.

First of all, exercise improves blood flow to the heart muscle itself through the growth of new capillaries—the smallest blood vessels that carry oxygen to the cells (in this case, to the cells of the heart muscle). Because oxygen is the food that nourishes the cells, improvement of the blood supply to the heart muscle strengthens the heart in the same way that increased blood supply to a leg or arm muscle strengthens those limbs. Exercise further stimulates the growth of new blood vessels to compensate for reduced blood flow through diseased vessels, like nature's own heart-bypass surgery.

The best measure of the health benefits of your exercise program is in the reduction of your heart rate—as measured in pulse beats—whether you are at rest or exercising. This slowing-down gives the pump portion of your heart a longer time to fill up between each beat and therefore increases the volume of blood moving through your system each time the heart pumps out its supply. A slower heart rate also has the effect of reducing blood pressure, which helps greatly in preventing heart attacks, strokes, and kidney failure.

You can easily measure the improvement in your heart rate yourself by simply taking your pulse. If you are working with a physician, he or she will also be able to measure increases in your red-blood-cell count that result from your exercise program. These cells transport oxygen from your lungs to muscle cells, which use it to produce energy for any form of physical activity. Now, as your red-blood-cell count increases, the total volume of fluid also rises to keep those red blood cells flowing smoothly through the blood vessels. In other words, people who exercise regularly can actually increase the volume of blood in their bodies by as much as one quart. In addition, exercise enhances the ability of each red blood cell to extract and transport oxygen.

In an almost complementary way, certain enzyme changes associated with exercise improve the capacity of the muscle cells to extract oxygen from the red blood cells.

There is also some evidence to indicate that the size of a person's arteries may actually increase with regular exercise. In the autopsy after his death from cancer, it was found that the coronary arteries of the great long-distance runner Clarence DeMar were two to three times the size normally expected in a man of 70 years of age. Of course, one must consider the possibility that DeMar's larger arteries were a congenital characteristic that made it possible for him to become the great distance runner he was. However, experiments with animals have shown that artery size does increase with regular exercise, and it would not seem unreasonable to extrapolate from this that the same might be true for humans.

Finally, there is also evidence that exercise increases what is called fibrinolytic activity—that is, the breakup of clotted or sludged blood in the system. This may be a protective mechanism which removes one of the factors that contribute to heart attacks.

In addition to benefiting the cardiovascular system, exercise brings about beneficial changes in the ways our bodies metabolize certain substances. In a sedentary person, for example, serum triglycerides—that is, a particular kind of blood fat associated with atherosclerosis—can be unusually high. (Atherosclerosis is a condition in which the arteries that carry blood to the major organs are narrowed and weakened.) This serum triglyceride is dramatically reduced in persons who exercise regularly.

In recent years there has been much discussion about blood fats, or cholesterol, and what can be done to reduce them. Actually, there are two types of blood fats: high-density lipoproteins (HDL) and low-density lipoproteins (LDL). To simplify, LDL is considered to be "bad" blood fat because a high level of it contributes to hardening of the arteries, high blood pressure, heart attacks, strokes, and kidney failure. On the other hand, HDL is considered "good" blood fat, partly because its presence has the effect of scrubbing the arteries, keeping them open and healthy so that they can continue to supply every cell of our bodies with blood. You increase "good" blood fats in the blood and decrease the amounts of "bad" fats through exercise.

A powerful argument for the need to continue exercise programs on a regular basis is this: Studies have found that patients with excessive low-density lipoproteins in the blood could reduce them to a healthy level through exercise, but when they stopped exercising for 48 hours, LDL levels immediately went up. In other words, exercise can't be taken once, like a pill or a surgical procedure, and then dropped. It must be incorporated into the person's regular lifestyle to produce lasting benefits.

Of course, exercise burns calories, resulting in weight loss and weight maintenance. After the desired weight is established, the triglycerides are immediately burned as fuel instead of being made into fat. Not only does the person's figure become more trim, but the harmful fats in the blood drop significantly.

Hormone levels—especially cortisol, growth hormone, plasmaglucogen, and catecholemines such as adrenalin—are elevated through regular exercise, and these raised hormone levels may be responsible for certain psychic effects of exercise—the "highs" that many athletes report. It is not fully understood how these hormones change our emotional states, but we do know that adrenalin has a biochemical role in preventing depression. There is much speculation in the medical community that these hormones, increased through a natural mechanism such as exercise, may constitute a powerful weapon against depression. Studies of exercise have shown not only antidepressive effects but also increased energy and diminished fatigue through improved hormone levels.

Last but not least, it has been shown that exercise allows borderline diabetics to maintain healthy blood-sugar levels without special diets or the need for supplementary insulin. This, of course, is also the result of hormonal changes stimulated by the person's increased physical activity on a regular basis.

WRITING YOUR EXERCISE PRESCRIPTION

Before launching into the rigors and glories of exercise, it's a good idea to discuss it with your physician, especially if you haven't been exercising regularly, if you are over 40, if you smoke, or if you have any sort of chronic health problem such as heart disease, high cholesterol, high blood pressure, or diabetes. An accurate evaluation of your exercise capacities can be made by taking an electrocardiogram while you are exercising on either a treadmill or a stationary bike. During this test, your heart is electronically monitored to detect abnormal heartbeats or the narrowing of arteries. This information will help you determine at what levels you should begin your exercise on the way to achieving your goals. In case your physician is not set up to provide you with this type of testing service, he or she can certainly refer you to someone in your community who is. In many cities, these services are available through hospitals, private gyms, and even organizations such as the YMCA.

If you are recuperating from any kind of infection, injury, or other illness, you should put off starting your exercise program until you are completely well. Most exercise specialists recommend walking as a way to gradually build up to a more vigorous program.

EQUIPMENT: FROM THE BASIC TO THE STATE OF THE ART

For the program we describe here you'll need an indoor bicycle with a speedometer, an odometer, and a device for varying the workload. The latter is usually a knob on the handlebars which, when turned, will apply pressure to a band around the wheel or to a brake rubbing aginst the rim of the wheel. This device makes it harder or easier to turn the pedals; the harder you pedal, the more energy you'll expend per minute of riding. In addition, you should have a watch or timer to measure the length of your workout.

You can also set up an indoor cycling system with what are called "bike rollers." These are operated by placing an ordinary ten-speed bike on a frame with rollers which turn in unison as you pedal. On the rollers, both front and rear wheels of the bike spin, providing a gyroscopic effect that allows the rider to stay up. The cyclist must learn to balance the bike on the rollers. Although there is no way of varying the workload, by equipping the bike with a speedometer/odometer you can measure the "distance" and speed of each workout. This lets you keep a record of each ride and duplicate workouts that meet your own particular needs. If you now own a good ten-speed bike, and your main interest is racing or riding on the road, consider bike rollers. By using your regular bike on rollers, you'll continue to use the muscles you employ on the road, whereas an exerciser will probably fit your body differently and therefore bring other muscles into play.

Indoor bicycles come in a variety of shapes, sizes, and prices. Depending on your pocketbook, you can spend anywhere from $150 to $3,000. The models shown on the following pages will give you an idea of the wide selection of indoor bicycles available today (See Figs. 8–1, 8–2, 8–3).

CYCLE TRAINING FOR INDOOR WHEELS

The program we present here is designed for people in good health, with no known health problems. We present it with the understanding that it is not a prescription for a rehabilitation program. As with all other exercise programs, we recommend that you consult your physician and get a complete medical checkup before beginning.

Fig. 8-1 This low-cost exerciser features a timer, a speedometer/odometer, and a friction tension adjustment for varying the workload. Sturdy and well-made, it sells for about $150.

Applying the Program

A healthy adult has an at-rest pulse of 70 or less beats per minute. Begin your program by taking your pulse after you have been inactive for ten minutes. If your at-rest heart rate is between 50 and 70, you are within the range of normalcy.

In order to exercise your heart, lungs, and vascular (blood-carrying) system, you'll want to exercise hard enough to raise your pulse rate to certain 164 minimum levels. The World Health Organization recommends the following exercise guidelines:

Age	Exercising Pulse Rate
20–29 years	160–170 beats per minute
30–39 years	150–160 beats per minute
40–49 years	140–150 beats per minute
50–59 years	130–140 beats per minute
60–up years	120–130 beats per minute

Fig. 8-2　Bike rollers let the outdoor cyclist work out indoors with his or her own bike. The cyclist must balance and steer to stay on the rollers, requiring some practice to master. Rollers approximate the feeling of outdoor cycling. Balance and control become highly developed. The lack of a tensioner limits muscular development, but the rollers definitely benefit the cardiovascular system. Cost is low—from $150 to $200. (Photo courtesy of Bicycling *magazine.)*

You can also use formulas for aerobic exercise levels, as provided in the previous chapter, to estimate your work levels. Learn to take your pulse while exercising, either at your wrist or at the carotid artery—a couple of inches to the right or left or your windpipe, just under your jaw line, as we described in Chapter 7.

Set your exerciser at a low workload level and get on. Pedal easily for three to five minutes to warm up. You should just begin to sweat.

Then begin pedaling at a rate of 60 to 75 revolutions per minute. (You can establish your rate by counting each time your right knee comes to the top of a stroke for each sweep of the second hand.) Take note of the speed

Fig. 8-3   *The Life Cycle is a top-of-the-line variety of stationary bikes, featuring space-age technology. A built-in computer and digital display give you instant readouts on everything from pulse rate to calories burned. Everything you need to know about your maximum heart rate, your progress over your last workout, and your present level of exertion (and more) are instantly available as you ride. The computer programs the machine to deliver varied workloads that approximate hills, valleys, and flat areas of a ride in the country. Cost is around $3,000.*

your speedometer needle registers when you are pedaling at the 60-75-rpm rate, and this will save you from having to count revolutions again.

   After five minutes, take your pulse as you continue to pedal. This is tricky at first, but with a little practice it'll become easy and automatic. Is your pulse rate below the exercising pulse rate for your age group, as described in the chart a few paragraphs back? If it is, increase your workload by tightening the adjustment knob on your exerciser. Is your pulse rate too high? Reduce the tension. Experiment until your workload is adjusted so that you can maintain your exercising pulse rate at the level matched to your age group.

Note the setting on your tensioner knob and the speed on your speedometer while you are pedaling at 60–75 rpm. These readings will give you accurate gauges for measuring the intensity of your workout each day.

Work out on your stationary bike for 20 minutes a day, three to five times each week. Do this for a month and you'll begin to notice changes in your body. For example, after a few weeks of riding you'll find that your pulse rate at rest will be lower than before you started working out. You'll bound upstairs feeling invigorated where you once panted for breath. Your heart muscle, lungs, and vascular system will have vastly improved. You'll easily perform work that only weeks before was a great effort. As your capacity improves, you'll find that you'll have to keep increasing the tension on your adjustment knob in order to keep your pulse to the exercising pulse rate recommended for your age group. Check your pulse rate at least every two weeks. Make adjustments for new work levels as you continue to improve.

You can also raise your pulse rate by the speed at which you pedal. Increasing the duration of your workout—that is, the period of time you exercise each day—will also increase your endurance.

For Outdoor Cyclists On Indoor Bikes

If you are an outdoor cyclist using a stationary bike to keep up your training levels in the winter months, you'll want to adjust the workloads to fit higher cadences than we have instructed above: i.e., if you ordinarily train outdoors at 90–100 rpm, set the tension on your indoor machine so that you can maintain your aerobic pulse rate at that cadence.

Because the stationary bike maintains a constant tension, while outdoor cycling usually gives you opportunities to coast, an hour of indoor cycling is usually more strenuous than an hour outdoors. As a rule of thumb, estimate that half an hour indoors will be approximately the same as a full hour outdoors.

Most noncompetitive cyclists who are in top shape seem to agree that half an hour on the stationary bike, three to five times a week, keeps them in shape for their favorite sport. Competitive cyclists double that, working at higher cadences with more tension to build strength and endurance.

When you're riding your own bike down the road, the air moving past you cools your body and keeps your body heat down. On a stationary bike you aren't moving, so your body temperature rises, you sweat more, you metabolize faster, and you burn more calories per minute than you do on the road. I like to take advantage of the higher body temperatures achieved on the stationary bike because that allows me to achieve a full workout in a short period of time. Other people like to reduce the heat by setting up fans to produce a cool breeze past their bodies as they work out. Schwinn sells a stationary bike called the "Air-Dyne"; instead of turning a wheel as you ride, you turn an air turbine that produces a good, stiff breeze to cool you. There's a similar device, called the "Road Machine," into which you can clamp your own bike.

What to Do About Boredom

Because the stationary bike *is* stationary, there is no passing scenery to keep you entertained, as you have when riding on the road. As a result, indoor cyclists are always seeking new ways to keep their workouts stimulating. Joel Hahn, a professional photographer, sets up an automatic slide projector and reviews pictures he's taken as he rides. Linda Henwood, a real-estate broker, watches the evening news on TV as she puts in her daily 20-minute workout. Pete Martin, a multi-media fanatic, listens to rock music on earphones while watching the afternoon cartoons on TV with the sound turned down. He claims that the visual rhythms of the cartoons match the rhythms he feels as he rides. He's particularly fond of the Road Runner cartoons. On a more serious side, Ralph Hanson, an attorney, has set up a book rack on his stationary bike, and he studies court cases as he rides.

Athletic clubs and gyms are adding the Life Cycle, a new breed of stationary bikes, to their equipment lists. Fully computerized, these new machines can calculate the physiological effects of the workout you're getting and read that information back to you on an electronic console mounted on the handlebars. The computer within the bike can be set to vary your workload—challenging you, for example, with a 12-minute work period that begins with an easy warmup, takes you through a series of progressively more difficult "hills," followed by a warmdown, or cooling-off period. Programs can be changed as your physical conditioning improves.

I work out regularly on such a machine. Because the program is varied by the computer, the workout itself keeps the cyclist interested. In addition, working out with other people at a gym or athletic club adds elements of interest and comradeship that help motivate the indoor cyclist.

Last Words

All the dietary ideas and suggestions offered in Chapter 7 apply equally to indoor cycling. Just as with outdoor cycle training, the physical demands of regular rigorous indoor cycling require that you treat your body kindly. That means reducing the amount of fatty foods and refined carbohydrates (white sugar and flour) in your diet and drinking plenty of fluids to replace those you lose in sweat as you exercise. For extra insurance, it doesn't hurt to take a vitamin/mineral supplement.

As we also mentioned in the previous chapter, you should pay careful attention to any signals from your body indicating that you are overdoing it. We've listed the symptoms you should watch for in Chapter 7. Use those as guidelines for when to lighten your workload.

Finally, be sure to make a regular habit of your exercise program, whether you are bicycling outdoors or indoors. Only 20 minutes a day three days each week is enough to ensure gradual improvement in your muscle tone and cardio-vascular system. That is the key to your physical growth. After only a few months of a regular program, you will find not only an improvement in your general health—fewer colds, etc.—but also whole new horizons of physical ability opening up to you. Taking a long scenic tour on your bicycle might be one of those new vistas.

NINE

TOURING THE WORLD ON TWO WHEELS

Touring is one of the most exciting and rewarding activities in the world of bicycling. Moving along under your own steam without depending on gasoline is the ultimate way to travel. Take it from those who know. In 1976, John Rakowski completed a round-the-world tour that took him a total of 15,660 miles on his bike. Writing in *Bicycling* magazine, Rakowski reflected on his 400 days on the road: "There was expectation at every curve of the road. What visitor awaited me? Would I have a stimulating conversation with someone at a village cafe? Or see an unusual building or monument? I arose each morning in anticipation of the day's events. One easily becomes optimistic when the whole world is there before him."

In 1964, Dr. Clifford Graves founded the International Bicycle Touring Society. At the age of 72 he was still cycle touring, having pedaled his bike through France, England, Ireland, Scotland, Hungary, Romania, Turkey, Japan, Norway, Denmark, Spain, Portugal, Yugoslavia, Czechoslovakia, Austria, Germany, and more than half of the United States. By his own calculations, he estimated that he'd traveled upwards of 250,000 miles in his 30 years of cycle touring.

One forgets the usual daily pressures and worries on a long bicycle tour. As Rakowski tells it: "I shed the bother of conventional time. I wore no watch, getting up and going to bed with the sun, eating when hungry and stopping to rest when tired. Although I believe mankind is too far removed from its past to be guided by instincts alone, I like to think that I had acquired more primitive rhythms, responding to the wants of the body on its terms rather than on the terms of society."

137

Many families take their children along on extended bicycle tours. In 1977, Tim Wilhelm and his wife Glenda traveled across the United States with their three-year-old son Erik and their nine-year-old daughter Kirsten. Kirsten rode her own bike, carried her own food, and was fully responsible for her own sleeping bag and clothes. Glenda pulled a small bicycle trailer (called a "Bugger") with son Erik in the back. Tim pulled a second trailer with a huge backpack, weighing 100 pounds, filled to the brim with their necessities. When asked if they'd do it again, or if they'd recommend the 66-day trip to other parents with children, the Wilhelms responded with an emphatic yes to each question.

Long-distance touring appeals to all ages. In 1975, to celebrate his 70th birthday, Ed "Foxy Grandpa" Delano rode from his home in Vallejo, California, to Québec, Canada—a total distance of 3,260 miles. He covered this distance in 34 days, averaging 94 miles a day on his bike. Ed described his ride in *Bicycling* magazine as follows: "I didn't make my stated 100 (miles) per day, either, missed that by about six miles. Didn't really think I could, but it was fun trying, and it was a spur to keep me moving and interested." In summing up his trip, and the huge town greeting he received upon his arrival in Québec, Ed portrayed his experience as "The greatest thing that ever happened to old Foxy Grandpa."

Cyclists who have made extended tours on their bikes almost unanimously report that riding off and on all day, for days on end, builds strength gradually, speeds up all aspects of the body's metabolism, and increases the capacities of the cardio-vascular system. What's more, these health benefits come almost as a subsidiary reward, a sidelight to the main attractions of sightseeing, meeting new people, discovering new places, enjoying a well-deserved meal at the end of a day's ride, sharing experiences you've had along

Scenic cycle camping with ten-speed tandems. (Photo courtesy of Bicycling *magazine.)*

the way, and feeling that the world belongs to you. As physical strength increases, you'll be adding years to your life. Your sleep cycles begin to improve, with sleep becoming deeper and longer than ever before. Chronic, nagging ailments diminish or vanish altogether. After a week on the road, you won't believe how healthy you look. Your skin will look bright and vital. Your body will look trim, and your clothes will fit you like a model's. Most of all, you'll feel great.

Touring is also one of the most psychologically healing activities there is. It gives you plenty of time to think, to figure out solutions to problems in your life, to contemplate nature, to plan ahead. It builds "staying power"— that is, the ability to persevere. There are few experiences more satisfying than to look back on a long bike trip you've made and realize what you've accomplished under your own power. It becomes the source of a very solid, fully justified sense of self-worth.

PLANNING YOUR TOUR

Careful planning is the key to success in cycle touring. Planning involves three basic considerations: route, companions and equipment.

Choosing a Route

Routing a bike tour gets easier each year. Not so long ago, planning a tour meant spending hours on the phone checking with other riders, the highway patrol, and the transportation department to figure out routes that accommodated cyclists. Nowadays, most states in the U.S. provide detailed route information, including maps clearly marking the roads and streets designated for bicycle traffic. Usually the department of transportation for each state is in charge of this. (At the end of this chapter you'll find a list of organizations where you can get complete bike-tour information for trips in both the United States and Europe.)

In the bicentennial summer of 1976, an organization known as "Bikecentennial" established a transcontinental route. (See Fig. 9–1.) Called the "Trans America Bicycle Trail," this network of rural roads linking Astoria, Oregon, with Yorktown, Virginia, saw over 4,000 cyclists in the bicentennial year alone. Said Eileen Connolly (who was in one of the first groups to complete the ride) in *Bicycling* magazine: "It was a dream of mine; one I came to fulfill in my lifetime. Sometimes now, months later, it seems like the kind of dream you have when you fall asleep. I wonder if it ever even took place. I rode across the country on a ten-speed bicycle!"

Bikecentennial, an ongoing organization based in Missoula, Montana, continues to develop new routes. For example, along the Trans America Bicycle Trail they've established shorter "loop" routes. These loops, each from

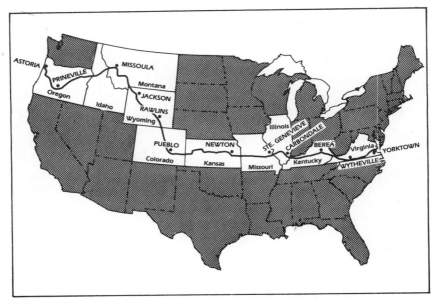

Fig. 9-1   The Bikecentennial Trans-America bicycle trail. (Courtesy of Bicycling *magazine.)*

350 to 500 miles in length, are designed for cyclists with only limited time for travel. Most of the loops can be completed in from eight to ten days by a cyclist of average strength. These loops have been developed, or are in the process of being developed, around several urban centers along the route. At the time of this writing, loops are in operation in Virginia, Kentucky, and Oregon.

Bikecentennial is also developing and sponsoring The Great River Route, running parallel to the Mississippi River from its source in northern Minnesota to the Louisiana delta. Other bike routes include The West Coast Route and The Great Parks Route, which links some of the great national parts of Canada and the United States.

In addition to Bikecentennial, American Youth Hostels and the Sierra Club also sponsor rides and have bicycle route information available.

The establishment of the Trans America Bicycle Trail has stirred the imaginations of cyclists and noncyclists alike. A recent issue of *Bicycling* magazine included a statement by Betty and Terry Noble, who live on the trail in the Bitter Root Valley in western Montana:

> The highlight of our summer was the Bikecentennial. The routing of this 4,100-mile trip was right past our house. We painted two signs, advertising the hope that people would stop for water, rest, and shade. Every afternoon

there would be bikers from all over the world, resting, napping, snacking out under the big maple tree. And what a delight these people were! There were students, doctors, a carpenter from Sweden, a musician from Mexico City, teachers, bike teams from Holland, and families.

Traveling thousands of miles across country on a bicycle may seem like an impossible feat for the average person. Yet a trip of any length becomes manageable if you simply break down the trip into small increments. Ride an hour, and you've covered 15 miles. Rest for a few minutes, enjoying your new surroundings. Ride again for 15 miles. Rest and enjoy yourself again. Do the same a third and a fourth time. Now take a look at what you've accomplished. In four hours of riding and resting, you've covered approximately 60 miles. Ride in this leisurely way for a week, and you'll have covered 420 miles— more than the distance from Los Angeles to San Francisco. In two weeks you've gone 840 miles. In a month you've gone 3,360 miles. In other words, traveling at a leisurely pace, you could traverse the United States in a month. And all this is within the range of the average person, starting out with only a few weeks of physical conditioning.

So whenever you think about taking a bike tour, think in terms of small increments, 15 miles at a stretch, three or four stretches each day. Focus on what you know you can do. The small increments add up quickly. You'll look back on a week of travel amazed at what you've done.

On my last transcontinental challenge, I covered upwards of 240 miles per day for 12 days on end. For the average person who is willing to spend a couple of months cycle training before a long tour, it is quite reasonable to think in terms of covering 75 to 80 miles each day. If you're willing to put in more hours in the saddle, you can, like Ed "Foxy Grandpa" Delano, cover a hundred miles a day without great difficulty.

Although you may want to ride at a more leisurely pace, it's important to recognize what can be done when you take the time to train and set goals for yourself. Also, knowing that it is humanly possible to cycle 250 to 300 miles in a single day makes more moderate goals seem less formidable.

But let's put athletic accomplishments aside for the time being and focus on something else. For most people, the real joy of cycle touring is found in a sense of closeness with the countryside. In a car you *see* the countryside as you pass through. On a bike you *live* with the countryside. Its sights, sounds, and smells surround you. Your muscles respond to its terrain, challenged on the uphills, relaxed and grateful on the downhills. You know the wind across the plains in the evenings, the heat of the sun at midday, the cool breezes across the ocean or a river in the late afternoon.

There are many ways to tour on a bike. Your first tour might be an afternoon jaunt to a park or recreational area a couple of hours' ride from your home. Or you might want to plan a trip with friends to a picturesque area a full day's ride away, where you'd stay the night in a motel and spend the next day riding home at a leisurely pace. You might want to take a month-long transcontinental tour or a tour of foreign countries. There are few limits to bicycle touring. In fact, the only real limits are those created in our own minds.

Companionship on the Ride

When planning a trip with other people, be sure to consider the biking skills and strengths of each rider. Two riders of quite different riding levels touring together can spoil the trip for both, since one rider will always be left a little behind. Although it may seem logical for the fast rider to slow down and keep pace with the slower rider, it really doesn't work that way. Slowing down one's ideal pace can be as fatiguing and frustrating to the faster rider as trying to ride faster is for the slower one. We recommend that if your strengths aren't matched, you plan to ride with others so that everyone has a riding partner whose pace and riding capacities are similar to their own.

In a larger group there are usually riders of various skills, allowing each person to enjoy the companionship of others while riding at his or her own pace. On longer tours lasting for more than a few days, the strengths of the slower riders improve and the faster riders often settle down to a more moderate pace. Thus the group tends to draw closer together the longer the tour.

Cycle touring provides direct and immediate experience of the landscape's beauty. (Photo courtesy of Bicycling *magazine.)*

If you're planning to take a bicycle tour with children, you'll have to make some special allowances and provisions. James and Carol Griffin, who have toured extensively with preteens, observed that kids can easily get bored and lose their motivation to keep plugging along. It helps to plan rest stops at places of interest along the way where the kids can find something to do. Variety keeps their interest up, as does logging in the miles you've traveled. Kids like the sense of accomplishment that comes from seeing how far you've come each day. And if the going gets rough, especially up hills, it might be best to get off and walk so that the child doesn't feel discouraged by the demands of the trip and want to give up. James and Carol found that they could easily travel 50 and 60 miles a day, with children of seven and ten years of age, and still have plenty of time to stop along the way.

For younger children, most experienced families have found that a bicycle trailer such as the "Bugger" works better than a child carrier fastened to the frame of the bike itself. The Bugger weighs about 30 pounds, rides well, and affords the younger child comfort and safety that other carrying systems won't allow. When they took their trip to Baja California, Steve Johnson set up his bicycle with an especially low gear to ease the task of drawing the bike trailer, with his son aboard, up the long Mexican hills.

Most preteens will be able to handle part of their own food, extra clothes, and a sleeping bag. You should count on carrying the rest for them: things like a flashlight, cooking utensils, basic foodstuffs, etc. In this case, consider using a bike trailer just for carrying the extra equipment. People who have done so say they can carry more weight more safely and with less effort in a trailer, such as the Bugger, than they can on the bicycle itself. Even though you have the best quality racks and *panniers* (carrying bags), the bike will have a tendency to be wobbly and unstable if you load it down with more than 40 pounds of equipment.

Choosing, Equipping, and Preparing Your Touring Bike

Except for short (one day or less) jaunts, three-speed or one-speed bikes are of little use. You *can* tour on them, but you'll pay the price lugging around a heavy machine with limited gearing. The longer the distance you'll be riding, the more you'll appreciate the refinements of the ten-speed bike.

The ideal touring bike (Fig. 9–2) is a medium- to high-quality ten-speed with dropped handlebars, rigid luggage carriers front and rear, and a comfortable seat on which you've already ridden *at least* a hundred miles. The bike should be equipped with metal pedals and toe clips, two water bottles with rigid brackets bolted to the frame or handlebars, and a good-quality tire pump.

Fig. 9-2   Touring bikes have special gear setups designed for carrying loads over varying terrain and fittings for rigid luggage racks.

There are people who use 15-speed setups on their touring bikes, but we don't recommend such an arrangement. We feel that the additional mechanical complexities, and the accompanying problems of derailleur adjustment, don't justify the extra gear ranges you gain. Instead, we recommend the following ten-speed setup:

Freewheel cluster (rear wheel)—13, 16, 19, 24, and 28 teeth.
Chainwheels (at crank)—34 teeth for inner sprocket, 48 teeth for outer sprocket.

This arrangement gives you a broad range of gear ratios. Shifting will be smooth and easy and chain wear minimal. You'll have a low gear of approximately 32 inches—quite sufficient for pulling you and your baggage up a long, steep grade. Top gear will be close to 100 inches, which at a cadence of 70 revolutions per minute will carry you forward at 22 miles per hour.

There used to be great controversy over which kinds of tires were best for touring. Some argued in favor of sewups because they were lighter and had less rolling resistance than clinchers. Some argued in favor of clinchers because they could be patched more easily on the road than sewups. Today the controversy has all but vanished, since advanced technology has brought us clinchers that are light in weight, have low rolling resistance, and still have the advantage of easy patching on the road.

Before you buy tires, determine what kind of load you'll be carrying. If you plan to stay in motels and carry only a tiny bundle of clothes and toilet articles with you, consider equipping your bike with ultra-light, narrow-tread clinchers. These tires will reward you with high performance comparable to the narrow-tread sewups found on racing bikes.

If you plan to carry more than 30 pounds, camping along the way, choose wider, high-pressure (minimum 85 psi) clinchers. With heavier loads the wider tire gives you better performance and stability than you'd get with the narrow tire.

Before leaving on any tour, make certain that the tire pump you have will easily inflate your particular brand of tires to their maximum pressure. Inexpensive pumps just won't handle the new high-pressure tires.

Safety equipment for night riding. Large safety reflectors on your wheels, which can be purchased at any bike shop, help make you visible to motorists on those occasions when you must ride at night. A red reflector on the rear luggage rack and a white one on the front also help.

Electric lights on bicycles are only marginally useful. Few help *you* see, though they do alert motorists to your presence. A very bright strobe light with red or amber lenses, about the size of a cigarette pack, can be purchased from yachting equipment suppliers for around $50. Visible for two to five miles, this is the only light available that gives you a fighting chance riding at night.

About panniers and luggage racks. For less than $10 you can buy a student's carrying rack that mounts over the back wheel of your bike and has two flimsy stabilizer struts that bolt to the frame at the rear axle. Although these are adequate for carrying your books to class, or for picking up a loaf of bread at the grocery store, they are of no use whatsoever to the serious bike tourist. They'll wobble back and forth under a load, stressing the metal to the breaking point and stealing your energy as your muscles make minute adjustments for the wobble they cause mile after mile.

Touring racks cost about twice as much as student's racks, and the construction is entirely different. Whereas student racks are riveted together and have only one stabilizer strut on each side, touring racks are welded together and have two—and sometimes three—stabilizer struts on each side. Touring racks are engineered for carrying loads from 15 pounds up to about a hundred. They are made of high-quality aluminum alloy (as seen in the American-made Blackburn racks) or rubber-coated steel (as seen in the English-made Karrymore racks). After being bolted to the frame, the touring racks become an integral part of the bike.

Touring racks are made for both the front and rear wheels. If you plan to carry more than 25 pounds of gear, it is a good idea to distribute that load between the front and rear of the bike rather than putting the whole load over the rear wheel. The bike will handle much better if you do this. Following his tour to Baja California, Steve Johnson reports that the bike handles best with approximately two-thirds of the load over the rear wheel and the other third over the front.

Panniers—that is, the fabric part of your carrying system—come in a variety of sizes and styles. The best ones have many of the same design features you'd expect to find in a good-quality backpack: zippered pockets, double straps to hold down all flap-style closures, adjustable straps for keeping the load tight and compact, and strong, waterproof synthetic fabrics used in the construction. Look for names like Kirtland, Eclipse, Bellweather, and Cannondale. If you're into sewing, you should also take a look at the pannier kits made by Frostline Kits.

Not all panniers fit all carrying racks. Before you actually give the store your money, make certain that the panniers and racks are fully compatible. The pannier manufacturers whose products require a particular kind of rack usually say so on a card attached to the pannier set. But don't count on this. Be fussy and make sure your total carrying system fits neatly and snugly together.

Some tourists like handlebar bags. They're fine for light items such as your map, a featherweight windbreaker, a small camera, and such. But since the weight carried in the handlebar bag is relatively high up on the bike, a heavy load will make the bike hard to handle, especially on fast downhills.

For best handling and maximum stability in your touring bike, always pack it with the heaviest objects lowest. For example, pack your stove and cooking utensils into the bottom portions of your rear panniers, keeping them as close to the axle as you can. Pack the lighter objects, such as sleeping bag and clothing, higher. This keeps the center of gravity low, and a low center of gravity contributes to stability on the road.

If you are planning to combine bike touring with trips on trains, planes, or buses, investigate the new panniers, which slip easily on or off a special rack. Eclipse is the company that pioneered this system.

Pre-tour servicing. Before any extended tour, make sure your bike is in good condition. If you take it to a shop for servicing, tell the mechanic about the tour you've planned so that he or she will know what to check out. Here is a checklist to guide you:

1. *All bearings:* Inspect the bearings in the headset, the wheels, the bottom bracket, and the little cogs on the rear derailleur. Check the freewheel for the condition of the ratchet as well as the bearings. Any worn bearings should be replaced, greased, and adjusted.
2. *Wheels:* Both wheels should be trued; they should neither wobble nor hop. Bent or broken spokes and worn or damaged tires and tubes should be replaced.
3. *Cables:* Inspect—and replace if necessary—the front and rear brake cables and the front and rear derailleur cables.
4. *Pedals:* Inspect the condition of each pedal. Remove them from the cranks and spin the pedal axles with your fingers. Service bearings or replace whole units that run rough.

5.   *Gears:* Inspect the condition of the chainwheels (front) and sprockets (rear). If you find bent or broken teeth, replace that unit.
6.   *Derailleurs:* Inspect the front and rear derailleurs. Replace or repair them if excess wear is discovered. Adjust as needed.
7.   *Brakes:* Inspect the brake levers, brake pads, and brake calipers. Replace parts whenever excessive wear is discovered.

Tool kit for the road. Whenever you go on an extended bike trip, be sure to carry tools and spare parts for making emergency repairs. Here's a list of items we recommend you take along:

Tire patch kit
Extra tube
Six-inch crescent wrench
Small screwdriver
Four extra spokes
Two brake pads
One rear derailleur cable (can be cut off to fit front if needed)
One spoke wrench
One rear brake cable (inner wire only)
One spare pedal strap
One chain rivet tool
An extra piece of bike chain, six links long, for repairs
Two tire irons
Allen wrenches to fit all bolts tightened this way
And remember your bike pump!

This kit will allow you to make most repairs that come up along the road, setting you on your way again—at least to the nearest town where you can find a competent bike mechanic.

THE NUTS AND BOLTS OF TOUR PREPARATION

Physical Conditioning for the Tour

Long-distance bike touring is certainly within the physical capacities of most people, assuming they're in basically good health. But unless you adequately prepare yourself, the first several days of your trip can be unpleasant indeed, perhaps even causing you to call an early halt to your planned tour.

Start getting in shape at least 30 days before your trip. Build up gradually, using the programs we describe in the chapters on "Cycle Training," and/or "Stationary Bicycling."

Before leaving for your trip, you should be riding the equivalent of 25 miles a day at least three days per week. A couple of times before you actually start your trip, a longer training tour—perhaps on a weekend—of 50 or 60 miles should be undertaken. Look for training routes that will approximate the kind of terrain you'll be riding on your trip. By the time you leave, you'll know your body's reasonable limits and will be able to choose a daily pace that will be comfortable for you and a reasonable distance to cover.

Dressing the Part

The first principle of dressing for the road is *Be Visible!* The second principle is *Be Comfortable!* Wear a brightly colored bicycle jersey and cycling shorts with a chamois-lined crotch, and you'll have the ultimate outfit for touring. Several manufacturers are now marketing shorts with chamois lining for bicyclists that look more conventional than cyclist's shorts. You may be more comfortable with these, especially since they can be worn with a T-shirt and not attract a lot of attention in town.

A good pair of cycling gloves will help cushion your hands on the bars. And, of course, don't go anywhere without a safety helmet. You'll undoubtedly want sunglasses to keep both the sun and the bugs out of your eyes. For further information on cycle clothing, see Chapter 12.

Here's a checklist of clothes you will want to carry along with you in addition to your riding clothes:

Two pairs of socks
Two changes of underwear
One pair of dress shoes (canvas boat shoes or sandals are lightweight)
One pair of wash-and-wear slacks or a skirt
One long-sleeved sport shirt, blouse, or light sweater
One warm sweater
One poncho or windbreaker
One swimsuit
One set of "Duofold"-type long underwear when cold weather threatens

You might want to add to this list, but it represents the bare minimum necessary. Stay as close to these requirements as you can to limit load weight.

Personal Articles

The following checklist is, again, a bare-bones minimum. Add to it with discretion.

First-aid kit (see your local bike shop for approved kit)
Sewing kit

Insect repellent
Toilet paper
Towelettes (individually wrapped paper towels with soap built in)
Small metal mirror
Toothbrush and toothpaste
Small bottle of liquid soap
Bath towel
Comb or small hairbrush
Shaving gear for men

If you're like most of us, you'll add a camera and film to this list. High-quality 35-mm miniature cameras made by Pentax, Olympus, and others weigh only ounces and produce excellent pictures.

Cycle Camping or Cycle Touring?

Cycle touring usually means going first-class where your accommodations are concerned—that is, sleeping in motels or hotels and eating your meals in restaurants. If you like to ride fast and light, and you've got money to spend, this is the best way to go.

Cycle camping, however, has its advantages. Although you need to carry a bigger load than the cycle tourer, you are not limited to staying in towns or near organized recreational areas. You can set up your tent nearly anywhere you wish.

If you do your own cooking along the way, plan your stops so you can either ride to town for provisions or carry them only a short way to your campsite.

The list below is for the complete cycle-camper. The entire camp setup weighs about 12 to 14 pounds.

One bike lock
One one-person tent—4 pounds
One 4 × 8-ft plastic dropcloth (moisture barrier under tent)—4 ounces
One sleeping bag—3 pounds
One Ensolite pad (mattress)—1 pound
One backpacking stove—2 pounds
Fuel bottle (full)—10 ounces
Knife, fork, and spoon—3 ounces
"Boy Scout Knife"—4 ounces
Nestling pot, pan, and dish—6 ounces
Waterproof matchbox and matches—2 ounces
One dishtowel—1 ounce
One plastic scrub pad—1 ounce

Twenty folds of paper towel—1 ounce
Handlebar light (to double as camp light)—8 ounces
Three polyethylene bags (for food storage)—1 ounce

Use this as your bare-bones checklist, adding to it only while bearing in mind that your personal energy will have to propel it across the miles.

Food for Travel

Food is to the bike tourer what gasoline is to the car. A cyclist needs certain kinds of food, however, and on the road one's eating habits may change radically from what he or she is accustomed to. As I learned when I first started cycling, stopping for a $10 full-course meal in the middle of the day can be an absolute disaster. During the course of the day's ride, your body turns all its energy reserves to muscular activity. That energy just isn't going to be available for digesting a big meal. You'll end up feeling bogged down, tired, in no mood to ride, or, if you're unlucky, downright sick.

Most seasoned bike tourists eat lightly in the middle of the day, staying as close as they can to a "natural" diet. This often means eating apples, oranges, carrots, or bananas available at vegetable stands or small grocery stores along the way. In their fresh form, these are easily digested and high in nutrients.

The seasoned bike tourer begins the day with a light meal. Avoid coffee and caffeine drinks, since they act as diuretics and can leech your system of vitamins and minerals required by your body for vigorous physical activity. If you need a hot drink to get you started in the morning, try herb teas—such as licorice root, Gotu Kola, dandelion, and Yellow Dock—available in most health food stores in tea bags which are easy to carry and prepare.

Instead of bacon and eggs in the morning, try Granola or other whole-grain cereals. Eat them with fruit juices instead of milk. The juices keep better in your panniers and are better for you than milk.

As you ride, munch and nibble. Eat foods rich in unrefined carbohydrates. I carry a small packet of mixed dried fruits and nuts in the pocket of my jersey. A good combination is raisins, dried apricots, dates, figs, peanuts, and almonds. A banana, orange, or apple may supplement this for variety. Nibble away sparingly, replenishing your energy supplies as you go. In this way, your body needn't store calories as extra body weight, but immediately processes the foods for the energy needed by your muscle cells. A salad, a bowl of soup, or a light vegetarian sandwich for lunch will keep your energies high and your appetite satisfied.

Avoid candy bars at all costs. Many bike tourers have learned this lesson the hard way. After eating a candy bar, your blood sugar rises astronomically, making you feel great for a short time. Then the body's chemistry goes to work trying to restore balance, sending insulin into the bloodstream. A few miles down the road, you begin to feel slightly depressed. You become sluggish, tired, ready to call it a day. And all because you fell for the old myth that "Candy is quick energy."

At the end of the day a big meal is great. In fact, you can use that as your motivational lift. It's your reward for logging all those miles. You deserve it. If you're camping, prepare a large meal with friends—a banquet with all the good companionship and spirit of a celebration. Eat what satisfies you the most. Your body will have ample time to digest it, turning it into energy reserves for the next day's ride.

It's a good idea to take vitamins and minerals on your tour. They will insure you against a possible vitamin or mineral deficiency, since sweating and exercising drain your body of nutrients you may not use in your usual daily life. Your body can best assimilate these micro-nutrients when they're taken with food, not on an empty stomach.

Don't take salt supplements. Most people get far more than they need in their daily diet. At the same time, drink plenty of fluids, replacing the water you lose by sweating. Keep in mind that as you ride, evaporation may carry away moisture from your body, giving you the wrong impression about how much fluid you're losing as you ride. On a long tour, keep two bottles of water on your bike, and sip away at the water before you actually feel a profound thirst. Dehydration can be serious to the cycle tourer riding in a warm climate, and it is something to be guarded against at all times. By some process which physiologists don't fully understand, seasoned tourists who keep in top shape summer and winter eventually develop metabolisms that retain fluids, requiring less replenishment during a long ride than most of us require. However, this is the exception rather than the rule.

RIDING TECHNIQUES FOR THE TOURIST

A loaded bike will handle much differently than an unloaded one. Banking steeply around turns is treacherous. Coming to a stop takes longer. And, of course, climbing hills takes a bit more energy. Steve and Lena Johnson's recommendation is to load up your bike and make a few trial runs close to home before you leave on your tour. Note the way the bike turns, the way it handles on downhills, and how it feels to climb hills with the extra weight.

Hal Bennett has one rule which he passes on to all tourists: *Never pedal when you don't have to.* If you're an experienced bike tourist you'll know this already, but, as simple as it sounds, beginners often don't grasp this until it's pointed out to them.

Take advantage of downhills to relax your legs, or stand up on the pedals and get the weight off your buttocks. Similarly, if you've got a tailwind, let it blow you along, pedaling at an easy rate while nature gives you this welcome assist. If you encounter a long, flat stretch of road with little or no wind to buck, don't worry about speed. Find your most comfortable gear and enjoy a leisurely pace for awhile.

Always think in terms of making things easy for yourself. Unlike cycle training programs, where you're trying to cram a lot of physical output into a short time, as a tourist you'll be putting in a lot of distance over a long period of time. By conserving your energy whenever you can, you'll find you can put in several more miles a day before feeling that you just have to stop.

"Listen" to your body as you ride. On long tours it is important to keep your motor—that's you—in good shape. When touring in a car the experienced motorist keeps his or her eyes and ears open for any complaints from the engine. Often, observing a climbing temperature gauge or a drop in oil pressure can prevent a major breakdown. The same goes for you when you're cycling.

When something starts to ache or hurt, recognize that this is a message from your body. It is telling you to do something, change something in order to make the pain go away. It is time to pay attention. Look for changes you can make to feel better.

Is saddle soreness necessary? *Some* discomfort is part of cycling, but don't jump to conclusions. Does the saddle fit you correctly? On a long tour, for example, a plastic "cushioned" saddle can turn into a torture rack. Sure it felt good when you were just riding around town, but touring is a different proposition. The next chance you get, try out a better model; Brooks, Ideal, and Avocet are all good. Or are you sore because your saddle isn't broken in yet? Or is the height adjustment off? Or are the seams in your clothes irritating you in the crotch area? As you ride, try to figure out what's causing the discomfort. And then do something to improve your situation.

Knee pain is another complaint of bike tourists. Often it means you're cycling in too high a gear. Drop down a gear or two. Learn to *spin*, and reduce your discomfort. If you're hurting, stop and rest. Knock off for the day. Enjoy the scenery while your knees heal up.

Stinging or numb sensations in your hands are caused by the handlebars pressing into the nerves of your hands. To alleviate this condition, wear padded cycling gloves or equip your bars with the new foam-rubber "Grab-Ons." Also, change the position of your hands frequently. Figure out ways to grip your handlebars that will distribute the pressure over the widest surface, in this way minimizing the irritation and limiting it to any one spot on your hands.

Numb crotch is another complaint of cyclists, especially men. Again, pay attention. Shift positions on the saddle as you ride. Try a new angle or new height on the saddle. And, if adjustments fail to correct the problem, try a new saddle—or simply stop cycling for a day and give your posterior a rest.

TRAVELING WITH THE COMMON CARRIERS

In the U.S. one might get the impression that buses, trains, and airline companies would rather not deal with bicycles. In spite of themselves, they do make concessions—in part because, according to the laws of interstate commerce, they are required to.

In traveling in the U.S. you'll find that bringing your bike along usually causes the ticket agent a lot of anxiety. However, most airlines provide cardboard boxes for bikes. You usually are required to remove wheels, pedals, and handlebars, tying these loose parts to the frame so they won't get lost. Usually you are not charged for extra handling, but this seems to depend on the policy of the airline and the mood of the ticket agent at the time.

Amtrak sometimes lets you bring your bike aboard intact. If you insist, they sometimes even allow you to escort your assembled bike to the baggage car. At other times they want the bike dismantled, as the airlines do, and boxed. Plan to arrive at the railroad station an hour ahead of time to get all this together. And plan to supply your own box (obtained from a bike shop beforehand). You may or may not be charged for shipping your bike with you; this policy varies from one station to the next.

Buses require that your bike be dismantled and boxed. This is understandable, considering the size of the luggage compartments on buses. Properly boxed, your bike can travel on the bus with you at no extra cost.

The European railroads generally have the bicycle problem worked out so smoothly you hardly need to give it a second thought. Bikes are hung on bike hooks in the baggage car, and there is no concern about dismantling them. Small fees (about the price of a glass of beer) are charged in some European countries for this service.

Europeans have combined bike and train travel for so long that no one gives a second thought to bringing a cycle along. Things continue to improve in the U.S., and—with the growing popularity of the bike—airlines, trains, and buses continue to make more and more reasonable provisions. So have faith, U.S. bike tourists. Things will get straightened out in the end. For now we recommend researching the policies of the common carriers you plan to use well in advance. Don't depend on rumors or word-of-mouth information. Contact the carriers directly.

ORGANIZATIONS TO HELP THE BIKE TOURIST

Whenever you're planning a tour, contact the department of transportation in each state where you want to travel. The address of each state agency is listed in a handy booklet called *The Cyclists' Yellow Pages*, available from Bikecentennial. Federal policies in the past few years have encouraged each state to accommodate bicycles in the name of fuel conservation. Many states will supply you with detailed bike routes for the areas you want to visit. California and Colorado are the forerunners in this. Very complete maps, including cross-sections of the topography, are supplied for many locales. The following organizations will prove valuable resources too:

American Youth Hostels: Membership fee of $10. Handbooks, route information, lists of hostels are available to members. *Address:* American Youth Hostels, Delaplane, VA 22025.

Bicycle Institute of America: They'll send you a free directory of all bicycle clubs in the U.S. Then contact individual clubs along your route for road info. *Address:* Bicycle Institute of America, 122 E. 42nd St., New York, NY 10017.

Bikecentennial: Develops and organizes bike tours across country, providing road information, scenery information, etc. Provides printed material on many bike subjects, including a monthly newsletter. Also publishes *The Cyclists' Yellow Pages*—a listing of national cycling associations, state agencies that provide cycle touring information and general information about routes, camping, and hostels. Membership fee is $12. *Address:* Bikecentennial, P.O. Box 8303, Missoula, MT 59807.

Cyclists' Touring Club: Touring information for British Isles and Europe. Has travel service and handbook of bed and breakfast places. Membership is $8 but going up at the time of this writing. *Address:* Cyclists' Touring Club, Cotterell House, 69 Meadrow, Godalming, Surrey, England GU7 3HS.

International Bicycle Touring Society: Organizes bike tours outside the U.S. *Address:* International Bicycle Touring Society, 846 Prospect St., La Jolla, CA 92037.

League of American Wheelmen: Dates back to 1880. Membership fee is $10 and includes "L.A.W. Bulletin." Information on tours, commuting, racing, and legislation. *Address:* L.A.W., 10 E. Read St., Baltimore, MD 21202.

TEN

THE WORLD OF CYCLE RACING

The world's first official bicycle race was held on May 31, 1868. Pedaling his 100-pound, iron-wheeled "Ordinary" over a rough gravel path in a park, James Moore, an Englishman, established his place in bicycling history by crossing the finish line ahead of the other contestants. The following year, this same bicyclist won the world's first long-distance trial, riding the 83 miles from Paris to Rouen in 10 hours, 25 minutes. At a scorching average speed of a little under eight miles per hour, he amazed the world.

France was the center of the world cycling competition almost from the start. In 1903, the world's greatest sporting event, the Tour de France, took place for the first time. The 2,600-mile course winds through villages and city streets, up through 7,500-foot mountain passes in the Alps and the Pyrenees— a test of human endurance that lasts for 22 days. This race is run with teams, each team including experts in sprinting and mountain climbing. Although several team members contribute to the win, the final glory goes to the first person across the finish line. It is customary, however, for the winner to turn over the entire winnings—as much as $25,000—to teammates.

The history of cycle racing in Great Britain is a curious one. Although there have been many great world-class British bicycle racers, organized racing had a rocky beginning in England. From 1890 until 1942 there were no "mass-start" races in Great Britain. The police, appalled by large groups of men racing on bicycles through the countryside, often arrested the racers for dangerous driving, which, of course, did little to encourage the sport.

Then a man by the name of F. T. Bidlake figured out a way to get around the police. Instead of having 50 men starting in a pack, Bidlake sent the racers off at intervals of one minute, timing each participant individually. This style of racing—called the "time-trial" race—has since become recognized the world over. "Mass-start" races were not officially allowed in Great Britain until 1942.

Bicycle racing has a colorful history, and in Europe it is the most popular competitive sport. In France, England, Spain, Switzerland, and Belgium, thousands of spectators line the streets for days, as racers, working in teams or individually, compete over distances ranging from a few miles to nearly 3,000 miles.

One of the world's best-known bicycle-racing heroes is the Belgian-born Eddy Merckx. In the early 1970s, at the height of his career, this man's paycheck from his Italian sponsors topped $10,000 per month! With advertising contracts, personal appearances, and prize money, it is estimated that he earned $500,000 per year, making him the highest-paid athlete in European history. During 1971, Merckx won 50 races, including the classic Tour de France for the third year in a row.

Not until 1958, however, were women officially recognized in the sport of cycle racing when British racing women got the women's world championships established. In 1969, a California woman by the name of Audrey McElmury went to Czechoslovakia and brought back America's first Gold Medal for world-class cycling competition in nearly 57 years.

Colorado's Red Zinger race. (Photo courtesy of Bicycling *magazine.)*

Colorado's Red Zinger race, 1979. (Photo courtesy of Bicyling *magazine.)*

Curiously enough, bike racing in the U.S. and Canada has not enjoyed the popularity it has in Europe. Yet this was not always true. Indeed, world-class cycling, with different nations competing against each other, started in Chicago in 1893, with the Chicago-born Arthur Zimmerman taking a first place in the popular one-mile race. Up until the early 1930s, bicycle racing enjoyed greater popularity in the U.S. than baseball and horse racing.

Then, for nearly 50 years, bicycle racing fell into relative obscurity in the Western Hemisphere as auto racing overshadowed the bike. But in recent years there has been a growing interest in bike racing, with Canada's Tour de la Nouvelle France and the United States' Red Zinger competitions. The latter, held in Colorado, draws racers from all over the world. Similarly, after an interval of 75 years, Montreal hosted the world cycling championships in 1974; in 1976 the same city became the site of the Olympic bike races.

Over the years many different forms of racing have evolved, challenging the athletic efforts of men and women of all ages. The following are the main racing events officially sanctioned by world-class cycle-racing organizations.

TIME TRIALS

This is the form of racing invented by F. T. Bidlake in 1942 to avoid conflicts with the police over "mass-start" races. Any number of cyclists can enter this race; each one is started at a different time. Usually there is a minute's space between racers. In the end, the person with the lowest elapsed time takes the prize.

Wherever you find bike clubs the world over, you'll find time trials. They usually take place on the open road, starting very early in the morning on days when traffic is light, such as Sundays and holidays.

Time trials are staged in terms of distances of 10, 20, 30, 50, or 100 miles; durations of 12 or 24 hours; or hill climbs from 300 yards to 3 miles, depending on the grade.

Average speeds are highest in the 10-to-30-mile category. Racers may cycle at speeds around 27 miles per hour, which they sustain for an hour without letup.

MASS-START RACING

Mass-start racing is when all the participants start in one pack. In some of the European classics, such as Canada's Tour de la Nouvelle France, or Belgium's Het Volk, there are literally thousands of participants. With each racer pitted against all the others and the prize going to the first athlete to cross the finish line, such races generate a great deal of excitement.

Mass-start races come in a variety of shapes and sizes. A *criterium*, for example, may be held in a populated area, with a mile-long circuit of road sealed off from regular traffic for the duration of the race. Often taking place in small towns, these races—which last only a few hours—draw huge crowds of excited onlookers.

Other mass-start races, such as the Tour de France, take as long as 22 days to complete, yet there is never any lack of spectators to cheer on their favorite heroes.

Professional entrants in the great European road races are usually members of teams sponsored by various companies. It is not uncommon for the riders' jerseys to carry names like Perrier, Cinzano, or Michelin, along with names like Peugeot, Simplex, and Campagnolo, which are more directly associated with the bicycle industry.

TRACK RACING

Nowhere in cycle racing are the wits and tactical abilities of the participants more important than in track events. Official tracks range in size from the smallest, in Ontario, Canada, with 13 laps to the mile, to the largest, in London, England, with about three laps per mile.

Tracks may be banked or flat. Depending on the size of the oval, the banks may be shallow or steep. On the Ontario track, the banks slope up at a dizzying 55 degrees on the turns.

Track racers use stripped-down racing bikes (Fig. 10–1) with a fixed gear and no brakes. These machines weigh from 16 to 20 pounds and are designed so that the cyclists must crouch very low over their front wheels, maximizing muscular control and power for sprinting.

There are several types of track races: sprint, pursuit, scratch, Devil-take-the-hindmost, unknown distance, Madison, and motor-paced riding. Let's describe each one briefly.

Sprint

This race takes place over 800- to 1,000-meter courses, but only the last 200 meters of the race count. Until that point, it's all tactical. Sprint races usually involve two or three cyclists who are so closely matched physically that the only way to win is by outwitting one's opponents. One tactic is to act as though you're going all out, forcing your opponent to put on the steam and waste his or her best efforts before you've actually made your best move. While he or she gets thoroughly worn out, you are waiting for the last minute to put on your reserve power and pass your opponent in the last 200 meters. Another tactic is to box in your opponent on the turns, maintaining your slight edge not by sprinting, but by outmaneuvering your challenger and preventing him or her from passing you.

Fig. 10-1   The track racing bike has a lean, tight look about it. Notice how close the wheels run to the frame, making for a stiff bike with minimum flex or "whip." Notice the relationship between the height of the seat and the handlebars, placing the rider in a deep crouch for maximum power. (Photo courtesy of Bicycling magazine.)

Pursuit

In this race, two riders start on opposite sides of the oval track. On a signal from the judges, each rider tries to catch up with, or pass, the other, usually over a distance of about 4,000 meters. Because riders are so closely matched in the official races, they seldom do catch up with each other, and the winner is determined by the clock—sometimes by hundredths or even thousandths of seconds.

Similar principles are applied in team pursuits, involving teams of up to eight riders each. Any racer passed by another is eliminated. The prize goes to the cyclist with the best time who is still on the track after completing the full distance of the race.

Scratch

This competition is run like a horse race, with all racers beginning on the same line. The first one across the finish line wins. Scratch races are generallly three, five, or ten miles long.

Devil-Take-the-Hindmost

As each circuit is completed, the last rider in each lap is eliminated. On the last lap of the race there's a mad sprint to the finish line, with the first rider across taking the prize.

Unknown Distance

When the race begins, the cyclists don't know how long they'll have to ride. Suddenly a gong is sounded, signaling the last lap. Wit, muscle, and courage explode on the track as each rider presses himself or herself to the limit to be the first one across the finish line.

Madison

Although it has been rebuilt several times, New York's Madison Square Garden was originally constructed, at the turn of the century, for bicycle racing. One form of bicycle racing still takes its name from that place. The original Madison races were six-day affairs, with riders dropping of exhaustion toward the ends of the races, causing dramatic and sometimes bloody crashes. Thousands of spectators came to watch the racers, just as they came to watch the infamous marathon dances of the era. Although the original version of the Madison is banned, the race is still run with paired riders; one rider rests while the other races, shifting back and forth in this manner for as long as six days.

Motor-Paced Riding

This race involves two cycles, one motor-driven and one pedaled. Riding ahead, a special motorcycle breaks the wind, creating a slipstream and reducing air resistance for the teammate pedaling inches behind. Speeds of up to 50 miles an hour are often reached on small, banked tracks.

Track racing is one of the most exciting and tense sports you can experience as an onlooker. In many ways it's a perfect spectator sport, since you can see the entire track from the grandstands as you urge on your favorite riders. The race itself calls for mental discipline as well as brute strength, as riders seek new ways to psych out their opponents or maneuver into position for the final assault on the finish line.

CYCLE-CROSS RACING

Originally this race was invented in Europe as a way of staying in shape during the off-season, but now it's become a serious event in itself, with athletes specializing in this single form of racing. The length of the race varies from one to eight miles. The racers go over hills, through streams, over fallen trees and boulders, and through mud, sand, tall grasses, and woods. The rider rides whenever possible. But when the going gets rough you simply have to hop off and carry your bike. It's a wonderful sport if you like to wallow in the mud, plunge head first into freezing-cold creeks, scramble up hills too steep to climb on a bike, and do all this in a frenzy of competition with a dozen or more other riders.

ULTRA-MARATHON

There is one other type of organized bicycle racing, and that is what I call "ultra-marathon time trials." These events take the cyclist to the outer limits of physical and mental endurance. The long-distance cyclist can be compared to an ultra-marathon runner, who runs continuously for 24 to 48 hours. But whereas the runner may be competing for a full day or two, the ultra-marathon cyclist may be competing for periods up to two weeks. I am talking, of course, of competitions like the transcontinental ride in which I participated.

The United States Cycling Federation recognizes the Transcontinental ride as the longest event—in terms of miles covered—on the record books. USCF rules state that a cyclist must ride from coast to coast, either west to east or east to west, with the terminal points of the ride being the New York City Hall on the East Coast and either San Francisco or Santa Monica, California, on the West Coast.

There are different categories of ultra-marathon: (1) Solo—that is, one

The end of the road: John Marino's 1978 arrival in New York City. (Photo courtesy of Liaison Agency.)

person unassisted and riding without the aid of windfoils or any other device to cut wind resistance; (2) two or more riders, riding as a team on separate bikes and taking turns riding in front to draft the other rider, giving the rider in the rear a period of relief from the wind; and (3) one cyclist riding solo, with a motorcycle riding just ahead to break the wind for the bicyclist. Within these categories, records are also kept for cyclists riding tandem bikes.

At the present time, Kevin and Kris Kvale, of Minneapolis, Minnesota, hold the record in the second category (two or more bicycles drafting each other) with a time of 14 days, 9 hours, and 19 minutes (August 9, 1977).

Similarly, four men from Southern California—Brooks McKinney, Bruce Hall, Pete Penseyres, and Rob Templin—hold the record for the dual tandem ride, with a time of 10 days, 21 hours, and 49 minutes (June 27, 1979).

I hold the world's record for the solo category for crossing the continent in 12 days, 3 hours, and 41 minutes (June 28, 1980)—a record I took from my friend Paul Cornish, also a Californian.

Another notable ultra-marathon for cyclists in the U.S. is the ride from Seattle, Washington, to San Diego, California, a distance of 1,600 miles. This record is currently held by Michael Shermer, from Tustin, California, who covered the distance in 7 days, 8 hours, and 28 minutes (September 22, 1980).

The spoils of victory: John Marino after his 1980 ride. (Photo by Jim Posarik, courtesy of Liaison Agency.)

You do not have to belong to a team or pass any tests to enter these competitions. As an ultra-marathon cyclist, you make all decisions on your own—including which route to take and when to leave—in challenging a record. The one thing that is required is a tremendous amount of preparation. This involves not only getting your own body in shape, but also putting together a "support team": people you can trust to follow along behind you and take care of such things as food preparation, sleeping facilities, and mechanical work on the bike.

My own transcontinental rides have demanded a lifelong commitment— a commitment that has necessitated great sacrifices in all areas of my life. In spite of the fact that I am a college graduate with a teaching credential, I have worked odd jobs at night, sold vacuum cleaners from door to door, and worked as a custodian so that I could have my days free to train. Every cent I earned— and then some—went toward achieving my goal. So if you are considering a transcontinental challenge, be prepared to give your life over to it. The goal can be achieved in no other way.

The real rewards of the long-distance challenge may well be invisible to the general public. It is not one's name in the record books that excites the marathoner, but something much deeper and more personal. It is the satisfaction of pushing onself to the outer limits, of proving one more time that the limits we perceive are never absolute. Perhaps in all forms of athletic competition the ultimate goals are to explore the physical and mental potentials of the human race, to redefine our capacities over and over again.

WHERE DO YOU GET STARTED?

To become a serious contender in the world of bicycle racing, you must train 12 months out of the year. This means riding 50 to 150 miles a day, five to seven days a week, regardless of the weather. When you absolutely can't train because of snow or ice, get on an indoor bicycle or take up an alternative sport such as speed-skating, which develops leg muscles that are important in bicycling and maintains the capacity of the cardiovascular system. Weight lifting or weight training is also popular with serious competitive cyclists.

There are many opportunities open for the aspiring cycle racer. Bicycle clubs in your community sponsor races and/or training rides. You can get the names of local clubs through your bike shop or by writing to:

Bicycle Institute of America
122 East 42nd Street
New York, NY 10017

In the U.S., the League of American Wheelmen sponsors both local and national bicycling events. Membership in that club provides you with a monthly magazine of touring and racing events. Write to:

League of American Wheelmen
10 E. Read St.
Baltimore, MD 21202

Information about the Olympic bike-racing programs, the Amateur Athletic Union, and the Union Cycliste Internationale (the world governing body for bike racing) is available from:

United States Cycling Federation
Box 669
Wall Street Station
New York, NY 10005

or:

Velo-News
Box 1257
Brattleboro, VT 05301

Names and addresses of local bike clubs change from year to year as new officers are elected. For this reason, you should ask at your local bike shop for the most current information and addresses of clubs in your area. Most bike shops have a bulletin board on which are posted cycling events and the dates of club meetings.

ELEVEN

DO'S AND DON'T'S FOR CYCLING SAFETY

Traveling around on a (relatively) fragile bike in the midst of automobile traffic might seem like a hazardous enterprise, and, of course, accidents do occur. Yet, United States Department of Transportation studies on bicycling accidents show that only one in five bicycle accidents involves another vehicle. This means that four out of five accidents* are caused by the bike rider and can, therefore, be avoided by following some precautions. Now I don't mean to sound like a police officer, but the many do's and don't's that fill this chapter are the best way I know for laying out ground rules to keep needless injury from ruining your riding pleasure.

Mechanical failures cause from 5 to 8 percent of adult bicycle accidents. In the final analysis most of these resulted not so much from the bike's failure as from the rider's failure to undertake needed repairs. Talk to any experienced bicycle mechanic, and he or she will tell you stories that will amaze you. Lou Wright, a bicycle mechanic in San Jose, says it isn't at all unusual for people to bring in bikes they have been riding for years with wobbly wheels, loose handlebars, no brakes, and even cracked frames. A peculiar psychology seems to be at work here. Some people who ride bikes apparently never see them as real vehicles, but treat them as toys, just as they did when they were children.

It is essential that, as an adult, you take your bike seriously. Learn to recognize mechanical problems early on. When something rattles, feels loose, feels too tight, squeaks, or just doesn't do what you want it to do, stop. Figure out what's wrong and fix it. Or take it to your bike mechanic and have it

---

*Twenty percent of all the injury accidents reported each year involve children, who are given to flying off curbs into immovable objects, falling on the pavement while doing wheelies, and losing control because of lack of experience.

checked out. Bicycle repairs are relatively inexpensive. Even major ones are far less expensive than medical treatment for a fractured wrist or other bodily injury, which could be the result of a fall or collision caused by a mechanical failure.

In addition, 20 to 30 percent of all cycle accidents occur because the rider hasn't mastered basic riding skills. Some of these happen in the first weeks of riding—often because the fledgling rider has no one, not even a book like this one, to help in the learning process. With good instruction, either from a book or a more experienced rider, many such accidents can be avoided. In Chapter 5 we discussed basic riding techniques, particularly braking, which play a crucial role in safe riding.

Going too fast (especially down hills), skidding on wet or oily pavement, and losing control in loose gravel—each claims its share of injuries. Accidents can be minimized by using safety equipment whenever you ride: this includes an approved helmet, shatterproof glasses, riding gloves, and toe clips.

TANGLING WITH MOTOR VEHICLES

On the basis of data published by the National Highway Safety Administration in 1978, we can pinpoint the scenarios that most commonly lead to injury accidents between bicycles and motor vehicles. Take a moment to study these situations. It will increase your ability to perceive the potential for an accident and take action to avoid it. We list them in order of the most common situations first:

1. The bicyclist rides from a driveway or alley into a street. The driver of an approaching car, his vision obstructed by a parked car, a tree, or a hedge, fails to see the cyclist and strikes him. Most cyclists injured in this way are children.

2. The bicyclist runs through a stop sign, or fails to slow down or stop for a signal light, and is struck by cross traffic.

3. A motorist wants to enter the street from a driveway, gas station, or parking lot. He or she stops, looks both ways, but fails to see a bicycle approaching from the side. The bicyclist, meanwhile, sees the car and makes the assumption that the driver has seen him. Both operators proceed, with the car striking the bike or vice versa.

4. A motorist stops at a stop street. He fails to see a cyclist approaching the intersection from the left or right, often because he is looking for larger objects—that is, trucks or cars. He starts out, but strikes the cyclist. In these cases as in the one above, the cyclist sometimes mistakenly assumes that the motorist has seen him. In about two-thirds of the cases the cyclist is found to have been riding on the wrong side of the street, against the flow of traffic, presenting the motorist with an unexpected situation.

5. The bicyclist is rear-ended by a motor vehicle whose driver failed to see him. (This accounts for about 25 percent of all bicycle fatalities.) Approximately 70 percent of these accidents happen in rural areas. And they frequently happen at night on narrow roads that have no bikepaths marked. Often the cyclist is riding farther out in the road than he normally would because it's nighttime, he either has no lights or has inadequate ones, and, because he can't see well, he's afraid to hug the shoulder. Motorists involved frequently say they didn't expect to see a bike at such a late hour and didn't notice the biker until it was too late to avoid a collision. Some of the motorists involved in these accidents proved to be under the influence of alcohol. In some cases reflectors or lights might have helped the motorist see the cyclist; in other cases it didn't help or wouldn't have helped.

6. The bicyclist is riding on the right side of the road. He decides he wants to make a left turn. Without checking traffic behind him, he starts his turn and rides directly into the path of a car that was preparing to pass him. In most cases the motorist has neither the time nor the space to avoid hitting the cyclist. In interviews after these accidents, cyclists gave two basic reasons for not checking traffic before making the turn:
    a. The cyclist hadn't learned how to turn his head to look behind him without losing control and veering into traffic. He thought about looking, but, because he hadn't developed this skill, he was afraid to try.
    b. The cyclist believed he could tell if a car was approaching from behind him by judging the sound of the traffic. But peripheral sounds— wind, a smooth street surface, or a particularly quiet motor vehicle— provided him with the wrong signals.

7. A motorist stops at an intersection and waits to make a left turn. He sees what he believes to be a break in traffic, proceeds with his turn, and strikes an approaching cyclist. In some cases, the driver's view of the cyclist was obscured by a motor vehicle directly in front of the cyclist. In other cases, the cylist saw the vehicle waiting to turn but was going too fast to stop or avoid the collision.

Picture each of these situations in your mind. Try to figure out what you'd do to avoid trouble when and if you were confronted with the same set of circumstances in real life. Imagine the potential accident and then imagine you on your bike safely averting the encounter. Having once gone over it in your mind, you actually program yourself both to be alert to the potential for an accident and to take action to avoid it.

Now, one last proviso before I get to my road rules. It is important to understand that off-street bicycle pathways are not the ultimate answer to safety problems. According to the Federal Highway Administration there is an injury accident—serious enough to require medical care—from a collision or fall once every 12,600 bicycle miles on off-street bikepaths. On streets with no special provisions for bikes, the rate is only one every 28,700 bicycle miles. And on streets with marked bike lanes, where bikes share the road with motor vehicles, the rate is only one every 40,300 bicycle miles. In other words, there are over three times more injury accidents on off-street bikepaths than on marked roadways where bikes and cars share space.

Riding on an off-street bikepath usually means sharing the space with joggers, children on bikes, walkers, and inexperienced adult riders. Some accident analysts have suggested that overconfidence on the part of the cyclists may contribute to accidents on bikepaths. People let down their guard, get careless, and aren't mentally prepared for hazardous encounters. In addition, many bikepaths are poorly designed—often by people who are not cyclists themselves and have no understanding of the unique problems faced by cyclists.

If you must use off-street bikepaths, keep alert at all times. Recognize that even though you're free of the menace of motor vehicles, you're riding where you are *most prone to accidents*. Be on the lookout for walkers and joggers and for children making abrupt, unexpected moves on bikes. Keep your speed slow and your eyes open.

RULES FOR THE CYCLIST'S SURVIVAL

The following set of road rules has been gleaned from our own experiences on the road and those of our cycle-riding friends.

Pay attention. Many accidents could be avoided if the cyclist paid attention to the flow of traffic, the condition of the road, and the terrain. All your senses help you stay out of trouble on the road. Vision is clearly the most important, but other senses play a role too. The sound of an engine behind you can help you judge the size of the vehicle, its speed, and whether or not the operator is driving recklessly. A car horn may be either a greeting or an order for you to get out of the way. The smell of exhaust fumes tells you to keep your distance from a bus or truck. The smell of asphalt tells you to beware of fresh or heat-softened pavement, which can gum up your tires. You can feel the vibrations of a heavy vehicle approaching from behind. You feel the wind of a bus passing you. Your senses and mental abilities work together when you're alert. Daydreaming detaches your mind from your senses, disconnecting you from the signals that would warn you of danger.

Ride predictably. Many accidents happen because bicyclists fail to observe traffic regulations. There is only one reason for traffic regulations, and that is to make it possible for each driver to predict what the other will do—at least to some extent. If you don't know official traffic regulations, go to the Department of Motor Vehicles and get a booklet that summarizes them. The rules will tell you what motorists are expecting. It's up to you to make your judgments accordingly.

Always signal your intentions to turn or stop. Extend your left arm straight out for a left turn; turn it up at the elbow for a right turn; and straighten it, pointing diagonally downward, for a stop.

Read motorists' minds. Whether driving a car or riding a bike, you are dealing with thousands of personalities. Each motorist is in a world of his own—and so are you. What seems right to you may seem totally wrong to the driver of a car approaching you, and vice versa. We often look at ourselves as the main event and everyone else as part of the sideshow. That's human nature. But if you assume that the drivers around you have things other than you on their minds, you'll make your decisions more cautiously and defensively. You won't make turns in front of drivers who *should* see you but in fact don't. You'll assume that they don't see you and make your turn accordingly. Although you may feel conspicuous, you're usually not. Instincts of self-survival dictate that we first notice those things that threaten our own life or limb, and give second priority to the things that don't. Because the bicyclist can't hurt the motorist, while a nearby truck can, he'll notice the truck first and the bike later—if at all. This has nothing to do with stupidity or insensitivity. The human mind automatically selects which information to process first and postpones the rest. While it is important to recognize the place you occupy in the motorist's mind, it's also important to recognize that most drivers will do their best where you're concerned. But, to avoid injury, you need to take full responsibility for your own defense.

Establish eye contact. Though it may not always be feasible, it's helpful to establish eye contact with motorists whenever you can. This works almost like magic. First, by seeking eye contact you immediately discover whether or not there's an obstacle preventing the driver from seeing you. This may be a tree, a bush, a parked car, or even a passenger in the driver's own car. Sometimes the obstacle is in the driver's head; he or she gazes out on the world with a glazed, empty expression—preoccupied with a conflict at work or at home, a new lover, plans for a vacation, or even how much nicer it would be to be riding a bike than driving a car. Frequently, however, when you establish eye contact and flash a smile you'll get open recognition of your presence. With the wave of a hand, the motorist may even signal you to take the right-of-way.

Keep a safe distance from the curb. Ride as far to the right side of the street as is *safe*, but don't ride in the gutter. The gutter is the 18-inch concrete strip that usually borders the street; the gap where the gutter and the asphalt meet is the seam. Changing weather expands and contracts the asphalt, causing the gap in the same to widen. Often this ridge is so rough that it causes the cyclist to lose control. If you ride in the gutter you have no room to escape from hazards such as glass, rocks, etc. If you ride too close to the curb, your wheel may rub the curb or your pedal may strike the top of the sidewalk. So always ride on the asphalt a comfortable distance to the left of the gutter and the seam. Twelve inches is usually sufficient. Of course, this depends largely on the width of the street and the amount of traffic. Most city streets are wide enough to accommodate bicycles.

Choose safe streets. If the traffic is too heavy and the street is narrow or lacks a bike lane, use an alternate route. The time of day can make a difference in traffic patterns. Some streets that are jammed from curb to curb during rush hour can be delightful, wide open, and even enjoyable to ride on at other times.

Watch for car doors opening. Be aware of doors opening from parked cars. Get in the habit of looking ahead into the cars before you pass them. If you see an occupant, expect the door to open. Adjust your speed through traffic so that you have room to swerve to your left should a car door be opened into your path. Check out the traffic to the rear frequently. Just a quick peek over your left shoulder will do; it only involves a quarter turn of your head. This can be done very fast. If you expect a door to open, focus on the seam between the door and the car body. The minute you see a change in this seam, stop or prepare to swerve. Don't hesitate to shout to warn the driver. Every cyclist should develop a good yell.

Don't weave. If cars are parked intermittently, don't weave into the empty spaces and then out again into traffic. This makes you very unpredictable to motorists, even though you may think you're being safe.

Always ride on the proper side of the street. Besides violating traffic laws, the wrong-way cyclist causes many accidents. Motorists do not expect a cyclist on the wrong side of the road. A motorist conditions his or her vision to look in the direction from which traffic is most likely to appear. Example: A driver is conditioned to look first to the left when leaving a driveway. The wrong-way cyclist, approaching from the right, may well go unnoticed. The biggest wrong-way riding offenders are youngsters under 16. They don't drive a car, and therefore they don't relate to the mental habits of the motorist.

Ride single-file in traffic areas. It's all right to cycle two abreast if you are not impeding traffic, but in traffic it's much safer to stay in single file.

Use caution where there's a potential for side traffic. An approaching driveway or street means a vehicle may cross your path. If a car or truck is waiting to enter traffic and the driver is looking your way, don't assume that he sees you. The motorist is looking for other cars, not bicycles, and besides, you may be in the motorist's blind spot. Make eye contact with the driver. Wave your hand as though to say "Hello." Many motorists misjudge the speed of bikes and pull in front of them, thinking they have plenty of time to complete a turn or enter a street. If you're a real bike athlete, you'll be especially annoyed by this problem because you'll be riding at speeds comparable to cars in city traffic—or about twice the speed of most cyclists.

Watch out for pedestrians. Since a bicycle is a vehicle, always yield the right-of-way to pedestrians. Also, don't hesitate to shout a warning to a pedestrian if you think you could be a hazard to each other. Be pleasant in your comments. You'll get back whatever you put out.

Keep your head high. Keep your eyes moving, scanning the road ahead, at all times. Develop as "big" a picture as you can. A youngster riding his Stingray on the sidewalk might suddenly swerve and fly off the curb into your path. With your head up high and your eyes sweeping the area ahead, you'll see the potential for trouble long before it happens.

Keep your hands free. Do not carry items that will interfere with your vision or your ability to handle your bike safely. Riding in traffic with one hand on the bars and the other holding a grocery bag is dangerous and foolhardy. Get yourself a bike rack and panniers or a backpack if there's something you want to carry.

Use caution at intersections. Always check cross traffic before passing through an intersection, even if the light is green. There may be a vehicle running a red light, or a pedestrian who didn't make it across the street in time, or an animal, or another cyclist either running the light or cutting it too close. Give yourself space to avoid collisions. Similarly, when waiting at a red light, don't dart out into the intersection when the light turns green without first looking in both directions. The law states that you must wait for both vehicles and pedestrians to clear the intersection before you proceed, even if your light is green.

Use caution in parking lots. Be very careful when riding through parking lots. Cars are frequently backing out of spaces, sometimes very quickly. They are looking for other cars, not bikes. If you wear toe straps, loosen them while riding in parking lots so that you'll have your feet free to keep from falling in case you need to stop fast. Watch for signals from cars—such as backup lights turning on—that will warn you what a car is preparing to do. But don't depend on that 100 percent, since backup lights don't always work.

Be on the lookout for sewer grates. Narrow tires can jam between the bars of sewer grates on the side of the road. Similarly, be especially cautious of expansion joints in steel deck bridges and approaches to bridges.

Watch the car passing you. A vehicle that has passed on your left may then turn to the right directly into your path. This happens to most cyclists at one time or another. The motorist either misjudges your speed or doesn't see you. Recognizing this possibility, always keep an eye on the right front tire of the car passing you. The moment you see it turn toward you, assume that the auto is about to cut you off. Slow down or stop to avoid a crash.

Never take the blinking lights of a vehicle's turn signals seriously. A motorist can change his or her mind at the last minute. Or the driver may not even know the signal is on.

Use skill and caution in turning left. A cyclist should only execute a left turn from the left lane if he or she is experienced and comfortable in doing so. The maneuver is legal providing the bike doesn't impede the flow of traffic.

Use practical and safe judgment when getting into the left lane, remembering that you must yield the right-of-way when changing lanes. If the traffic is heavy, and getting over into the turn lane would require a vehicle to slow down for you, forget it. Don't assume that cars have to stop for you. In this case they don't! If the intersection has two left-turn lanes, always use the lane on the right and complete your turn as close to the right side of the street as is safe. Watch for cars turning right, and yield to pedestrians. Another way to execute your left turn (Fig. 11–1) is to continue straight across the original intersection, stop, and turn your bike 90 degrees to the left; then wait for the green light and proceed with the flow of traffic.

Use caution in crossing railroad tracks. When you see tracks, slow down before crossing. Often the rails are an inch or two above the road surface. Crossing too fast can cause your wheel to bottom out on the track, which can dent the rim or ruin a tire or both. Always cross at a right angle to prevent your front wheel from getting caught in the track groove. It's best to get up off your seat the instant you cross the tracks. This takes weight off the bike to provide a softer crossing.

Ride clear of debris. Glass, rocks, twigs, cans, nails, wire, potholes, and even wet leaves in the road are hazards. They can ruin a tire, cause you to lose control, or both.

Beware of dogs. Dogs have long presented a problem to bikers, especially on country roads where dogs are often allowed to run free. A dog may do any of several things: (1) Run alongside you but not leave the property; (2) leap at you only once, then turn around and go back; (3) try to snap at your legs,

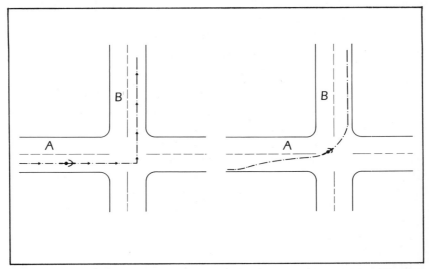

Fig. 11-1   When you want to turn from A Street to B Street, try the tactic on the left instead of the one on the right. It takes a little longer but is safer.

feet, or wheels; or (4) dart across in front of you. Only rarely will an animal jump on you or run into your bike—but it has happened. There are several things you can do to discourage dogs:

Yell at the dog—say "No" or "Stay." Be very firm, as though you were giving an order to your own animal. Dogs perceive confidence and more often than not respect authority.

If yelling doesn't stop the dog, *use some repellent.* A well-aimed squirt of water from a water bottle can be effective.

Outrun the dog. In most cases the dog isn't really trying to hurt you; he's trying to chase you away. It gives his ego a big boost to see you go.

Never try to kick a dog. He'll take this as an attack and become very serious about biting you.

Watch out for gravel. Gravel is very hazardous, especially when it is scattered across pavement, because it can cause your bike to skid out from under you. It is particularly hazardous when turning; make your turns gingerly. Use your rear brake only in gravel.

Monitor downhill speeds. Do not take downhills with reckless abandon. Know the limits of your bike. The higher the quality of the bike, the faster the speeds it can handle. Occasionally, on a fast downhill run, you may experience what is called wheel wobble as the bike oscillates or vibrates excessively. Though experts aren't completely sure of the cause, wheel wobble can result from improper wheel balance, slight imperfections in frame construction or design, placement of loads on the bike, intensity of sidewinds, or the texture of the road. If this ever happens to you, tighten your knees in close to the top tube, grasp the handlebars firmly on the hooks, and apply the rear brake gently and smoothly. Easy pressure on the front brake will then reduce your speed, and the vibration will stop.

Watch out for side-view mirrors on large vehicles. Note the extension of side mirrors on campers and pickup trucks. A passing vehicle can unwittingly bump you with a protruding mirror. Recreational vehicles and trucks from rental agencies are bigger hazards than semi's. The drivers of RV's and rentals are generally inexperienced and may not realize how far out their mirrors extend. It may even be the first time they've ever driven anything larger than the family car. And drivers of RV's are subject to many distractions: kids in the camper, scenery, maps, or a nervous, nagging husband or wife. It's always best to assume that they don't know you're there.

Note the number of occupants in a vehicle. Passengers in the back seat mean poor rear vision for the driver, who may also be less alert to traffic because he or she is conversing with friends. Beware of happy sightseers. Such things as conversation, scenery, or consulting a map are distractions that can take the driver's attention away from the road and from you.

"Understand" trucks. Professional truck drivers are the most skilled drivers on the road. Learn to respect them, if for no other reason than that they outweight you a million to one. Besides, driving those 18-wheel rigs through traffic, and on narrow roads, isn't exactly a piece of cake. A trucker behind the wheel is a person hard at work. From the trucker's point of view, that job is far more important than some bike rider out on a lark. Understand the peculiar problems of the truck driver: Momentum is a major factor. A truck can have as many as 18 gears, and when it's fully loaded the driver may have to go through all of them to get up to highway speeds. After that, drivers don't like to lose speed, since that means losing time, and going through all those gears again is hard work. Keep this in mind when riding your bike. It may be far easier for the cyclist to give a little than for the trucker to slow down. If you hear a large truck approaching, check out the conditions ahead. Is another vehicle coming in the opposite direction, making it impossible for the truck to pass in the opposing lane? Are you approaching a curve or the crest of a hill, making it dangerous for a truck to pass? Slow down and get off the road if necessary. You'll be surprised at how many "thank you's" you'll hear in the form of quick double blasts on the trucks' air horns.

Dress for the road. We've saved this rule for the last, hoping the reader would remember it longest. Wear an approved bicycle helmet—white or yellow for greatest visibility. Wear bright colors—an orange, red, or yellow jersey, for example. Wear riding gloves, both to cushion your grip on the handlebars and to protect the palms of your hands in the event of a fall. Equip your bike with toe clips; though it will take a little practice before you feel secure in them, they will prevent your feet from slipping off the pedals and will increase your speed and power. Lastly, wear shatterproof sunglasses to shield you from the sun and to prevent bugs, dirt, and small stones flung by car and truck wheels from injuring your eyes.

These are the basic "Rules of Riding," but we're not through yet. There are others which apply whenever you ride with a group.

RULES FOR SAFE GROUP RIDING

Group riding is a very enjoyable pastime. It gives you a chance to enjoy the company of people who share a common interest, to generate new friendships, and to exchange thoughts and information. When you're climbing those steep hills and look over and see your partner straining and sweating as much as you, it somehow makes it easier. And after a ride you've got friends with whom you can recap the experience.

Here are a few handy tips used in cycling clubs.

Ride single-file unless traffic permits otherwise. Traffic should not have to slow down for you.

Use hand signals to indicate hazards. An emphatic point of your finger warns riders behind you to stay clear of a hole, a branch from a tree, broken glass, etc.

Group riding presents the possibility for *drafting.* Drafting (riding close behind another cyclist) provides about a 20-percent advantage to the rider behind because the lead rider is bucking the wind resistance. Competitive racers will draft as close as one inch from wheel to wheel. The closer you can get to the lead rider, the greater the effect drafting will have. It's customary for the riders doing this to trade off the lead position. After the leader has "paid his dues" for whatever length of time he wishes, he pulls to the left and drops back to the rear position. The second rider is now the leader. When drafting, ride steady and straight. Don't make any sudden moves without signaling first. The leader can ride very hard for a short period and then pull out. The pace line or "pack" can always move faster than a single rider. If you want to draft the rider in front of you, first ask permission unless this has been arranged beforehand.

Use your voice to warn other riders of your intentions: "Passing on your left," "Let's turn left at the next intersection," etc. Make it a rule to always pass another cyclist on the left. That way your fellow cyclists know what to expect.

Signal your intention to stop by extending a hand downward with an open palm.

Hand-signal all right or left turns.

Offer assistance if needed. If you pass a cyclist who has stopped, make sure he or she is all right.

Obey all traffic laws. This is very important. It is not okay to break the law simply because you have the strength of numbers. We've heard stories of police stopping 20 riders in a pack and citing each one individually. Besides, 15 cyclists running a stop sign isn't exactly great PR. Waiting motorists see this and immediately lower their opinion of cyclists.

Tell other cyclists if they are riding dangerously, or if their bikes are unsafe. And don't take offense at comments or suggestions if you are on the receiving end. It's the best way to learn.

The camaraderie on group rides is terrific. It doesn't matter how old you are. Everyone from 8 to 80 can take part. Round up the family and friends, jump on your bikes, and head off for a long, enjoyable ride, coaching each new participant on the rules of group riding before you mount up.

MOTHER NATURE AND THE QUESTION OF SAFETY

Sometimes it's not motorists or other cyclists who threaten your safety so much as the forces of nature: rain, wind, fog, darkness, and the heat of the desert. On a bicycle you're obviously much more vulnerable to the natural elements than you would be in your car or at home with a good book. If you're an avid cyclist you'll want to acquaint yourself with potential natural hazards and the best ways to handle them.

Rain

The first thing most people think about when rain is mentioned is getting wet. That's not the first thing a cyclist thinks about, however.

Streets become slippery in the rain, and certain areas of the road are much worse than others. When the rain begins, and for about half an hour afterwards, water lies on top of the oil scum that has been accumulating on the roads, from the undersides of cars, since the last rain. For that period of time the streets can be as slippery as ice, especially in parking areas and at intersections where cars stand for long periods dripping oil onto the street.

Use special caution on city streets in the rain. Plan to get under cover or get off your bike and walk it for at least the first 20 minutes or half hour after the rains start, or until grease and oil films begin to wash away.

Gas stations become particularly treacherous in the rain. The combination of gas and oil spilled on the concrete aprons becomes as slick as a freshly waxed floor. If you're a seasoned cyclist, you've probably learned this lesson the hard way. If you're a new rider, you may be spared that experience by our warnings. Never take short cuts through gas stations in the rain.

Anything metal—manhole covers, railroad or streetcar tracks—becomes slippery in the rain, as do cobblestones and bricks used for crosswalks.

If at all possible, don't ride through puddles. You never know exactly how deep they are or what's at the bottom. Hidden beneath the water there might be broken glass, nails, or a sharp piece of metal that could ruin a tire.

If you've got to ride up steep hills in the rain, be aware that your rear wheel may spin on the wet pavement, causing you to lose forward motion and perhaps fall. If you have any doubts about a particular hill, get off and walk the bike up.

Bicycle brakes work poorly when they're wet. Water on the rims prevents friction—and friction is what makes you stop. Aluminum-alloy rims are more porous and therefore stop better than steel rims in the rain. And brake pads made by Mathausser are among the few brake pads engineered to stop effectively in rain. Gently touch your brakes from time to time, barely rubbing the rims. This helps to clear the water from the rims and leaves them relatively dry should you need to stop suddenly. And, of course, avoid braking too hard in the rain. With slippery streets it is easy to "lock up" the wheel, the result being a skid and a fall.

During a rain, the light can be very misleading; that is, the sky is dark, and with this darkness ground shadows fade or disappear. As a result it becomes difficult to judge distances.

If you are touring when it rains, you may have to continue riding in the rain for a considerable distance. Along the way the sun may pass in and out of the clouds. This can happen suddenly. One moment you're in the dark, the next you're in the sun. It takes a few moments for the retina of your eyes to adjust to these changes, and during that period of adjustment you may have difficulty seeing clearly.

Never forget that you become less visible in the rain. If you must ride in the rain, make yourself as visible as you can by wearing bright colors and using lights if you have them.

After riding in the rain, always wipe off your bike while it's still wet. Otherwise, dirt dries and hardens, making cleaning a real chore.

And what about your body getting wet? Most bicyclists consider that issue of the lowest priority, which should give you an idea of how important the issues of personal safety become. There is clothing to help you stay comfortable while riding in the rain. You'll find this discussed in the chapter which follows.

Wind

Most people wish for money, fame, or love. The bicyclist wishes for a tailwind. And most cyclists, if given the choice, would much prefer rain to a strong headwind.

Wind can sap a rider's energy very quickly, especially if it's combined with heat. What happens is this: The heat makes you perspire, but the wind dries your skin. You can become overheated and dehydrated very quickly unless you are careful to continually drink water.

Gusts of wind can be dangerous unless you are prepared for them. Side gusts are the worst, since they can blow you into the ditch or, worse yet, into the traffic lane. When they come, lean into them to counteract this force.

Be especially alert for winds when riding in mountains or hilly country. In such country the wind can seem to come from all directions at once. One moment it's still, the next moment the wind is in your face. A mile down the road it's at your back, and ten minutes later a gust hits you from the side.

Don't forget that Mother Nature isn't the only source of wind. Large trucks and buses also produce rapid air currents. As a bus is passing you, for example, there'll be a moment of stillness; then as it goes by there's a sudden blast, followed by a suction that wants to draw you out into the road. These winds aren't usually a big problem—you learn to correct for them automatically—but they can be alarming on your first few miles of touring.

When you combine winds, especially headwinds, with heavy bus and truck traffic, the results can be exhausting and nerve-racking. If you feel yourself pushed and pulled around on the road by all this wind action, find yourself a place to rest out of the weather and take a break.

When you have to ride in a wind, get as low as you can on the bike. Rest your hands on the lowest part of the handlebars. Wear tight clothes to minimize wind resistance and flapping. And get into your lower gears. Every few minutes, straighten up for a few seconds to allow blood to circulate to your midsection. Focus on the white line along the bike lane 20 or 30 feet in front of you. Look up now and then to check traffic or the condition of the road.

Finally, winds play games with your senses. It is difficult to judge the directions of sounds, and because of this you can become disoriented or even dizzy. When it's windy, assume that your ears are probably going to deceive you. Use your eyes to make judgments about traffic. Don't depend entirely on your ears.

In most areas of the country, winds are fairly predictable. The same areas can be windy in September and dead still in February. If you are planning a long tour, check with members of bike clubs near where you're going. Tell your contact when you're planning to be there, and ask about the wind.

Darkness

A full 25 percent of all bicycle fatalities take place at night on narrow country roads. Based on those figures, we feel it is wise to avoid such rides if at all possible, but, if you must ride at night, do everything you can to be visible. There are several precautions you can take: Wear white or fluorescent colors that reflect the headlights of motor vehicles that may be approaching from any direction. Bike shops and hardware stores carry fluorescent tape that can be applied to your clothing, your bike, and your cycling shoes. Reflective devices on your pedals, feet, or ankles are especially good, because the movement of your feet attracts more attention than the same reflective devices on the frame of your bike.

Make sure you have large reflectors on your bike—a red reflector in the rear and a white one in front. Each wheel should have a reflector mounted on the spokes to make you visible to drivers approaching from the side. Reflectors on your pedals also help. Never deliberately plan to cycle in the dark, but be prepared for that event in case you ever have to.

What about lighting systems? Bicycle lighting systems are only marginally effective. At best they only help you become a little more visible to motorists. We know of none that supply you with enough light to safely illuminate your way at speeds over ten miles an hour. There are two types of lighting systems—those that run on batteries and those that work from a small generator driven off the tire of your bike. In addition, there are blinking lights to fasten to the bike or your clothing. We describe these and others in more detail in the next chapter.

Fog

We have one suggestion about riding in the fog: DON'T! There just isn't a way to make it safe. If you're in the city, take public transportation, or call a friend to drive you to your destination. If you're touring and you have your camping gear with you, stop and set up camp. Do everything you can to avoid riding in the fog.

Desert Conditions

The prime danger of riding in a desert is dehydration. The heat and the dryness of the air deplete your body fluids. The symptoms are progressive: You begin with a dry mouth, nose, and eyelids; then your skin becomes pale and clammy; next come dizziness and hallucination; weakness and nausea follow quickly.

Dehydration can happen within a few hours or a few days. The best treatment is prevention. Realize that you can act to prevent it, if you act wisely. Conserve your energy in hot weather. Ride slowly and steadily, maintining a comfortable, almost leisurely pace. Get up with the first light of dawn—sometimes 3:00 or 4:00 A.M. in the Western Hemisphere—and put in most of your riding hours before 10:00 in the morning.

Dr. George Sheehan, author of the *Encyclopedia of Athletic Medicine*, has the following to say about dehydration: "There is now general agreement about what to do: fluids, fluids, and more fluids. This is the first priority. The amounts of fluid lost and therefore needing to be replaced can be astounding."

Drink small amounts of water frequently, rather than large amounts occasionally. Don't wait until you feel thirsty to drink. That's too late. Rather, drink enough water to keep your mouth always a little moist.

Studies by the U.S. Army have shown that most people require three to seven days to adjust to heat. Even great competitive athletes who live in cold climates are temporarily devastated by heat initially. Contrary to what some people think, adjustment to heat is not facilitated by the numerous electrolyte-replacement drinks—such as Gatorade and ERG—that are on the market. These drinks basically consist of sodium, potassium, and dextrose* for quick energy. The original electrolytes are lost in sweating, so it becomes necessary to replace them. However, restoration of electrolytes does not speed up your body's adjustment to hot weather.

One of the best ways to prevent dehydration is by eating fruits. (Oranges, bananas, apples, and pears are excellent.) These contain large quantities of water as well as the vitamins and minerals you need in hot climates. Natural fruit juices are terrific in the heat. Celery helps prevent sodium loss. Tomato

*Dextrose is a sugar added to these drinks for quick energy.

juice diluted with a little water provides good quantities of sodium and potassium.

Before you venture into the desert, mix up whatever you are going to drink along the way: electrolyte-replacement drinks, fruit juice, or plain water. Freeze it inside your water bottles (it's good to travel with at least two) the night before you leave and remove them from the freezer just as you're leaving. The drinks will stay cold for several hours this way, and they will help keep your body temperature down. When the water gets hot, don't drink it. It may increase your body temperature and accelerate sweating. Wet your lips and tongue periodically. Use some of the water to wet down your neck, head, and chest.

Before you depart, know where you can get drinking water along the way. This is psychologically important. You'll know how to pace yourself better. Make sure the water is drinkable.

If you are planning a long trip that necessitates crossing a desert, but doesn't end there, consider sending some of your supplies ahead so you won't have to pedal this extra burden across the burning wastelands. Send your things to an appropriately located Post Office, addressed to yourself at General Delivery. Or ship the supplies by bus; the rate is usually reasonable, and you can pick up your packages at a bus station located along your route. If you're really worried about the heat, or simply don't want to face it, take the bus ahead with your bike.

Watch the pressure in your tires as you proceed. Heat will cause the air inside to expand, increasing the pressure. Let about ten pounds of air out when you begin, and then check it every couple of hours as you go.

Although we urge reasonable precautions, don't be afraid of the desert. It can be extremely beautiful. In the U.S. the roads across the deserts are well traveled, so that even if you get into some kind of trouble on your bike, it isn't difficult to hail a passing motorist and get a ride—bike and all.

Finally, wear a white helmet to keep the sun off your head. Wear good sunglasses, and use sunscreen on your face or any other bare-skin areas that need protection. You'll find that your arms, the tops of your thighs, and the backs of your calves get the most exposure.

THE JOY OF SAFETY

Keep abreast of the latest information, legislation, and products that can make bicycling safer. As an increasingly large number of people take to their bikes for commuting, touring, physical fitness, and casual recreation, we'll be seeing more and more safety developments. One way to keep informed is by joining a local bike club. Bike clubs wield a surprising amount of political clout, and through them cyclists are able to prod state and local politicians into ordering bikepaths, setting up bike routes through cities, and establishing policies to allow cyclists to bring their machines aboard public-transportation vehicles.

One of the oldest bike clubs in the U.S. is the League of American Wheelmen, whose address we gave you in the chapter on touring. Members of this group, established in 1880, were responsible for getting legislation passed and funding made available to grade and surface roads back at the turn of the century. It was not motorists but bicyclists, lobbying as a group, who were responsible for this important innovation. Similarly, bicycle clubs exercising their political clout have been responsible for getting highway departments across the nation to add bike lanes to interstate routes and mark them accordingly.

By riding with bike clubs, you have the opportunity to travel with people who are roadwise. Information is exchanged in an easy way, and the new rider learns much through simple observation.

Another good resource for learning more about safety is by subscribing to a magazine or newsletter devoted to bicycling. Sometimes newsletters are published by local bike clubs. You can find out about these by asking the people at your local bike shop. At the time of this writing, there's only one national magazine that's devoted to the cyclist:

*Bicycling**
33 East Minor St.
Emmaus, PA 18049

After the basic principles are learned, as we've outlined them in this chapter, defensive riding becomes second nature. You'll practice safety techniques in an easy and relaxed way. As experience develops, you'll know exactly what to do in crowded traffic or when adverse weather conditions strike. Fears are replaced by knowledge, and judgments about riding safety come quickly and easily. At that point, the whole joy of bicycling opens up to you.

*(*Bicycling* magazine now incorporates *Bike World* magazine.)

TWELVE

THE WELL-DRESSED CYCLIST

I n recent years the design of cycle clothing, especially jerseys, has been heavily influenced by the world of high fashion. Bold colors, dramatic stripes, and high-quality knit fabrics have brought a new dimension to cycling clothes. With the new design innovations, nothing has been lost in function; as with most other athletic clothing, there's a clear logic to the designs that have evolved over the years, and that tradition has been maintained.

A number of practical considerations have dictated designs in cycle clothing: low wind resistance, ability to adjust clothes to regulate the body temperature as exercise raises it, and freedom from binding or chafing as the cyclist pedals.

Cycling gloves, shoes, and helmet—each has its own set of design problems. Gloves should be well ventilated while providing padding against road vibration and a sure grip on the handlebars. Helmets must be protective, light in weight, and cool. Shoes must be light, cool, and strong enough to protect the cyclist's feet from injury by the steel pedals after miles and miles of pedaling.

The clothing that has evolved for cycling competition is useful for racer and tourist alike. If you're a tourist, you'll want to add to your wardrobe certain garments that protect you from the weather or make you more visible in traffic.

Cycle clothing is comparable in price to similar garments for everyday use. A jersey is about the same price as a knit sweater, for example, and, like sweaters, jerseys come in a variety of fibers, from polyesters to lamb's wool. Naturally the price varies accordingly. Cycling shorts may be a few dollars more than a good pair of casual pants.

BASIC CLOTHING

Helmets: Put Your Money on Your Head

I consider my helmet to be the most important and essential article of bicycle clothing I own. Helmets rank right along with automobile seatbelts in terms of providing crucial protection. With a helmet, a potentially life-threatening accident can be limited to a minor mishap.

Helmets designed specifically for bicyclists are manufactured by Bell, MSR, Pro-tec, and Skid-Lid. A few bike shops still stock the kind designed for racers 50 years ago, featuring strips of padded leather that line the top of your head. In a fall these can protect you, to some degree, from abrasions, but they're of little more use than a baseball cap for protection from concussion or a fractured skull. Reflecting on their ultimate function, cyclists have given them a well-deserved nickname: "hairnets."

Basically, all helmets are constructed such that they are light in weight to prevent neck fatigue, yet strong enough to cushion and absorb the impact of a blow to the head. The best helmets are made of a durable Lexan shell to resist shock and abrasion and lined with absorbing material to "give" upon impact. (See Figure 12–1.)

The main problem with bicycle helmets—getting people to wear them—has little to do with technology. People argue that the weight on their heads gives them a pain in the neck. Others argue that the helmets are too hot. And a few make no excuse except that wearing a helmet is too much bother. None of the arguments holds up, however. Helmets actually provide shade from the intense rays of the sun. Most are equipped with absorption material to prevent perspiration from getting into your eyes. After you've worn a good bicycle helmet for a few days you'll never even notice it's there. And, once you get into the habit of wearing one, you'll feel naked without it.

The Jersey

The upper part of your body is the largest area visible to motorists as you ride on the street. Take advantage of that fact by wearing the brightest, most attractive jersey you can find. They come in a variety of colors, from grey to shocking pink, and in recent years there has been a move toward colorful stripes similar to those used in ski sweaters. The combination of bright colors and an aesthetically arresting appearance will go a long way toward making motorists aware of your presence. So consider these choices ultimately as safety features in addition to their importance in establishing a positive image of the bicyclist in the public mind.

As for function, the design which has evolved for bicycle jerseys is perfection itself. Tight-fitting, the jersey has low wind resistance. A zipper at the

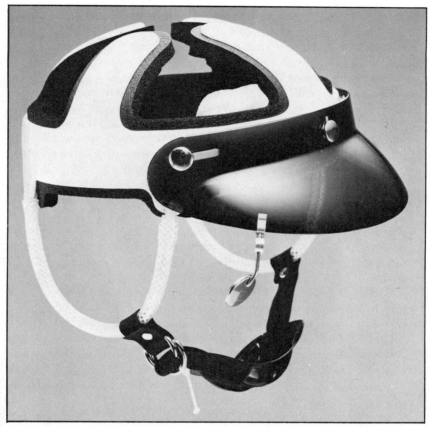

Fig. 12-1 The design of this bicycle helmet, the Skid-Lid, incorporates both safety and comfort. The ventilation openings keep the rider's head cool.

neck is easily adjusted while you're riding, providing more or less ventilation as you go.

The jersey is long in the waist so it doesn't ride up as you bear down. A wide pocket across the back gives you a safe place to store your wallet, a piece of fruit for your lunch, and even a tire patch kit. Located in the rear, the pocket is out of the way, and, even when it's bulging with a spare sewup tire, it won't interfere with your performance. A few jerseys are made with small breast pockets in addition to the one in the back.

The knit fabric comes in both wool and polyester, the wool usually costing about twice the price of the synthetic. Many cyclists actually prefer the synthetic fibers because they can be tossed into the washing machine with other clothes and tumble-dried, at low heat, at the end of a ride. Wool jerseys require the same kind of care as any good-quality wool product—that is, hand-washing in cool water and drip-drying.

In really hot weather, a tee-shirt may be all you want or need. But be careful about riding bare-chested. Your back gets a lot more exposure to the sun when you're on your bike than when you're walking or jogging. It's better to wear a tee-shirt so that you don't accidentally sunburn yourself and ruin the rest of your ride. As they say, an ounce of prevention . . . .

In cold weather, a good combination of shirts will keep you comfortable: a cotton tee-shirt under a wool jersey, with a snug-fitting nylon windbreaker over it. As you exercise, and your body temperature rises, you can shed first one and then the other garment to adjust your comfort.

Cycling Shorts

When you start riding you'll probably wear a pair of jeans or running shorts—whatever you have around. But if you substantially increase the number of miles you ride in a day, you'll find that the seams on regular pants chafe your legs.

Cycling shorts are designed to overcome this problem. They are made of stretchy fabric which fits skintight, eliminating chafing in the thighs. And smooth seams prevent irritation of the sensitive skin of the crotch.

Cycling shorts are usually longer than conventional shorts, with legs extending to the middle or lower middle of the thigh. The greater length prevents the fabric from riding up on your legs and bunching in the crotch as you ride. And cycling shorts are lined with soft chamois, which minimizes abrasion in the sensitive genital areas.

Shorts come in both synthetic and natural fibers, both of which are fine as long as they are stretchy and comfortable. Because of the chamois liner in the crotch, you'll have to take special care in laundering. Washing shorts in cool water with baby shampoo instead of detergents gets them clean, leaves no irritating chemicals behind, and isn't hard on the chamois. Always smooth out the chamois with your hand while still wet, before you hang the shorts up to dry indoors, out of direct sun. Do not put them in the dryer. Afterwards, work the chamois with your hand until it's soft and rub in some baby oil or chamois fat (available in bike shops) to preserve the leather and reduce friction.

Cycling shorts are designed to be worn without underwear, but some people prefer to have fabric next to their skin. Men's underwear is usually constructed with seams in the crotch, which can become quite uncomfortable after 20 miles of riding. However, women's cotton underwear is all but seamless and can be worn beneath riding shorts for extra comfort.

Although cycling shorts have elastic at the waist and are worn with the jersey over them, many cyclists wear them with suspenders, which prevents the waist from slipping down during a ride.

Leg and Arm Warmers

On an early morning ride the air may be cold enough so that your bare arms and legs need some extra protection. For this there are arm and leg warmers—simple sleeves of fabric that fit snugly and can be slipped on and off in seconds. As you exercise and heat up, your body generates enough heat to keep you comfortable, and at that point you can remove the sleeves, fold them up, and slip them in the pocket of your jersey. Although many bike shops carry both arm and leg warmers, adequate arm warmers can be improvised by cutting the arms from an old sweatshirt.

For longer rides in cold weather, it's usually advisable to anchor the tops of the leg warmers to your shorts with a safety pin. You may also want to install Velcro tabs or small snaps as more permanent fasteners.

Cycling Shoes

Traditional cycling shoes are made of leather, often perforated for ventilation. They are very light in weight but sturdy. There's no heel, and the soles are of leather. The bottom of the shoe is reinforced with an inner metal shank that protects your foot from the metal of the rat-trap pedal. This design is extremely effective for pedaling, but impossible for walking. Using this model of cycling shoes, you'll have to carry an extra pair of shoes for any walk-stops you make.

A pair of good cycling shoes weighs in the range of 1½ to 2 pounds—the lighter the better. The weight is important because, with every turn of the cranks, you're lifting the weight of your shoe a little over a foot. If you're pedaling at 75 revolutions per minute, you lift that weight, once for each foot, 4,500 times every hour.

A good shoe is designed to fit snugly into a pedal equipped with a toe clip. For maximum efficiency, a metal or plastic cleat can be fastened to the bottom of the shoe. This holds your shoe firmly in the pedal, minimizing twisting movements that might otherwise waste energy, maintaining your foot on the pedal in the most effective position, and allowing you to pull up on the backstroke without having your foot slip from the pedal.

In recent years a canvas-and-rubber touring shoe has appeared on the market. The ridged rubber sole works quite well with a rat-trap pedal and toe clip, providing enough traction to prevent it from slipping easily from the pedal. And the canvas uppers allow your feet to breathe, keeping them reasonably cool. These new touring shoes can double as town shoes or camp shoes, saving you the trouble—to say nothing of the weight—of carrying a second pair of shoes in your panniers. The touring shoes are reinforced with a steel shank and have an adequate heel for comfortable walking.

Whatever you do, don't try to cycle distances of more than five miles in tennis shoes. Most "sneakers" are much too soft on the bottom, and without this necessary support you can injure your feet.

Gloves

Gloves seem like a luxury until you've gotten into the habit of riding with them. Cycling gloves, which look like regular gloves with the fingers cut off, usually have backs made of a coarse weave and palms of leather.

The best cycling gloves are padded to absorb road shock transmitted to the handlebars. In addition, they give you a good grip and prevent your hands from slipping when they're sweaty.

Recently a couple of companies have begun marketing high-quality foam-rubber padding that fits snugly over your handlebars and is so effective against road shock that gloves become obsolete. Many cyclists favor this arrangement. The foam-rubber padding is comfortable without being squishy, and being able to ride without gloves means two less pieces of loose equipment to lose or misplace. The choice is really a personal matter.

Safety Vests

A nylon roadworker's vest with a highly visible surface—usually shocking pink or orange—can be purchased at most hardware stores for very little money. This will make you more visible on the road when you don't have a bright jersey or tee-shirt to wear. Roadworker's vests are favored by commuters who cycle to work in their work clothes, as they're easy to put on and take off and can be folded up and stuck in a pocket.

PROTECTION FROM THE WIND AND RAIN

Cyclists who are in top physical condition often ride in the rain with no more than a jersey and shorts. By maintaining a high rate of physical output, their bodies generate enough heat to protect them from chilling. Upon arriving at their destination, they take a hot shower and change into dry clothes before their bodies have a chance to cool off.

For tourers, commuters, and recreational riders, there is raingear to help out. If you want a lightweight rain jacket to get you no further than ten miles, almost any good-quality, waterproof nylon jacket will do. The trouble with most fabrics that keep out the rain, however, is that they also hold in your body heat and moisture. These fabrics, which don't "breathe," will remind you of a Swedish sauna after only a few miles. This can be fine if it's chilly outside, but if you have to stay in that portable sauna for more than half an hour you'll begin to feel as though you're suffocating.

A new fabric, called Gore-tex®, to a great extent solves this problem.

This miracle fabric is a laminate—two layers of different materials bonded to one another. The inner membrane was originally invented by a physician for making artificial valves for the human heart. The secret of the Gore-tex laminate is a synthetic resin called Polytetrafluoroethylene. When bonded to fabrics such as nylon, Gore-tex forms a microporous membrane that allows the gaseous moistures from your body to escape while blocking water and rain droplets from entering. That means that rain can't get in, but your body can breathe.

Gore-tex rain togs are the best there is. Several companies make rain jackets suitable for biking. Early Winters, a company that makes many different kinds of sports clothes, makes a jacket designed specifically for cyclists.

Any jacket you buy for cycling should have a smooth front; the fewer the pockets and zippers, the better. When you're moving forward, water can be driven through zippers and even through the tiny holes made in the process of stitching the fabric together. Seams can be sealed against the rain with a plastic seam sealer that comes in a tube, but zippers can't be, and front pockets tend to collect water.

A hood on the jacket keeps your head dry and prevents the rain from trickling down the back of your neck. But check out the hood before you buy. When you turn your head, the hood should turn with you, or you'll find yourself staring at the inside of the hood instead of the road.

Gore-tex chaps pull up over your legs, providing sufficient protection while still allowing plenty of ventilation. Full pants are also available in Gore-tex.

Nylon booties and mittens complete your raingear ensemble, the whole outfit going a long way toward keeping you dry and relatively comfortable.

Riding very far in the rain isn't advisable regardless of how well prepared you are. The extra fabric will feel cumbersome and constricting. And even with Gore-tex you can get overly heated and damp from an accumulation of your own heat and moisture, so even as you're putting on your raingear you should be making plans to stop a few miles down the road.

If you have a leather saddle, protect it from the water with a plastic sack (such as a bread sack) when you must ride in the rain.

When it rains, skies get gloomy and visibility is reduced. So whatever raingear you're purchasing, get the brightest colors you can find. Orange, yellow, and red are especially useful in making it easier for motorists to see you.

COLD-WEATHER CYCLING

When the temperature drops, the cyclist is presented with a new set of problems: how to stay warm and still be able to move. Heavy winter clothing may be a good protection against the cold, but it makes pedaling a bike almost impossible.

In cold weather, pay particular attention to your toes, face, fingers, and neck. Wool mittens or gloves are good, and if the temperature gets really cold a good pair of ski gloves or motorcycle gloves will keep your fingers warm while still allowing you to control the brakes and shifters. Wool socks are a must, and if you're a fanatic you can even buy cycling shoes made for winter riding.

A knit ski hat worn under your bike helmet will help keep your head warm, and, if your helmet is vented, blocking the vents with little chunks of foam rubber will also help. A knit ski mask, with holes for the eyes, nose, and mouth, goes a long way toward keeping your face from freezing.

Instead of wearing a heavy coat, try wearing several layers of clothing, such as a duofold insulated underwear top, followed by a long-sleeved wool ski sweater or jersey, followed by a snug-fitting windbreaker. If your chest gets cold from the force of the wind, a piece of newspaper folded under your jersey will make you more comfortable. Layered clothing is better than a single warm garment because you can shed whatever layers you need to be comfortable after you've started to heat up from exercise. With a heavy coat you get damp from your own perspiration, and eventually that makes you feel chilled and clammy.

For pants, you can use leg warmers with your cycling shorts. And if it's *very* cold, wear warmup pants designed for joggers.

When you're cycling in cold weather, always consider the chill factor of the wind passing over your body as a result of your forward motion. Your movement at ten miles per hour reduces the apparent temperature to just the same extent as a ten-mile-per-hour wind. When you add the wind *you're* creating to the wind Mother Nature is making, things get even chillier. If you're cycling at ten miles per hour in a ten-mile-per-hour wind, figure the chill factor as being just the same as a 20-mile-per-hour wind.

As the weather gets cold and wet, equip your bicycle with panniers or a handlebar bag to carry the extra clothes you might need. Any good-quality handlebar bag will do. If you prefer panniers, see the chapter on touring, which describes the best carrying systems to get.

A CATALOG OF
ACCESSORIES

Much of the initial excitement of buying a new bike comes in choosing accessories, those intriguing little pieces of equipment that can improve your enjoyment of the sport. Because bicyclists must be particularly aware of weight and durability, most accessories reflect the essence of simplicity in engineering and design. These features make the search for the perfect accessory to fit your needs all the more enticing.

TOE CLIPS

Your pedaling efficiency and power can be increased by about 20 percent with the addition of toe clips to your bike. (See Fig. 13–1.) Add another 10 percent of efficiency if you add cleats to your shoes.

After you become a confident rider you'll see, particularly if you ride without cleats, there's no danger of getting your foot caught in the toe clips—a common anxiety of beginning riders. An adjustable quick-release strap lets you keep them as snug as you wish, though you can still release your foot instantly when you come to a stop.

If you wear cleats on your shoes, the strap on your toe clips must be released before you can pull out your foot. This takes some practice. You have to lean down, flip the quick-release buckle on the strap, and pull your foot free. This sounds precarious and tricky, but it really isn't hard to learn. We don't recommend it for beginning riders because it's just that much more to remember. And many experienced riders, especially commuters and tourers, use the clips without cleats.

When you install toe clips on your pedals, make certain you get the right size. They come in small, medium, and large. The size determines how far

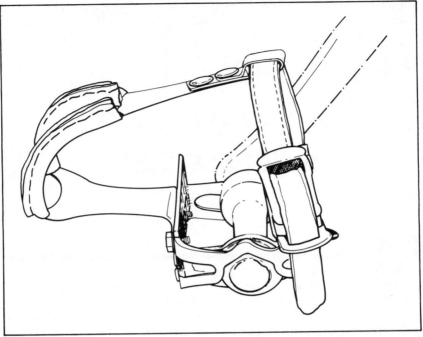

Fig. 13-1   Toe clips can increase your pedaling efficiency by 30 to 50 percent.

forward on the pedal your foot will ride. (The ball of your foot should be directly over the axle of the pedal.)

If your toe clips are too long, allowing your foot to slip too far forward on the pedal, you may injure your instep, and your pedaling efficiency will be reduced. If the toe clip is too short, you can end up with tendonitis in your Achilles tendon. So make certain you've got the proper size.

AIR PUMP

A good-quality hand pump is a must. (See Fig. 13–2.) But be careful to buy one that is compatible with the valves on your inner tubes. There are two types of valves: Shraeder and Presta. If you have any doubts as to which type you have, take your bike with you when you buy the pump.

There are both plastic-bodied and metal-bodied pumps. Most cyclists prefer the plastic pump because metal ones dent, and, once dented, the plunger may not function properly. However, there are some high-quality metal pumps available these days, and if you exercise reasonable care they'll provide many years of good service.

Fig. 13-2 Every bicycle should have a good air pump mounted on the frame as standard equipment.

Buy the best pump you can afford. Cheap pumps are a source of frazzled nerves, and they usually end up being thrown into a ditch or beaten into a twisted mass after you have fruitlessly attempted to inflate a flat tire on the road away from home.

A pump usually comes with clips to mount it to the frame of your bike. The best place to put it is on the seat tube; there it won't interfere with your shift levers. Some people mount the pump under the top tube. We have found this inconvenient. Every time you grab the top tube to carry your bike over a curb or up some steps, the pump is dislodged.

Pumps come in different sizes to match the size of the bike frame. Silca of Italy makes a pump with an indentation on the handle so that no extra clip is required to hold it fast to the frame. These also come in various colors to coordinate with the color of your frame.

WATER BOTTLE

If you're planning any kind of tour, or regular rides of more than a couple of miles in hot weather, buy yourself a water bottle and a water-bottle cage to hold the bottle to the frame. Mount the cage on the down tube, out of the way of the shifters but still within easy reach. Water-bottle cages can also be purchased to mount on your handlebars. The bottles are of plastic. Although water bottles come in colors, we suggest white, which keeps your water cool by reflecting the sun's rays. Even a color like bright orange can raise the temperature to lukewarm after half an hour in the sun. Long-distance tourists mount two and sometimes three water bottles on their bikes.

TOOL KIT

The need to carry a tool kit varies. For example, if you're never more than a few miles from home, a bike shop, or a telephone, a tool kit is probably unnecessary. If you're going on a tour that will take you several days' ride from home and you have totally overhauled your bike (we advise this) before you leave, the chances of your having any mechanical problems other than a flat tire are slim. Many people carry tool kits for years and never actually need to use them, although they often get out the tools to fuss with their bikes while killing time in camp.

In all my years of riding, I have never required more than the following for daily rides of 20 to 50 miles:

> Three aluminum tire irons (omit if you use sewup tires)
> Six-inch crescent wrench
> One small screwdriver
> One patch kit (if you use sewup tires, subtract the patch kit and carry an extra tire rolled up under your saddle)
> Two extra spokes taped to the chainstays of your bike frame
> Three towelette packets to clean the grease off your hands

On long tours (i.e., trips lasting more than a couple of days), add these tools to the above list:

> One pair of ignition pliers
> Three to six Allen wrenches to fit the Allen-wrench bolts on your bike (common sizes are 3, 5, 6, 7, 9, and 10 mm; carry only those you need)
> One chain tool to remove and replace chain rivets for repairs
> One length of three or four links of chain for chain repairs

Two thin cone wrenches to adjust the wheel bearings on your bike (carry
only the sizes you need)
One inner tube
One tire (folding type is available for clinchers)
One derailleur cable
One long brake cable
One yoke cable if your bike has center-pull brakes
One pair of rubber brake pads
One toe strap for toe clips
One freewheel remover

Obviously, if you don't know how to use any of these, either learn how
or don't bother carrying them. One bicycling friend of ours—a man who
stubbornly refuses to make the smallest effort to learn the difference between
a screwdriver and a floorjack—has invented what he calls the "Universal Tool
Kit." This consists of one thumb and one dime: the thumb for hitching a ride
home or to the nearest bike shop, and the dime for making a phone call to a
friend in case he can't hitch a ride.

The "Day-Ride Tool Kit" can be carried in the pocket of your jersey or
in a small pouch fastened to the back of your seat. The larger kit is usually
carried in the panniers, or a handlebar bag, when you're touring.

REFLECTORS

People who own fancy racing bikes practically go into apoplexy when you talk
about adding reflectors. To the purist, fastening reflectors to the wheels, pedals, and frame is a sin never to be committed because it clutters up the clean
lines of a racing bike. Sin or not, if you're riding at night (even if there's only
a slim chance of your having to), reflectors can save your life.

If you commute by bike, there probably are times—especially in the
autumn—when you get caught riding in the dark. For that reason, reflectors
should be standard equipment for you.

Set up your bike with a white reflector in front if you don't have a
headlight. Have a 2-inch red reflector in the rear. Have spoke reflectors
mounted on at least one wheel. Put reflectors on your pedals or put reflective
tape on your cycling shoes to create a highly visible reflection that bobs up
and down as you pedal. Reflectors are easy to install, and they don't interfere
with your bike's operation.

LIGHTS

We've already discussed bicycle lights briefly in the chapter on safety. Figs.
13–3 through 13–5 will give you a better picture of what's available.

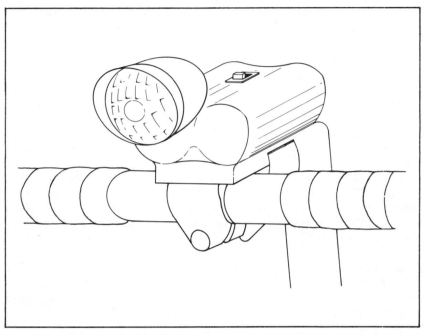

Fig. 13-3   *Clip-on lights like this "Cat Eye" or the more popular "Wonderlite" can double as camp lights for touring. They make you visible to observant motorists and shed enough light to prevent you from running into immovable objects.*

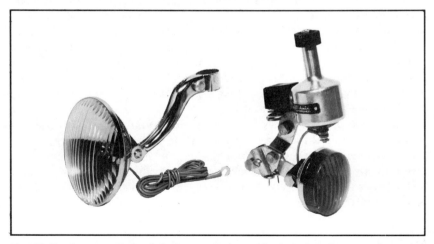

Fig. 13-4   *Generator lights help drivers see you in the dark, but they go out when you stop. They cause a drag on your wheel and are not completely dependable.*

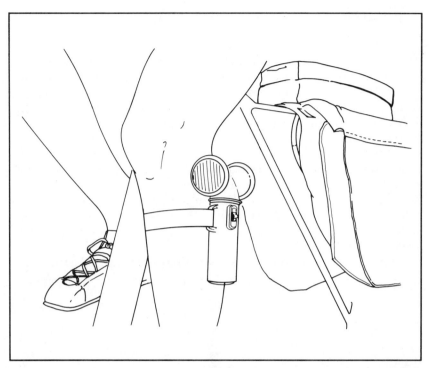

Fig. 13-5 Leg lights have a red lens shining backwards and a clear lens shining forward. Strap them to your leg or ankle—not your arm—and they create a fairly visible bobbing light for observant motorists to see. They do little or nothing to help you see in the dark.

There are two other lighting systems worth mentioning here, although neither one of them is a standard bicycle item.

Yachting supply stores carry a lightweight emergency strobe light that sells for about $50 and is about the size of a pack of cigarettes. They come with red, amber, green, and clear lenses and can be seen for miles. They're very powerful and compact, clip to your clothing, and are one of the few ways you can really make yourself visible to drivers.

If you're commuting in the dark regularly, and if you're also mechanically skilled, you might consider making your own lighting system. Buy a headlight and taillight made for a moped or other small motorcycle. Add a storage battery—also for a motorcycle—and purchase a small battery charger. With a little ingenuity you can rig up a very respectable system. Keep the battery charger at home and recharge your battery overnight. The total initial cost will be high (around $75), but if you're doing a lot of night riding there really isn't anything better.

MEASURING YOUR PERFORMANCE

A variety of odometers and speedometers is currently available for cyclists. Odometers are relatively inexpensive and are handy for keeping track of your daily miles in training and touring. There are two types of odometers, both of which mount on the front axle of your bike. One type counts the miles by a "finger" that fastens to the spokes; it makes a clicking sound as you go, which can be annoying on a long downhill. A second type, made by Huret, is belt-driven and silent.

Speedometer/odometers that mount on the handlebars are available. Some have a gear mechanism that attaches to the hub, and others have a small friction wheel that rubs against the tire.

Try to get an odometer with both an accumulative mileage counter and a trip counter that can be turned back. The Huret odometer has both these features, letting you measure either a single ride or the total miles you've ridden your bike.

The most intriguing device for measuring performance is the Pacer 2000,

Fig. 13-6 *This handlebar-mounted computer tells you speed, cadence, elapsed time, average speed, and even pulse rate.*

made by Veltec, Inc. (See Figure 13–6). This digital electronic miracle weighs ounces and measures distance; pedaling cadence; elapsed time in seconds, minutes, and hours; average speed; and miles per hour. Nonfriction electronic sensors pick up the signals to calculate all this information from your front wheel and crank-set. The device fastens to the handlebars with Velcro strips. The Pacer 2000 is also available with a heart rate indicator. An elastic belt fits around your chest with three contacts which pick up your heart beat. A small wire connects to the Pacer, giving you a constant reading of your heart rate.

HANDLEBAR PADDING

Most bicyclists, until now, have taped their handlebars for a cushioned grip. However, you now have a second option, in the form of rubber sleeves applied to the bars. If you have trouble with your hands—irritation of the nerves, etc.—you will find that the sleeves do provide considerably more comfort than tape. They are applied by removing the handbrakes and old tape, soaping up the handlebars, and pushing the sleeves into place. After the soap and water dry, the sleeves become very secure.

Hal Bennett always had pain in his right wrist after riding for more than 15 or 20 miles—the result of a fractured wrist suffered in a motorcycle accident 15 years before. When he installed the foam sleeves on his bike, he found that the pain went away. In addition, he found that the sleeves made riding gloves quite unnecessary.

CAR RACK

There are two types of racks available for carrying your bike on your car. The first—for large and intermediate cars only—fastens to the trunk of your car, and the second lets you mount your bike on the roof.

We recommend the roof rack for several reasons. First, the rack that hangs from your trunk puts your bike in a vulnerable position. If another car even tapped your rear bumper at a stoplight, it could do damage to the wheels and frame. Second, the roof rack is less accessible to bicycle thieves looking for a score.

Most roof racks allow the bikes to be mounted upside down. With wheels in the air your car takes on a strange appearance indeed, but the bikes are secure there. You won't have to bother with them every time you open the trunk, either.

If you can carry your bike on your car, sightseeing takes on a whole new dimension. On weekend trips to new places you can take to your bike when you arrive and explore the territory on two wheels. On your bike you'll discover worlds you would miss in your car. After once establishing the routine, you'll look upon the family car as incomplete without a bicycle rack.

FOURTEEN

PREVENTING AND
TREATING INJURIES

Bicyclists are amazingly free of serious injuries directly associated with their sport. Most athletic injuries are caused by twisting or torqueing the limbs past their limits, as in breaking a leg skiing or getting shin splints from running on pavement. The limits to bodily movement imposed by the bicycle frame eliminate torqueing and pounding. The only vigorous athletic activity with less potential for injury is swimming.

Most bicycle injuries—other than injuries received in a fall—are the result of using wrong or improperly adjusted equipment. Or you might experience discomfort as a result of pushing yourself too hard, a problem that is certainly not exclusive to cycling. In by far the largest number of cases, resting, relaxing, and then returning to cycling when you feel better is the appropriate course of treatment.

We want to emphasize the fact that injury prevention is the key to painless, trouble-free biking. Warmup exercises, as described in Chapter 7, prevent injury and discomfort in all sports, and by exercising to warm up you decrease the possibility of hurting yourself. Warmups are as much a part of bicycling as the ride itself. The problems and injuries experienced by bicyclists fall into three categories: general aches and pains, pre-existing medical conditions that can be aggravated by bicycling, and, of course, injuries received in a fall. What follows is prevention and treatment advice for the cyclist's most common complaints.

203

ACHES AND PAINS

Muscular Aches and Pains

Muscular aches and pains are experienced in most forms of physical activity when you are first starting out. They should be respected as signs of overuse—that is, as indications that you are trying to do too much too soon.

Rest and relaxation are the best tonics for these complaints. Massage or a sauna will help relax muscles, as will soaking in a hot tub.

Prevention: Do warmup exercises (described in Chapter 7). Recognize that you must be patient and allow your body to adjust to the new activity gradually.

Saddle Sores

Pressure, combined with heat and perspiration, causes the condition known as saddle sores. Rest and relaxation are the main course of treatment.

Prevention: Use a leather saddle rather than a plastic one. Leather will breathe, allowing heat and moisture to escape. Also try altering the seat angle or height. Often a $\frac{1}{16}$ inch adjustment solves the saddle sore problem. While riding, move around or get up off your saddle from time to time to allow your posterior to restore itself. Good-quality cycling shorts with a chamois-lined crotch will reduce friction, thus eliminating one of the main causes of this complaint. Always break in a good leather saddle slowly over the course of weeks, especially before a long ride.

Muscle Cramps

Muscle cramps can occur while riding and also in the evening after a long ride. Both types can be caused by overuse—that is, by riding harder than your body was conditioned to ride. Conditioned athletes can also get cramps while riding that result from a deficiency in certain minerals which are lost in perspiration. Professional cyclists are careful to keep up their potassium and sodium levels by drinking fresh fruit juices and eating bananas. Dehydration can also cause cramps.

Prevention: Ride within your physical capacities and make certain you get enough water. If you are exerting yourself for a race or a long tour, drink fresh juices for the minerals they contain.

Knee Pains

Irritation of the cartilage on the underside of the kneecap—felt as knee pain—results mainly from pedaling in gears that are too high. The pain usually increases when you straighten out the leg. The treatment is rest and relaxation for a day or two until the discomfort goes away.

Prevention: Learn to "spin" your pedals (see Chapter 7). Check seat height and other adjustments to make certain they are correct, and stay in lower gears.

Neck Pains

New cyclists may experience some neck pain until their neck and shoulder muscles are conditioned to the riding position, which requires you to twist your head back from time to time to check out the traffic.

Prevention: You can eliminate the main cause of this discomfort by wearing a small mirror (available in bike shops) that attaches to your glasses or helmet. This device lets you watch traffic behind you without twisting your head to look back.

Shoulder Pains

Most shoulder pains are caused by riding a bike with an improper seat or handlebar adjustment, which causes the rider to overuse the shoulder muscles. The treatment is rest and relaxation, massage by a friend, or hot baths.

Prevention: Make certain the bike is properly adjusted. (See Chapter 4.)

Numb or Tingling Hands

The continuous pressure of the handlebars against the ulnar nerve in the hand can produce numbness in the fourth and fifth fingers. Normal sensations will return if you give your hands a rest. Permanent damage to this nerve is rare and results only from ignoring early symptoms.

Prevention: (1) change hand positions frequently as you ride; (2) wear riding gloves or install padding on your handlebars; (3) adjust your handlebars higher and closer to your saddle for a more upright riding position, which will take weight off your hands; (4) avoid rough road surfaces when you can; (5) reduce pressure in your front tire five to ten pounds to provide a cushier ride; (6) whenever you get a chance try out other bikes, investigate the possibility that your bike frame just isn't a comfortable one (there is great variation in bike frames where comfort is concerned).

Numb Penis

This condition is caused by the saddle pressing against the pubic bones and cutting off the circulation of blood to the penis. It is rarely serious, although it can make a person rather nervous.

The treatment is rest and relaxation. Sensation will return by morning.

Prevention: Pay attention to your riding position, and make certain your bike is adjusted properly. Try tilting the nose of the saddle down slightly. Stand up frequently while riding to relieve pressure.

Sore Feet

The single most common cause of sore feet is cycling in sneakers. The soreness is the result of bruising the sole of the foot by pressing against the hard pedal without adequate foot protection. Treatment is rest and relaxation until the pain goes away.

Prevention: Wear cycling shoes or shoes with firm soles that protect the foot from being bruised by the pedal.

Tendinitis

Although it is rare, cyclists occasionally report having pain in the Achilles' tendon—that long tendon that extends from your heel into your calf muscle. This pain can result from climbing a grade that is too steep for your level of conditioning or from using toe clips that are too short (the latter forces the tendon to do work that the bones should do). This condition can also occur in people whose Achilles' tendons have become shortened by wearing high-heeled shoes. The stretching required in pedaling a bike can cause pain or discomfort in such shortened tendons. Treatment is rest and relaxation, but icepacks will help reduce inflammation.

Prevention: Correct the length of your toe clips. To alleviate the short-tendon problem, raise your seat half an inch or so to compensate. Stretching exercises to lengthen the tendon can be recommended by physiotherapists.

PRE-EXISTING MEDICAL PROBLEMS

Back Pain

In the general population back pain is the second most common cause of disability. Back pain often results from stressful situations that cause the back muscles to tense up, from improper use of the back muscles in lifting, or from posture that puts undue strain on the back—not from bicycling. Instead, many people with existing back pain—including myself—find that bicycling actually relieves their condition by keeping the back muscles stretched and supple. If you do find your back pain worsened during cycling, try moving the saddle forward or back, or otherwise experiment with your riding position.

Treat back pain by relaxing and getting plenty of rest on a *firm* surface. The worst position for back pain is sitting, since the muscles can't relax.

Prevention: Prevention is rather simple, but it does require some changes of old habits and the development of some new ones. First, always do warmup exercises, such as those we describe in the "Cycle Training" chapter, before riding. Second, avoid lifting heavy objects. Third, after the pain has gone away, you can strengthen your back and abdominal muscles by doing the following exercises:

Lie on your back on the floor. Bring first your left, then your right, then both knees to your chest. Hug your knees to your chest. Put your feet back down on the floor and relax.

With your legs straight, lift them both three to six inches from the floor. Hold them off the floor for a count of three. Do ten or fifteen such leg lifts and then relax. Increase the number of lifts you do each day as your abdominal muscles increase in strength.

Support your weight at your shoulders and heels and raise your buttocks off the floor. This conditions your buttock and abdominal muscles to work along with your back muscles.

Prostatitis

Prostatitis is an inflammation of the prostate gland—a gland located just below the bladder which secretes a fluid that empties into a man's seminal ducts during ejaculation. There is no doubt that people with chronic prostatitis may notice that their condition is aggravated by bicycle riding or any other activity that exposes them to vibration in the rectal area.

Treatment may include antibiotics, since sometimes prostatitis is caused by bacterial infection. Hot baths for 15 to 20 minutes at a time, two to three times a day, frequently relieve the inflammation causing the pain. Often, prostate massage (get instructions from your physician) or frequent ejaculation can help resolve the problem.

Prevention: Avoid caffeine, alcohol, and any other stimulants that act as diuretics. Cyclists with chronic prostatitis have discovered that changing saddles sometimes relieves the problem. For some people a wider seat brings relief, whereas for others it's a narrower seat. You'll need to experiment. Also, try tipping the nose of the saddle downward. Take every opportunity to get up off the saddle while riding—while climbing hills, while pedaling along a flat piece of road, etc.

Hemorrhoids

There's a popular myth that bicycling can cause hemorrhoids. However, no medical research supports this idea. Hemorrhoids are enlargements of the blood veins in the rectal area that are like varicose veins. The actual cause is not well understood, but it probably relates to a combination of heredity and poor bowel habits. If you are a hemorrhoid sufferer, avoid sitting during flare-ups and cut down on your cycling until you feel better.

The usual treatment for hemorrhoids is frequent warm baths. Avoid straining to evacuate bowels.

Prevention: The hemorrhoid sufferer will often benefit from a diet that is high in fiber—even supplemented by bran or other fibers—to increase the frequency and bulkiness of stools. Ointments or suppositories relieve symptoms, but changes in diet and bowel habits address the cause.

If you have an existing disease for which you are now getting treatment, you should work with your physician to design an exercise program to benefit you. Most chronic diseases respond to exercise in specific and predictable ways. Some responses are positive and some negative, and articulating the limits with each disease is beyond the range of this book.

In general, bicycling is excellent exercise, and for a person in good health it can be an important part of any preventive program. If you have a chronic disease and are interested in exploring how cycling can contribute to rehabilitation, talk it over with your physician. If your physician isn't knowledgeable about using exercise in the treatment of chronic disease, there are physicians who are: Most doctors can refer you to other physicians who specialize in this field.

ABOUT ACCIDENTS

Most bicycle accidents are minor ones caused by the cyclist and involving no other persons or vehicles. Losing control when the front wheel skids while crossing a railroad track; the tire catching in a metal grating; skidding in the rain or on loose gravel spilled on the pavement—all are examples of what are usually described as operator-caused bicycle accidents.

The resulting fall may inflict bruises, abrasions, or pulled muscles, all of which require nothing more than first aid and rest. But it is important, even in those situations, to know how to handle yourself for the moment. Getting back on your bike and immediately riding off might cause more serious damage to an injured part. For example, a pulled muscle—stressed when it is still tight from the original injury—can become a more serious sprain if you continue to use it.

People who have experienced accidents such as these know that there is a period of time immediately following a fall when you feel out of touch with your body. This is a normal response to trauma. Often the reflex is to jump back on your bike and ride off before checking out your body or your bike. Your mind races off in a thousand different directions at once. Adrenaline is pumping through your veins at a crazy rate. You're only vaguely aware of pain, and somehow the only message that gets through is "Get out of there as fast as you can."

To prevent further injury, sit down and fully relax yourself. Do this consciously. Lean against a tree or a nearby building. Take a deep breath, hold it, let it out slowly. Do this two or three times. It will help you relax in a very real way. Then count your breaths until you reach 50 or 60. You'll feel the world come back into focus as you do these things. Then start evaluating any injuries. Starting with your feet and working up to the top of your head, ask yourself how each area of your body feels—just as though you were taking an inventory. Once everything checks out, get up and walk around slowly. If you have pains that you don't understand, or if you are particularly anxious, summon help. Get a friend to come and pick you up, or rally the aid of a passerby.

If your body checks out all right, go on to check out your bike. Check the handlebars to see that they are straight. Check front and rear brakes to make certain they're in proper working order. Lift first the front of the bike and then the rear, spinning each wheel in turn to see that it isn't wobbling. Make certain that both tires are inflated. Check the seat and the derailleurs and the pedals. When you are certain that everything is in safe working order, get back on and ride slowly for the first half mile or more. Ease yourself into the ride. Only when your confidence in your body begins to return—and you are certain the bike is mechanically safe—should you resume your normal riding pace.

FIFTEEN

KEEPING YOUR BIKE IN TOP SHAPE

Keeping your bike in top condition is essential to your continued riding pleasure. A wobbly wheel or loose pedal bearings can easily cause needless anxiety while sapping your energy. Regular bicycle maintenance also goes a long way toward preventing or minimizing costly repairs.

Luckily, bicycle maintenance is easy, and most of it can be done by anyone, with or without mechanical skill. The instructions that follow will help you keep your bike in top running condition between yearly tuneups by a skilled mechanic. For those of you who wish to do your own yearly overhaul and repairs, there are many excellent manuals available at your local bike shop. Instead of duplicating that information here, we've tried to stick to the basics.

The first rule of bicycle maintenance is "Keep your bike clean!" Grit tends to build up on moving parts, and, unless you clean it off, it has a way of getting into bearing surfaces and wearing them out before their time. Never use water to clean your bike. Use a solvent, such as kerosene (be careful, it's highly flammable), Bullshot, or WD-40. Avoid getting these solvents on brake pads and tires.

TIRE REPAIRS

When you begin riding more than a few miles a week, you will inevitably have a flat tire sooner or later. You can postpone this eventuality by keeping your tires inflated to pressures recommended by the manufacturer; replacing your tires before the treads are worn thin; avoiding glass and metal objects in the road; and brushing your tires off with your riding gloves whenever you stop to rest to remove any tiny, sharp stones or glass that may be sticking to the tread and working their way into the rubber.

When you do get a flat tire on the road, you either change the tire or patch it, depending on whether your bike has clinchers or sewups. We'll describe the latter first.

Changing Sewup Tires

Tools required: Pump and spare tire.

Sewup tires are easier and faster to change on the road than clinchers. That's one reason why they were invented. With the tube sewn into the tire casing, both are easily removable as a unit.

Sewup tires are glued to the wheels of your bike. Begin by removing the wheel, which is usually accomplished by means of a quick-release lever (Fig. 15–1).

If your brakes rub against the tire, release the brake's quick release, located on the brake lever or the brake assembly itself. This release mechanism is different on different brakes, so if you don't know how to operate yours, get specific instructions from your bike shop.

Locate the tire valve and release any pressure that may still be in the tire.

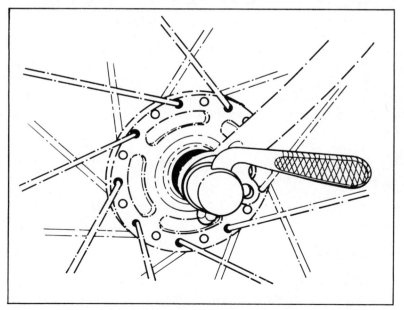

Fig. 15-1   Quick-release levers greatly simplify the task of changing a tire.

Then start removing the tire on the side of the wheel opposite the valve by pulling it away from the metal rim. The glue used is a rubber-based adhesive that maintains a tackiness for months and sometimes years, so the tire is usually easy to peel from the rim.

To replace the punctured tire with your spare, first insert the valve stem in the hole provided for it in the rim. Press the rim against a tree, a wall, or a clean patch of ground so you can stretch the tire onto it. (Be careful not to pick up rocks and stones while you're doing this.) Starting at the valve stem, work the tire onto the rim evenly by stretching it around the wheel with both hands at once. Never use any kind of metal object or pry bar on a sewup tire. Not only is it unnecessary, but it can also destroy a good tire.

Inflate the tire to about half-pressure and check the tire to make certain it's mounted evenly on the rim. At low pressure, it is easy to twist the tire right or left to align it on the wheel.

Replace the tire on the frame. Lock the quick-release skewers in place on the axle. Re-engage the release mechanisms on the brakes. Inflate the tire with your hand pump until it is up to proper pressure or feels hard when you press your thumb firmly against it. That's it—you're ready to go! With practice, the average person can change a sewup tire on the road in less than five minutes.

About spares: Unless you plan to carry a spare tire with you, you're defeating the purpose of having a bike equipped with sewups. A spare weighs only ounces and can be clipped under the seat with a spare toe strap or one of several simple carrying devices sold for this purpose.

It's a good idea to get an old rim from your bike shop's junk bin to use for "seasoning" spare sewup tires. When you buy a new tire, glue it to the rim, inflate it, and let it stretch into shape. Whenever you need a fresh spare to carry on your bike, remove the seasoned tire and put it under the seat. A seasoned tire is much easier to install on the road than an unseasoned one.

If you season new tires in this way, you won't have to carry rim cement with you on your bike because the tire will already have its own glue on it. Having to work with glue on the road is about as much fun as removing chewing gum from your child's hair—you end up with sticky fingers that pick up dirt, hair, and grime and just won't wipe off. The glue on the tire will be tacky to the touch by the time you need it, but it won't come off on your hands.

Patching sewup tires takes time and patience. For instructions, consult complete repair manual, which you can purchase from most bicycle shops.

Changing Clincher Tires

Tools required: Pump, patch kit, two tire irons, and a 6-inch crescent wrench if you have bolt-on axles.

Wheels with clincher tires may be equipped with either quick-release axles or bolt-ons. In either case, remove the wheel from the frame. Begin by releasing the quick-release mechanism of the brake—a device that will be located either on the hand lever on the handlebars or on the brake caliper over the wheel. Each company has a slightly different design for this, so if you can't figure out how to operate yours, take your bike to your local bike shop and ask for specific instructions.

Remove the wheel either by loosening the nuts that hold the axle to the frame or by releasing the quick-release skewer. Pump some air into the tire to locate the leak. Mark that area with a pencil, with a pen, or, if you don't have either of these, by scratching the tire with a stone.

Remove the tire from the rim. In some cases you'll be able to do this with your hands, but with the new high-pressure tires you may have to use tire irons.

Work one tire iron in between the rim and the side of the casing. Be careful not to catch the tube with the iron, as this can tear the rubber and cause another leak.

With one iron holding the tire, work the second iron around the rim until you've released one side of the tire from the rim for the full circumference of the wheel. Now you can reach in and remove the inner tube.

Inflate the tube with your pump and check for leaks. Mark the leak with a pen, pencil, or stone. Release the air from the tube.

Following the instructions that came with your patch kit, apply a patch over the hole in the tube and reinflate it. Check for leaks again. If you've run over a nail, the chances are good that you have two puncture holes—the first caused by the initial penetration, the second by the nail chewing up the tube as you rode for a few yards with the tire flat.

When you are satisfied that you've patched all the leaks, examine the inside of your tire casing. Run your fingers *very carefully* over the entire inside of the tire. You may find a nail or a shard of glass in there, so explore with caution or you'll puncture your finger, too. Examine the casing from the inside to see if there are any breaks or cuts that might pinch the tube. Temporary repairs can often be made by applying a regular tire patch over any break more than a quarter-inch long. But never trust such a repair job to carry you any farther than the nearest bike shop to buy a new tire.

Work one side of the tire casing onto the rim with your fingers. Then place the tube inside the casing, inflating it just enough to give it body. Smooth the tube neatly into the casing. Work the casing into the rim with your fingers, releasing air from the tube if necessary. Sometimes, especially with high-pressure clinchers, it may be necessary to work the last six or eight inches of the casing on with a tire iron. Do this only as a last resort, as it is easy to tear the tube using an iron. Be sure to check with your bike shop to determine whether or not you should use a tool on your particular type of tire.

Replace the wheel in the frame and inflate it to full pressure. Check to see that the quick release is re-engaged on the brake. Make certain that the axle nuts and skewers are tight. Then you're ready to go.

About spares: Some bicyclists carry a spare tube instead of a patch kit. Repairing the clincher on the road then requires no more than removing the punctured tube, examining the casing, and reassembling the whole. On a tour, it is also possible to purchase a spare casing that folds up to about the same size as a sewup tire.

WHEEL CHECKS

Wheels need to be kept "true"—that is, free of wobble. Regular checks of your wheels will help you prevent broken spokes and bent rims. Since the condition of the wheel affects the brakes, a wobbly wheel will cause you to lurch to a stop. On wet pavement or gravel, your wobbly wheel can even cause a dangerous skid.

To check your wheel, have someone lift one wheel at a time an inch or two from the ground. Spin the wheel and watch for side-to-side play (called "wobble"). If the wheel wobbles more than a 16th of an inch from center, it needs attention. As the wheel is spinning, watch for up-and-down movement also. This is called "hop." Again, more than $\frac{1}{16}$ inch of hop indicates that the wheel needs to be trued.

Any good bike shop will true a wheel for a nominal fee. There are books available to help you learn how to do this, but it does take a lot of practice to become good at it. Unless you're willing to put in several hours of practice, it's best to have the job done by your favorite bike mechanic.

Tightening Spokes

Tools required: A spoke wrench.

As you're checking your wheels, also check for loose or broken spokes. Every spoke in the wheel should "plink" when you pluck it as you'd pluck a stringed musical instrument. If a spoke wiggles instead of plinking, it's too loose. If the wheel hops or wobbles, there are probably one or more loose spokes. Tightening spokes is an integral part of truing a wheel. In fact, truing is accomplished by adjusting spoke tension.

However, sometimes you'll find one or two loose spokes even though the wheel is true. You can tighten these yourself if you use care. Tighten them by turning the spoke nipple clockwise (Fig. 15–2).

The best way to get the right tension is to snug up the spoke—that is, to tighten most of the looseness out and then continue to tighten the spoke, a quarter turn at a time. Tighten a quarter, spin the wheel to check for true, tighten another quarter turn, etc. If the wheel wobbles after the spoke is

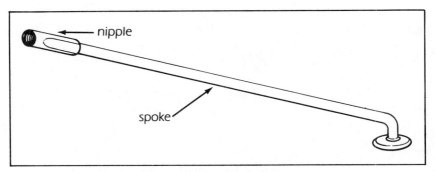

Fig. 15-2   To tighten a spoke, turn the nipple clockwise.

tightened, it means that you've tightened it too much. Back off on the tension until the wobble disappears again.

Pay particular attention to the rear wheel. Spokes in that wheel get much more stress than those in the front wheel. Spokes stretch or the wheel distorts as a result of the power you exert on it when you climb a hill.

If you're conscientious about adjusting loose spokes, and you develop a good feel for it, this simple maintenance procedure can save you many dollars in more expensive repairs.

Brake Shoes

Tools required: A 6-inch crescent wrench or a 10-mm box-end wrench.

Every time you apply your brakes, rubber blocks rub against the rim of the wheel to slow your bike down or bring it to a stop. Each time that happens, a little rubber is worn from the brake pads and in time they need to be replaced.

Usually it's very easy to tell when your brakes need attention; your bike doesn't respond to your squeezing of the brake levers. However, if that is your only criterion for testing the brakes, you may discover your need for repair or adjustment only after you've injured yourself or your bike or both.

Instead, we recommend inspecting your brakes regularly. With the hand lever in its released position, each brake pad should be ⅛ to ¼ inch from the rim, depending on how finely tuned you keep your bike. If they're set wider than that, your brake pads are probably worn and need to be replaced.

Check the alignment of the brakes on the rim. To do this, squeeze each brake lever and examine the way the pad lines up on the rim. If it's not centered on the braking surface, as shown in Figure 15–3, this indicates excess wear and a need for adjustment or replacement.

You'll notice that there's a slot in the brake caliper arm onto which the brake pads are bolted. You can center the pads on the braking surface of the rim by loosening the nuts that hold them and sliding the pad up or down. Be

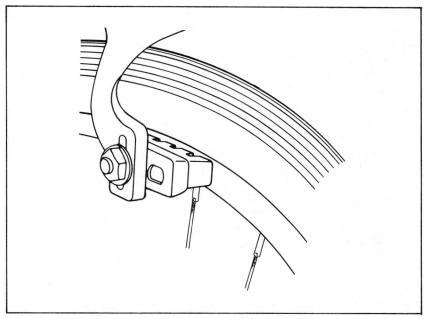

Fig. 15-3 When pressed against the rim, the brake pad should be centered on the braking surface.

sure to adjust the pads for the position they will be in when the hand lever is squeezed and the pads are fully engaged on the rim.

Cable adjustment is usually necessary after adjusting or replacing the brake pads. You can adjust either the outer cable or the inner cable. (The outer cable is like a tube; the inner cable runs inside it.) On side-pull brakes, the outer cable adjustment is located on the brake assembly itself; on center-pulls, it's on a clip above the brake assembly.

Adjust the outer cable by first loosening the locknut and then turning the adjusting barrel until the pads are from ⅛ to ¼ inch from the rim. Try the brakes by squeezing the hand-lever. When you're satisfied with your adjustment, tighten the locknut back in place.

Most minor adjustments can be accomplished with the outer cable adjustment. However, if the pads are badly worn or you are replacing them, you may need to adjust the inner cable. This is done by loosening the nut on the inner cable-adjustment bolt and either shortening or lengthening the cable. As you'll see when you get started, this is a three-handed job. Unless you're very good with your hands, have a friend help you or get a tool from your bike shop called a "third hand," which holds the brake pads against the rim while you adjust the cables.

Pads are easy to replace once you've mastered the technique described above. Each pad is held in place by a single nut. Unscrew that nut, drop out the old pad assembly, put in the new, and adjust. The only thing to watch is that some pad clips, or holders, are open on one end (Fig. 15–4). Whenever you put in new brake pads, *make certain that the closed end faces forward;* otherwise the pad can fly out of its clip while you're braking.

CHECKING BOTTOM BRACKET BEARINGS

Tools required: Wrenches designed for the specific make of bottom bracket (available from bike shops).

It is easy to overlook the bottom bracket bearings—that is, the bearings that carry the crankset of your bike. Unless you're doing a lot of wet-weather riding, these bearings won't require full servicing (disassembly and grease) more than once a year. But, to prevent bearing damage, you do need to check this adjustment every two or three months.

To check for play or looseness in the bearing, grasp either crank arm firmly and try to move it sideways. It should rotate freely without play. Then remove the chain from the front chainwheel and try spinning the crank. It should spin freely and smoothly. If you feel excessive side-play, looseness, or

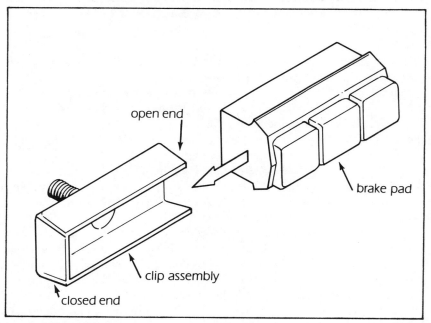

Fig. 15-4   Note that some brake-pad clips have one closed and one open end. The closed end should always face forward.

sloppiness in the bearing, it will need to be tightened. If the crank is hard to turn it will need to be loosened. If the crank turns roughly or you hear a gritty sound, that indicates that the bearings and parts need to be disassembled, examined for bearing damage, replaced if worn, greased, and reassembled.

Simple adjustments are done from the left side of the bike (Fig. 15–5). You begin by releasing the "lockring" and turning the "adjusting cup" to either tighten or loosen the bearing—clockwise to tighten, counterclockwise to loosen. Tighten the lockring and try the adjustment again. Sometimes the lockring will change the adjustment as it is tightened, requiring readjustment of the adjusting cup until the bearing runs smoothly with the lockring tight.

Each bottom bracket bearing is a little different, and each one requires tools designed specifically for it. Your bike shop can supply you with the right tools for adjustment. This will make the job easier than trying to improvise with household tools.

If you don't wish to do the mechanical work yourself, take your bike to your bike shop when you discover that bearing adjustments are needed. The few dollars you'll spend now can save you money in the long run.

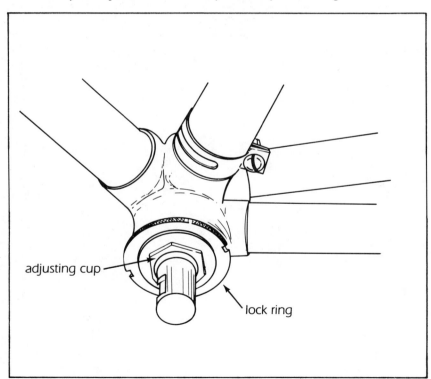

Fig. 15-5   Bottom bracket adjustments are made from the left side of the bike.

CHECKING PEDALS

Tools required: A wrench (preferably a pedal wrench) to fit the pedals on your bike.

One of the simplest maintenance checks you can make is also one of the most expensive if neglected. On occasion, the pedal spindle, which is threaded into the crank, unscrews slightly. You may not feel that it's loose. As you ride with a loose pedal, the threaded end of its spindle rocks back and forth in the crank arm. This can strip the threads in the crank arm, and, once the arm is stripped in this way, you have no choice but to buy a new one. If your bike has high-quality alloy cranks, the damage can be an expensive proposition indeed.

Put a wrench on the pedals and tighten them snugly into the crank arm. Note that the pedal on the right is tightened by turning it clockwise, while the pedal on the left is tightened by turning it in the opposite direction.

While you're at it, check the pedal bearings. Grasp the pedal and feel for any looseness in the bearing. Spin it and make certain it spins freely.

Mid- to high-quality pedal bearings can be both adjusted and greased. To adjust them, remove the outer dust cap (Fig. 15–6), behind which you'll find a locknut and bearing assembly similar to those you've become familiar with on the wheels and crankset. To adjust the pedal bearing, you loosen the locknut and adjust the cone (it is threaded like a nut) until the pedal runs free and smooth.

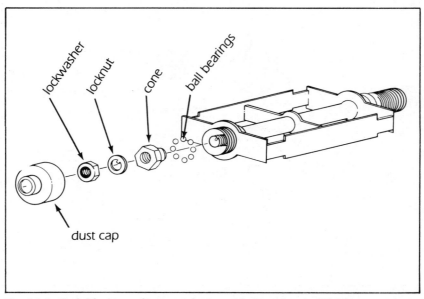

Fig. 15-6   Pedal bearing adjustment begins with the removal of the dust cap.

CHECKING HEADSET BEARINGS

Tools required: Wrenches to fit both the locknut and the adjusting nut of the headset.

The headset of your bicycle holds the bearings that support the front fork, allowing you to turn the front wheel. Unlike any other bearing, this one must resist the erratic pounding of the road. Because of the vibration transmitted to the headset, there is a tendency for the locknut and adjusting nut to loosen. For this reason, we recommend getting into the habit of checking the headset adjustment every time you ride. The procedure is so simple that you'll soon be doing it as a matter of course.

Straddle your bike as though getting ready to ride. Engage the front wheel brake and push the bike forward and back with the brake on. Do you feel any looseness in the headset? Does it make a clicking or rattling sound? In either case, it's time for an adjustment.

Loosen the locknut (Fig. 15–7) and turn the adjusting nut until the click or looseness goes away. Tighten the locknut against the adjusting nut to prevent it from working loose again. Now turn the front fork back and forth. Does it bind as you turn it? If so, the adjusting nut needs to be loosened.

When you can turn the fork smoothly from side to side while *not* producing a clicking noise in the headset, you'll know that the adjustment is correct.

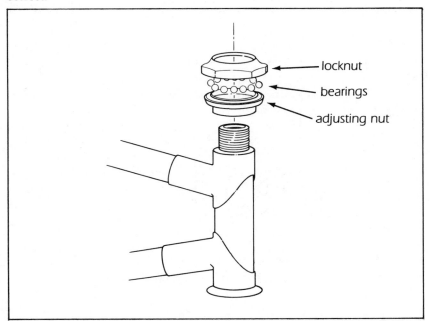

locknut

bearings

adjusting nut

Fig. 15-7   Adjust for looseness or binding in the headset by turning the adjusting nut.

CHECKING AND ADJUSTING WHEEL BEARINGS

Tools required: One cone wrench (a very thin open-end wrench which you can purchase at the bike shop). One wrench to turn the locknut.

Not all wheel bearings can be adjusted. Some high-quality bikes are equipped with bearings that are sealed at the factory. Even though you can't adjust these, you can check them, and if they're loose or otherwise defective they can be repaired by a bike shop or returned to the factory for new bearing assemblies.

To check your wheel bearings, lift the wheel a few inches off the ground and, grasping the tire, try to wiggle it from left to right. If the bearing feels loose, you'll want to adjust it or send the wheel into the shop for adjustment.

Spin the wheel and see how it goes. Does it roll freely and smoothly for a minute or two? If so, and if the above check revealed a snug bearing, you're in luck—the wheel bearing needs no adjustment. Does the bearing bind? If so, you'll need to adjust it.

To adjust the wheel bearings, remove the wheel from the frame. Fit the cone wrench into the adjusting nut as shown in Figure 15–8. Loosen the locknut. Now turn the adjusting cone until you can spin the axle in your fingers. Tighten the locknut against the adjusting cone to prevent it from coming loose. Put the wheel back on your bike and tighten it into place, either with the quick-release skewer or the axlenuts.

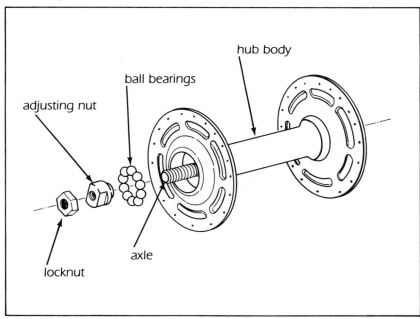

Fig. 15-8   Adjust the wheel bearings so that the axles spin smoothly when you turn them with your fingers.

CLEANING AND ADJUSTING DERAILLEURS

Tools required: Small screwdriver; spray can of Bullshot, WD-40, or similar lubricant/solvent; stiff ¼-inch paintbrush.

Because they are close to the road and pick up dust, as well as grease from the chain, derailleurs can get filthy. The combination of grease and road grit gums up the works and causes excessive wear, so it's important to clean off the grime from time to time.

Using a quarter-inch paintbrush, brush away any grit around the moving parts and adjustment screws of both front and rear derailleurs. Then spray each derailleur with Bullshot or WD-40. Wipe away any excess solvent along with the grease, using a soft rag.

Clean the outer surfaces of the guide pulleys of the rear derailleur in the same way. Then go over all the shift cables and shift levers with the paintbrush, solvent/lubricant spray, and soft rag. Doing this once every couple of months will go a long way toward preventing expensive repairs.

Adjusting the rear derailleur. Does the chain ever slip off the freewheel cogs when you're riding? Or does it refuse to go onto the smallest or largest cogs? If you have any of these problems, your rear derailleur needs adjustment.

Suspend the rear wheel of your bike in such a way that you can crank it by hand and shift gears. Now find the adjustment screws on the rear derailleur (Fig. 15–9). Sometimes these screws are marked with an "L" for low and an "H" for high. Remember that the high gear is the smallest one on the freewheel, the low gear the biggest.

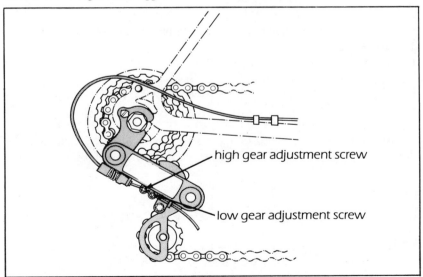

Fig. 15-9   Adjust for high and low gear positions on the rear derailleur by turning the adjustment screws as shown.

Turn the adjustment screw left or right until the chain centers perfectly on the corresponding cog. You'll see that the adjustment screws limit the travel of the derailleur cage, preventing the chain from slipping off the outer cogs. Altering the adjustment screws changes only these outer limits.

Adjusting the front derailleur. You will find the same two adjustment screws on the front derailleur. In this case, the screws limit the travel of the derailleur cage that positions the chain over the chainwheels.

After you have made your initial adjustments, crank the bike by hand, with the rear wheel suspended, and shift both front and rear derailleurs back and forth in various gear combinations. In certain extreme gear combinations you may discover that you need further adjustments.

CARING FOR AND ADJUSTING THREE-SPEED HUBS

Tools required: SAE 20-weight oil in a small oil can.

Three-speed rear hubs are among the most durable and easily adjusted pieces of equipment on bicycles. On the body of the three-speed hub you'll find an oil fitting with either a metal or a plastic dust cap. Monthly maintenance consists of opening this cap and feeding the hub three drops of 20-weight oil.

If your bicycle slips out of gear while you're pedaling, it can be fixed by means of an easy adjustment. On the right hand side of the bike you'll find a cable connected to a small chain going inside the hub (Fig. 15–10). Here's the procedure for adjusting the gears:

1. Move the gear control mounted on the handlebars to second gear.
2. Loosen the locknut.
3. Turn the cable connector until the shoulder of the gear indicator rod is perfectly aligned with the end of the axle.
4. Tighten the locknut against the cable connector. All gears are now in perfect adjustment.

Wipe the hub and its various surfaces clean. Clean the cable and the shift mechanism on the handlebars with a little solvent/lubricant such as Bullshot or WD-40.

CLEANING AND LUBRICATING THE CHAIN

Tools required: Bullshot or WD-40; chain lube or 20-weight oil; rags.

Chain care is extremely important. Each link of the chain pivots eight times every time the chain completes a circuit. In the average gear ranges of a ten-speed bike, the chain goes around at least 50 times per minute. Since your chain has approximately 115 links, there are 46,000 tiny oscillations per

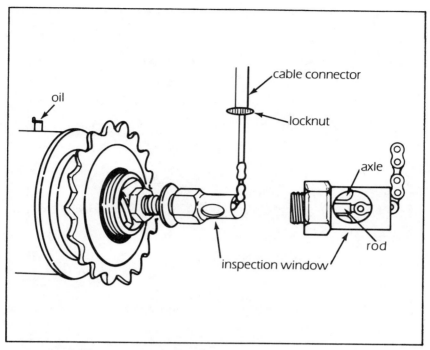

oil

cable connector

locknut

axle

rod

inspection window

Fig. 15-10   Three-speed hub adjustment.

minute. Any friction, therefore, is greatly magnified—the net result being more effort to move your bike forward.

Take a close look at the way your chain is constructed; it's a complex affair. Each link has bearing surfaces that must be kept working smoothly for maximum efficiency and effortless riding. The rollers must run freely in each inner bearing surface, and each rivet—acting as both a bearing and a connector between the side plates—must move freely to allow the chain to flex.

To test for optimal chain efficiency, take a paper match and press the unlighted head against any roller (Fig. 15–11). You should be able to rotate the roller using the match. If you can't, the chain needs to be thoroughly cleaned and lubricated.

Using a clean, soft rag and Bullshot or WD-40, alternately spray and wipe the full length of your chain. Spray, wipe, turn the crank forward to the next length, spray, wipe, etc., until the chain looks bright, clean, and slightly oily. Make the match test again on random links. When you are satisfied that the chain is clean, give it one more light spray without wiping it off with a rag. Let it dry for a few minutes and then treat the chain with 20-weight oil or chain lube. Wipe off the excess oil to avoid picking up dirt. Leave the bike standing for an hour or so, if convenient, to allow excess lubricant to drip off. Tip the bike to the right so the lubricant doesn't drip onto the tires and rims.

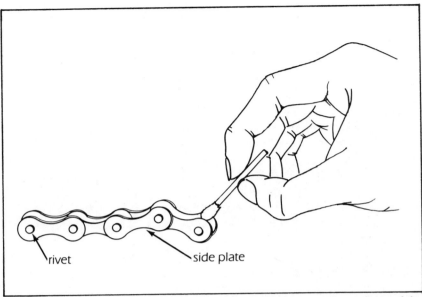

rivet   side plate

Fig. 15-11   An unlighted matchhead is a useful gauge for testing the condition of the chain rollers.

Whenever you use Bullshot, WD-40, or any other lubricant in a spray can, avoid getting it on the tires, rims, or brake pads, as it can affect braking performance. Also, some kinds of rubber and plastic may be adversely affected by lubricants.

Sometimes you'll hear people talking about their bicycle drive chains "stretching." This means that the inner bearing surfaces have worn down, accelerated by dirt clinging to the links. As the bearing surfaces wear out, the distances between their centers elongate. This, of course, results in the chain getting measurably longer. Because there are so many links in a chain, even the smallest amount of wear in each bearing surface is magnified. It is not unusual to find a worn chain as much as a link longer than a new one.

When a chain wears and stretches, the links no longer fit between the cogs of the gears. They ride high between the teeth, causing the teeth themselves to wear. So regular chain maintenance, including cleaning and lubrication, not only makes your ride more enjoyable, it saves wear and tear on expensive moving parts.

Whenever you suspect excess chain wear—because the bike is hard to shift or slips out of gear, or because the chain constantly rattles against the derailleur cages—have it examined by your bike mechanic. A new chain costs under $10 plus a few dollars for installation. In the long run, you'll save much more than that in worn chainwheels and sheer aggravation. However, a chain that receives regular cleaning and lubrication every two or three months should give you many years of trouble-free service, so your time in periodic maintenance will indeed be well spent.

TAPING HANDLEBARS

Tools required: No tools are needed, but two rolls of handlebar tape are required for a complete job.

For some reason many people are intimidated by the idea of taping their handlebars. The process is simple, however, and can be done in about half an hour even though you've never done it before.

There are several kinds of handlebar tape available: plastic, rubber, leather, and fabric. We recommend the fabric tape for two reasons. First, unlike rubber or plastic, fabric tape absorbs perspiration, keeping your grip on the handlebars solid and secure. Second, fabric tape has its own adhesive backing, making the job of wrapping the bars relatively easy.

Using fabric tape, start wrapping at the end of the bars (Fig. 15–12), going *counterclockwise* on the left bar and *clockwise* on the right. Make two complete turns as you start. This will prevent fraying at the ends. As you spiral up the bar, overlap each turn about a quarter inch.

Stretch the tape smoothly past the handbrakes and continue wrapping, as before, on the top bar. Stop the wrap two to three inches from the stem. Tape down the end of the fabric tape nearest the handlebar stem with a band of plastic electrician's tape to prevent fraying and unwrapping.

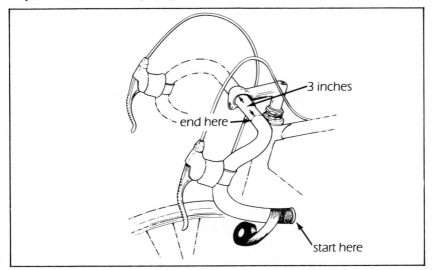

Fig. 15-12 *Make two complete turns to prevent fraying as you start wrapping handlebar tape from the ends of the handlebars.*

As many cyclists leave the old tape in place when retaping their handlebars, it is not unusual to find three or four layers of tape. The extra tape provides additional padding and insulation from road shock.

INSTALLING HANDLEBAR PADDING

What about Grab-ons and other insulated handlebar padding? To put on insulated sleeves, you must remove the hand brakes and clean all the old tape from the handlebars. Soap up the bars with shaving soap, or any other soap that will lather, and thus lubricate the sleeves as you work them over the bars. Keep the bars slippery and damp as you work. Then wipe off excess soap, replace your handbrakes, and you're ready to go.

INDEX